D0251121

"There is hope for your church! Any church can become healthy again, enjoy renewed vitality, and make a difference if you're willing to take the steps outlined in this practical and powerful book. As a successful pastor, church planter, researcher, and advisor to thousands of churches, Ed Stetzer speaks from a wealth of experience with all kinds of churches. Now, in one volume, your church can benefit from his wisdom. This book is a winner!"
— **Dr. Rick Warren**
   The Purpose-Driven Life, The Purpose-Driven Church

"I realized that I had given Ed Stetzer and Mike Dodson the ultimate compliment for their book when I asked my assistant to send the manuscript to my oldest son Sam who is beginning a new pastorate. *Comeback Churches* has the three greatest components that a book on the church could have. First and foremost, it is biblical. Second, it is well researched. And third, it is immensely practical and applicable. With the vast majority of the American churches in decline, this book should be in the hands of hundreds of thousands of pastors, staff, and church leaders. Simply stated, it is just that good."
— **Thom S. Rainer,** President and CEO
   LifeWay Christian Resources

"Finally, a book of practical advice that is based on research. I have seen it both ways—endless research with little advice or much advice with little facts. This book strikes the balance with perfection. I heartily recommend that every pastor study it with the church leadership. If your church (no matter the size) is mired in plateau or decline, or just needs a breath of fresh spiritual air, *Comeback Churches* will help!"
— **Elmer Towns,** Dean
   Liberty University

"This is the most helpful, practical book on church revitalization I've read this century. The authors show us how a comeback church is really a GoForth and GoForward church. I can't begin to do justice to this bountiful book. This is the book every author dreams of doing: the book that no one in the field can get around without going through."
— **Leonard Sweet,** Drew Theological School,
   George Fox University, www.wikiletics.com

"Here's hope—because there's real life here. *Comeback Churches* is more than a pep talk. It's rooted in the 'right stuff' to bring a congregation out of the dismal into the vital. I commend this book because it grounds everything in the dynamics of actual discipleship—the only timeless keys to true resurgence and revitalizing—light years beyond clever methods and stylized techniques. The authors show the way to the enduringly fruitful; a quality needful among us church leaders in a day when 'quick fix' approaches tempt, delude, and finally discourage too many."

— **Jack W. Hayford**
   President, International Foursquare Churches
   Chancellor, The King's College and Seminary

"Are your leaders courageous enough to engage in missional ministry? Does your church have the will to chart a new course of action to revitalize its life? Are you willing to invest the energy, time, and money to get off a long-term plateau? If so . . . read *Comeback Churches,* listen to its advice, and put the powerful insights into action this year! No one, to my knowledge, has done the hard research, presented the facts, and offered such sound advice as Ed Stetzer and Mike Dodson. Based on a study of more than three hundred churches that have successfully revitalized their ministries, *Comeback Churches* is the number-one book on turning around declining and plateauing church ministry."

— **Gary L. McIntosh,** D.Min., Ph.D.
   Professor of Christian Ministry & Leadership,
   Talbot School of Theology, Biola University

"A refreshing book by authors who know how to make research exciting and instructional. Leaders and members of nongrowing evangelical churches should read this book (it wouldn't hurt mainliners either)!"

— **Bill Easum**
   Easum, Bandy & Associates

"Finally, a book that brings together the knowledge of the scholar, the information of the researcher, the experience of the practitioner and the heart of the pastor! Ed Stetzer and Mike Dodson have provided a powerful tool for leaders who want to help their churches become missional but just don't know where to start. This book is wonderfully balanced between the spiritual, biblical, strategic, and practical. One of the most powerful features of the book is the use of comeback stories from leaders that most pastors have never heard of, yet most pastors can relate to. Frustrated leaders will come away from this book with renewed hope and a workable plan to lead their church toward robust life and community transformation. I hope that every pastor leading a church that is currently experiencing plateau or decline will read this book and apply its principles!"

— **Steven M. Pike**
Assemblies of God Division of U.S. Missions

"Ed Stetzer has nailed the major need in America. Churches are always in transition in this changing culture. Our greatest hope beyond launching new works is seeing churches come back alive with growth and vigor. This work has enormous potential to light the fire in thousands of churches. Read it . . . embrace its principles . . . join Jesus in growing His church! We have no other option."

— **Dr. Ronnie W. Floyd,** Senior Pastor
First Baptist Church of Springdale and the Church
at Pinnacle Hills, Arkansas

"Ed Stetzer and Mike Dodson could be called participant-observers. When it comes to leading churches from the brink of decline back to healthy Kingdom advance, they have been there and done that. But I prefer to call them practitioner-theologians, for they care deeply about biblical ecclesiology and how it finds root in faithful congregations of God's people today. This book should be read by every student preparing for pastoral ministry."

— **Timothy George**
Dean, Beeson Divinity School, Samford University and
Executive Editor, *Christianity Today*

"As a denominational leader, I am always looking for tools to help equip pastors to bring new life to established churches. *Comeback Churches* is a great resource that can help bring renewal to congregations and, ultimately, denominations as a whole."

— **Rev. Dr. Harry G. Gardner,** Executive Minister
Convention of Atlantic Baptist Churches, Canada

"*Comeback Churches* is written from a heart of passion for the renewing of the church. It is based upon biblical principles, and while it has a wealth of practical suggestions, it is not only a collection of 'quick fixes.' Written by experienced comeback leaders, this is a must-read for the pastor and layleaders who are sincerely concerned about revitalizing the church!"

— **Wayne W. Boyer,** Executive Director
Churches of God, General Conference

"*Comeback Churches* is not a good book. . . . It is a great book! The chapter on Intentional and Strategic Church Evangelism is the most important word to the local church that I have read in many years. If I could require that every pastor and church leader in America read one book, it would be this one. With *Comeback Churches,* Ed Stetzer further establishes himself as one of the most strategically important kingdom leaders of our day."

— **John Avant,** North American Mission Board

"Keeping one eye on the Bible and one eye on 'best practices' of more than three hundred comeback churches in the U.S., Ed Stetzer illustrates that it's possible to revitalize local congregations without losing sight of the important things that make a church a church: e.g., scriptural authority, biblical leadership, covenant community, and mission. Stetzer's sweep is broad. But his prescriptions aren't complex. They focus on the basic things like strategic and intentional prayer, outreach, and preaching. Church transformation, Stetzer would agree, is neither mechanical nor easy. But it can be achieved. Whether you're a coach or consultant who works with plateaued and declining churches or a pastor or church leader who desires to lead your church to the next level, you will benefit from a prayerful study of *Comeback Churches.*"

— **Jim Fann,** EFCA ChurchHealth Director

COMEBACK CHURCHES

HOW 300 CHURCHES TURNED AROUND AND YOURS CAN TOO

ED STETZER AND MIKE DODSON

PUBLISHING GROUP
Nashville, Tennessee

© 2007 by Ed Stetzer and Mike Dodson
All rights reserved
Printed in the United States of America

ISBN: 978-0-8054-4536-7

Published by B & H Publishing Group,
Nashville, Tennessee

Dewey Decimal Classification: 260
Subject Heading: CHURCH RENEWAL
CHURCH—RESEARCH

Unless otherwise designated, Scripture quotations are from the Holman Christian Standard Bible, copyright © 1999, 2000, 2002, 2003 by Holman Bible Publishers, Nashville, Tennessee; all rights reserved. Other Bible translations quoted are noted as NASB, New American Standard Bible, copyright © 1960, 1962, 1963, 1968, 1971, 1972, 1973, 1975, 1977, 1995 by The Lockman Foundation; NIV, New International Version, copyright © 1973, 1978, 1984 by International Bible Society; and NLT, New Living Translation, copyright © 1996, 2004 by Tyndale Charitable Trust, used by permission of Tyndale House Publishers.

9 10 11 12 13 14   17 16 15 14 13

Table of Contents

Dedication: viii
Preface: ix

Dedication

We are extremely grateful to 324 comeback churches, their leaders, and denominational agencies for taking the time to provide great insights and valuable information. Because of their commitment, others who desire to be renewed and revitalized will find practical strategies and help in the pages of this book.

We are also indebted to the NAMB Research Team, which Ed has the privilege of leading. Team members Richie Stanley, Marilynn Kelly, Chris Gaskin, Lizette Beard, and Jeff Farmer made phone calls, collected data, provided feedback, and served us and this project in so many practical ways. Also, we are indebted to Marvin Owen and Beau Abernathy for their help with the writing and editing process.

Finally, we are extremely grateful for the gift of our wives and children who often sacrifice so that we can fulfill the ministries that God has called us and allowed us to fulfill. They are a tremendous blessing from God!

—*For God's glory,*
    Ed Stetzer and Mike Dodson

Preface

In sports, we get excited about teams or players that make great comebacks, beat the odds, and do something that almost no one thought possible. The team that's down by an insurmountable point spread finds a way to overcome and win. The player who was washed up and rededicates him or herself and does whatever it takes to play at a high level once again, and triumph. We celebrate those comebacks because they inspire us to believe that seemingly impossible things really are possible. That's why we wrote this book. We believe that comebacks are not only needed in many churches but possible. Is it an easy road to travel? NO! Is it a journey worth taking? YES! *Comeback Churches* will help you make that journey.

If you have ever hiked in the mountains, you have discovered the thrill of reaching the peak, being able to see green valleys stretching out for miles, reaching a mountain meadow at the very moment a heavy snow shower starts to fall, or enjoying those hikes with a good friend. It's always hard work climbing those mountains, but it is always worth the effort.

There is nothing that compares to reaching majestic mountain peaks. However, life and ministry can be full of peaks and valleys, plateaus and decline. When we reach life's peaks or make that comeback, it can be fun, exhilarating, and fulfilling. Staying on the plateaus or being stuck in the valleys can be boring, frustrating, and disheartening. We can forget what it is like to reach the peaks. After expending energy on a ministry "climb" and personally experiencing the majesty of living life with a sense of mission and purpose, we can lose the joy of feeling refreshed, renewed, and revitalized.

Many churches that are stuck on a plateau or spiraling into decline can discover the joy of reaching the peak of revitalization. In many ways, the North American Church has forgotten the joy of climbing the mountain peaks of ministry. It has become overweight with modern techniques and methodologies and lost sight of its true mission and purpose to simply make more and better followers of Jesus Christ.

This is clearly evident based upon even a casual examination of the state of the churches. The statistics are alarming. Too many churches have come to rest on plateaus while others are stumbling into decline. Some decided to stay on a peak that was reached long ago, or others have lost their footing in ministry and are sliding down the mountainside of church decline.

Helping churches "come back" after being at a place of plateau or decline is the reason we are writing this book. We believe there is hope for some of the churches that have lost the joy of climbing the peaks of ministry and of making more and better followers of Jesus Christ. Therefore, we have studied more than three hundred churches that have recently experienced renewed growth after a significant period of plateau and/or decline. May God use the journey of these "comeback churches" to lead other churches to experience the exhilaration of reaching new peaks of mission and purpose. Enjoy the view—start climbing again!

The Research and Our Approach to This Book

Experience in ministry has been a great teacher for us. Our learning process has entailed many disappointments as well as victories and led to this question: **"What principles from *Comeback Churches* could guide pastors and churches down the path of revitalization?"** We sought to detect these biblical principles and understand how they enabled each church to be a comeback church.

Additionally, we recognized that we can learn from either our own experiences or from the experience of others. This book will help you learn from the experiences of three hundred comeback churches so that you do not have to pay the same price and endure the same hard lessons for the education. We are moved by another question: "What can be done to change the direction of churches that are merely existing or that are dying?" Are there specific steps that can be taken to move a church off the path of plateau/decline and back onto the road of renewal?

The overall effort was an attempt to describe the best practices of three hundred churches who met these criteria. It was not intended to prove that all revitalized churches always do certain things. As a qualitative study built on quantitative data, it can be a great help to look at your own church practice. For a helpful qualitative study, following a group of thirteen churches that went from good to great, see Thom Rainer's *Breakout Churches*. Ours is different in size and methodology, but we think both would be of great help.

Writing about comeback churches is important to us. Both authors have led churches that were in decline. It was a privilege because those churches chose not to stay in decline—they took up the challenge to grow again. You will hear some of those stories in this book.

Success can be difficult to define in any study, particularly one that involves spiritual matters. For us, it was not enough to know if a church "got bigger." We also wanted to know the impact on the kingdom of God. In other words, were men and women coming to faith in Christ because of this transformed church? We also tried to evaluate the spiritual dynamics that enabled the church to discover what God was already doing in the community.

Just as a healthy body temperature measures approximately 98.6 degrees, we measured factors like baptismal ratios and attendance figures to determine the health of an effective comeback. These criteria were chosen because they are common benchmarks used to indicate how well we are doing reaching people, both historically and biblically. In a few denominations, the benchmarks had to be adjusted due to differences in belief, ministry approach, and record keeping. Regardless, our focus was on church revitalization that led to more people coming to Christ and the church growing because of such.

The Participants in This Study

Thanks to the help of the research and church growth departments of several denominations, we were able to assemble a list of churches that met the turnaround criteria. This book would not be possible without the partnership of Assemblies of God, Baptist General Conference, the Christian and Missionary Alliance, Churches of God, General Conference, Church of the Nazarene, Convention of Atlantic Baptist Churches in Canada, the Evangelical Free Church of America, the Foursquare Church, the Wesleyan Church, and the Southern Baptist Convention's North American Mission Board. This study is a result of their passion for helping their churches transform lives and communities because of the gospel.

Key Factors of the Study

Our study is not intended to be the end of the revitalization discussion. Our study was focused on several key factors, not all important factors. First, though the study led to some consistent findings, we only addressed the results of the 324 churches that responded. In other words, many comeback churches across America were not identified and studied. This project studied a specific group of churches and their leaders whose names were provided by participating denominations.

Second, our study focused on comeback churches that were experiencing significant growth through conversion as measured by increasing attendance and a decreasing membership to baptism ratio. Where data differed between denominations, similar conversion criteria were used depending upon the denomination. Other churches may have grown numerically through transfer growth, but those churches were not the focus of this study.

Third, our process here is not just a technical description and reporting of how these churches turn around. Other resources may do a better job at that. Our intent here is not only to use the exploratory research project that we have conducted to undergird and inform, but also to use the experiences (ours and the study respondents') to inspire and guide. As you read, these experiences and the research findings will be woven together with one ultimate purpose in mind—to practically help pastors and churches that may be struggling in plateau-and-decline mode to experience revitalization. That is at the heart of our desire to write this book and why we did the research.

Background of the Study

The study took place over several months with the help of several researchers. Ed started writing a six-part series of articles on church revitalization and was planning a study on the topic at the Center for Missional Research (CMR). Mike was interested in the subject and wanted to do his doctor of missiology dissertation on the subject, so Ed invited Mike to do his project in partnership with CMR; thus, the research began.

Mike and Jeff Farmer assisted Chris Gaskin, who did most of the phone work, including follow-up interviews for more information on specific topics. (The phone survey can be found at www.comebackchurches.com.) Beau Abernathy, Lizette Beard, Marvin Owen, and Marilynn Kelly contributed significantly to the final writing and research. All survey results were compiled by spring 2006. As the surveys were completed, the responses were calculated, analyzed, and compared.[1] The church leaders who responded to our survey also provided permission to be quoted in this book.

We developed the survey based on our knowledge of churches and how they grow. The lists we requested from other denominations were for only those churches that met the following criteria:

1. The church experienced five years of plateau and/or decline since 1995 (worship attendance grew less than 10% in a five-year period).
2. That decline or plateau was followed by significant growth over the past two to five years which included:
   a. A membership to baptism (conversion) ratio of 35:1 or lower each year and
   b. At least a 10 percent increase in attendance each year.

Once this identification and survey process was complete, 324 churches were evaluated by ranking the potential factors involved in their comeback. Responses in each statistical category were totaled and then divided by the number of respondents. This scaling system gave each category a number ranking between 1.0 and 5.0. The resulting ranking revealed which factors comeback church leaders identified as more critical for church renewal versus the factors they deemed to be less critical.

This book will use many statistics. However, our purpose and this book are about more than research or statistics. In almost every chapter, we use the statistics to inform but then use the rest of the chapter to illustrate and advise—providing, we hope, some suggestions so that you can implement best practices in your church context. **Let us say it again: this is not a book of statistics. It is ultimately a book of practical advice—advice from more than three hundred churches and advice from your two authors.**

Our prayer is that these findings will encourage and challenge you as you lead your church to accomplish all that God has envisioned for you and the local church where you serve.

Ed Stetzer, Ph.D.
Mike Dodson, D.Miss.

For more help with church revitalization,
or to examine the research project and findings
more thoroughly, go to www.comebackchurches.com.

Foundations

We know it is odd to have a chapter 0, but it is important to us, and we think it will be important to you so you can understand our presuppositions. Having a biblical, missional theology and view of the church is the underlying essence of the book—so we start here.

You will notice a few things about this book. Although it is multidenominational, those involved are evangelical, as we are. Of course, God is at work in mainline churches as well, and there are many Bible-focused and mission-shaped churches inside these denominations. However, we wanted to focus on churches where Scripture is an assumed priority. That value will be reflected in the pages of this book.

This is not only a book about research. This is about churches involved in the daily flow of life. Because we have combined our experiences with much statistics and research, we are unapologetic about giving counsel.

We begin this chapter by examining what a church should be. That is the goal, as we see it—a perspective found throughout the book.

Jesus loved the church and gave Himself for her (Eph. 5:25). He declared, "I will build My church" (Matt. 16:18), and allows us to join Him in its building. Following our Lord's command to make disciples of all the "nations" (Matt. 28:19–20) and to witness for Him throughout the world (Acts 1:8), the apostles planted churches, evangelized, and taught the new believers. The Letters to the Seven Churches in Revelation 2–3 reveal Christ's concern for the churches in Asia Minor and His desire to see them believe and behave appropriately. His passion and purpose for the church are evident throughout Scripture.

In Acts 20:28, Paul exhorted the elders of the church at Ephesus to be "shepherds of the church of God" (NIV), meaning that they should care for and guard the church. In 1 Corinthians 14, Paul encouraged the leaders in Corinth to edify, build up, and strengthen the church through worship. Without fail, Paul wrote of his prayers for the church. For these reasons, we're passionate about helping the hundreds of thousands of North American churches in plateau or decline. They may be a bride in distress, but they are still the bride of Christ.

Churches Should Be Biblical

Our goal in this work is to uphold biblical standards. I (Ed) recently presented a paper at the American Society of Church Growth, proposing that six criteria exist in all biblical churches. These six criteria are mentioned frequently and prominently in Scripture.

Criteria of a Biblical Church

We know that many readers will read this book to "save" their church, and that can be good. But clearly, you cannot "save" a church without focusing on the important things that make it a church—scriptural authority, biblical leadership, teaching and preaching, ordinances, covenant community, and mission.

Scriptural authority. The apostles continually appealed to the Old Testament as their authority in preaching and teaching. Peter's sermon in Acts 2 and Stephen's sermon in Acts 7 are dramatic examples. In his itinerant ministry, Paul customarily began ministering in the synagogue, showing from the Scriptures that Jesus must be the Messiah (Acts 17:2–3). In 2 Timothy 3:15–17, Paul established for all time the authority of the Scriptures in the life of the church.

Biblical leadership. Churches need leadership, a fact that is obvious in the New Testament. There are differences in those leadership positions, titles, and roles, but leadership is an integral part of God's plan for the church. The New Testament speaks of elders, bishops, pastors, deacons, evangelists, prophets, and apostles. The church may have organized itself differently in different places and at different times, but the churches *were organized and led by leaders.* These leaders all gave themselves to equipping the believers for ministry (Eph. 4:11–12). The Scriptures instruct believers to accord these leaders "double honor" (1 Tim. 5:17).

Preaching and teaching. People need to hear, read, study, apply, and meditate on God's Word (Rom. 10:14; John 8:32; 2 Tim. 2:15; etc.). The lost need to hear the truth of the gospel, and the redeemed need biblical instruction to grow to maturity. Sadly, for many modern believers *worship* has come to mean the singing and responses that precede the sermon. True worship is more than that and in a church service it includes both praise and preaching. The style and length of the sermon varies from culture to culture, but the preaching and teaching of God's Word has to be a transcultural constant.

Ordinances. The church at Jerusalem devoted itself to the "breaking of bread" (Acts 2:42). This references the Lord's Supper. Jesus' command to "do this in remembrance of me" and the apostle Paul's instructions in 1 Corinthians 11 show how important the Lord's Supper was, and is, to the church. Jesus commissioned His disciples to baptize the nations, and the book of Acts and the epistles show that the early church faithfully baptized new believers (Acts 2:41).

Covenant community. Biblically, the church is not comprised of some who are believers in covenant community and some who are not. The letter of James insists that all the believers be treated the same. As a covenant community, believers share several common ideals, as reflected in Acts 2:42–47. First, they share doctrinal convictions. Acts 2:42 says the believers "continued in the apostles' doctrine." They diligently learned the lessons taught by the apostles. They also devoted themselves to congregational prayer. They prayed for each other, bearing one another's burdens. They met the physical and financial needs of their fellow believers. When necessary, they exercised church discipline.

Mission. Churches are called to the mission of propagating the gospel. Scripture clearly and frequently teaches this. Mission includes the task of worldwide evangelism, social justice, meeting human needs, and many other activities. The acts of the early Christians demonstrate their understanding of Christ's expectations. Jesus' last words to His disciples, recorded in Acts and in each of the four Gospels, pertain to missions. Many churches today forget that the church did mission as it learned to apply its theology.

Churches Should Be Missional

The wrong question is whether your church is "traditional" or "contemporary" and which is better. The real issue is whether your church is biblically faithful, acting as the presence of Christ in the community at large, able to relate Christ to people in culture, and is on mission. In short, is your church "missional"?

The word "missional" has become more accepted, and that's good. It means that churches are asking hard questions about biblical ministry in community. So, what is a missional church? Why all the fuss over a word? Can't a church just do what it's done for over two millennia and not mess with semantics? It certainly can. But, the real fuss has nothing to do with a word but the emphasis created by *that* word. Churches are rediscovering the need to focus on the mission of God and be missionaries in their communities. Our hope is that this book will help you be missional in your context.

In its simplest form, the term "missional" is the noun "missionary" modified to be an adjective. Missional churches do what missionaries do, regardless of the context. They can parachute-drop into a village in India or go into a metropolitan U.S. city and be missional. If they do what missionaries do—study and learn language, become part of culture, proclaim the Good News, be the presence of Christ, and contextualize biblical life and church for that culture—they are missional churches.

A person can be missional in Afghanistan or at their Ameritrade office. Context does not change the baseline activities of a missionary, or a missional person. A "missional church" functions as a missionary in its community. It eats, breathes, and lives within its culture, while sowing seeds of love, kindness, grace, redemption, and Good News. Missional churches take Acts 1:8 literally, acting like missionaries in their own "Jerusalem, Judea, Samaria, and to the ends of the earth." Missional churches act faithfully and intentionally wherever God gives them opportunity.

One distinction of the missional church is that it gives focus to meeting needs inside and outside the church. It takes care of its own, but it also reaches out for the sake of the gospel. Leaders in some circles classify churches as attractional (we do everything in our power to "attract" non-Christians to us and our ministries) or missional (we send people and serve the community—whether the people we serve ever come to our church).

Fortunately, most churches don't view mission and attraction as mutually exclusive. Leaders increasingly understand how attraction-oriented churches can become more missional in allocating their resources and time. This perception is being fueled by ministers like Cincinnati Pastor Steve Sjogren and his focus on "servant evangelism" and ministries like the Dallas-based Leadership Network for equipping "externally-focused churches."

As Robert Lewis so pointedly asks in his book *The Church of Irresistible Influence,* if your church closed its doors today, would anyone but its own members notice? Would the city be saddened because such a great community-transformation partner—a missionary of impact—was gone? Or would it even miss a beat? It's a question that is taking the missional church discussion to a new level. It's more a matter of deeds than of any given word.

Characteristics of a Missional Church

Not all comeback churches look alike. Our study showed they came in all different shapes and sizes. We think that is a good thing. As Slaughter and Bird explained: "God's kingdom is not best represented by franchises of McChurch. If you focus your energies on copying someone else's methodologies or programs, you will miss something crucially important. . . . The Holy Spirit is empowering transformational leaders who demonstrate the kingdom of God in unique ways in each different community."[1]

So, what then, do missional churches look like? They are more than the characteristics below, but certainly they are:

Incarnational. Missional churches are deeply entrenched in their communities. They are not focused on their facilities, but on living, demonstrating, and offering biblical community to a lost world. They may look like Logos Church in Atlanta, where church planter Danny Presten has become part of the biker community he's trying to reach by working at a motorcycle store while planting this new church.

Incarnational can also mean a traditional church that lives out the mandate of Christ in a context where a traditional church is appropriate. The church does not exist for itself. Instead, the rural brick church in southern Michigan believes and lives as the presence of Christ in the community. An incarnational church functions as the "body of Christ" because it represents the presence of Christ in a community.

Indigenous. Missional churches are indigenous, taking root in the soil of their society and reflecting, appropriately, their culture. Indigenous churches look different from Seattle, to Senegal, to Singapore. We rejoice in an African church worshiping to African music, in African dress and with African enthusiasm, but that would be entirely inappropriate in a different setting.

Being indigenous is harder than it sounds, because almost all declining churches already have a culture. In most cases, the existing church culture is from a former era that is only meaningful to those in the church, not those in the community. We believe that the gospel is best lived out when churches are firmly rooted in their surrounding community's culture. They are driven by Scripture, but people from the community see people like them—just radically different in the way they live.

It's ironic that most evangelical churches are filled with people who live very much like the world but look different from it. It should be exactly the opposite. We should look similar to those in our community but act differently. Study after study has shown that North American evangelicals engage in the same lifestyles and sins as the unchurched. Yet, their church preferences are quite different than the world. In other words, we look different to the world, yet live the same as the world. How ironic that many churches have chosen to live the opposite of the biblical commands. Scripture teaches us to contend for the faith (Jude 3) and contextualize to culture (1 Cor. 9:22–23). That makes our churches indigenous to culture.

Intentional. Missional churches are intentional about their methodologies. In missional churches, biblical preaching, discipleship, baptism, and other functions are vital. But worship style, evangelistic methods, attire, service times, locations, and other matters are determined by their effectiveness in a specific cultural context.

Our churches struggle with being evangelistically effective because they are locked into a self-affirming subculture while the larger culture continues to move in other directions. The cultural distance between our churches and communities continues to widen, making it harder and harder to communicate the gospel. Being missional means moving intentionally beyond our church preferences, making missional decisions rather than preferential decisions. Today, people, churches, and denominations desperately need to apply the lens of intentional missiology to North America, not just international fields. The most effective comeback churches will be those that intentionally think like missionaries in their context.

Churches Can Become Missional

A missional church responds to the commands of Jesus by becoming incarnational, indigenous, and intentional in its context. When Jesus said, "As the Father has sent Me, I also send you" (John 20:21), the mandate was not for a select group of cross-cultural missionaries. It was a commission to you, to me, and to our churches. We have a sender (Jesus), a message (the gospel), and a people to whom we are sent (those in our culture). It is worth the effort to go beyond personal preferences and attractional methods to proclaim the gospel in our church services and outside the walls.

Tim Keller explained: "Some churches certainly did 'evangelism' as one ministry among many. But the church in the West had not become completely *'missional'*—adapting and reformulating absolutely everything it did in worship, discipleship, community, and service—so as to be engaged with the non-Christian society around it. It had not developed a 'missiology of western culture' the way it had done so for other non-believing cultures."[2]

The study of missions is called missiology. Missiology is birthed from our understanding about who Jesus is and what He sends us to do. So, who Christ is and how He was sent matters. It directs our missiology. How we "do" church is grounded in Scripture but applied in culture. Simply stated, missional churches are biblically faithful and culturally relevant.

Missionaries live at the intersection of Christology, Missiology, and Ecclesiology. All of these flow from, and are based on, Scripture. This concept is explained more fully in Ed Stetzer and David Putnam's book *Breaking the Missional Code.*

The source of our missionary identity in the church is found in the nature of the one, triune God who sends. God's missional nature explains the very existence of the church. God's people are sent by God to be on His mission. The apostle Peter explains, "But you are a chosen race, a royal priesthood, a holy nation, a people for His possession, so that you may proclaim the praises of the One who called you out of darkness into His marvelous light" (1 Pet. 2:9).

Church and ecclesiology. In *Perimeters of Light: Biblical Boundaries for the Emerging Church,* Elmer Towns and Ed Stetzer state that ecclesiology is not a blank slate taken from the cultural situation. Certain things need to be put in place for a biblical church to exist, such as some form of leadership structure and the practice of ordinances. Certainly, *how* we do some of those things is determined by the context, but *what* we do is determined by the Scriptures.

Strategy and missiology. Many comeback churches are different from each other, which is a good thing. These missional churches have learned to strategize intentionally for mission and ministry based on their context. They analyzed their communities and developed strategies to reach them. The most effective churches don't look for the latest tool from another context in developing their missional strategy. They recognize that their context is different than others', so their approach to ministry will be different. That's why we would ask you not to read this book and say "most churches did this," and then conclude that you must do it that way.

The Missional Matrix

The following diagram entitled "The Missional Matrix" may help explain the interaction of Christology, missiology, and ecclesiology.[3] The shaded circle illustrates the necessity of the scriptural and theological foundation, and its application enabled by the Holy Spirit. Missional churches begin and end with a solid foundation of accurate biblical theology. Only within this circle do Christology, ecclesiology, and missiology interact. Otherwise the church will be unbalanced and unscriptural.

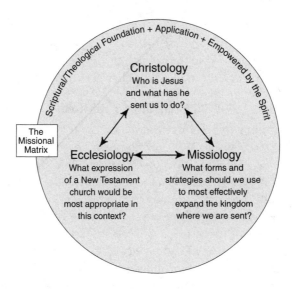

Missional leaders bring the gospel into a context by asking the question, "What cultural containers—church, worship style, small group ministry—will be most effective in this context?" Instead of importing one-size-fits-all styles and models, more pastors are genuinely asking the same questions raised by international missionaries:

- What style of worship/music will best help this group worship in spirit and truth?
- What evangelistic methods should I use here to reach the most people without compromising the gospel?
- What structure of church will best connect with this community?
- How can *this* church be God's missionary to *this* community?

Today, people are realizing that God uses different methods and models to reach different kinds of people. Yes, it is even OK to be traditional—as long as God is using your church to reach its community effectively. Every one of the models listed above is just a model. Models are tools, and too often tools become rules.

Missional churches look different from community to community, but if they faithfully proclaim the word and reach their communities, we should celebrate them. The answer is not to make all churches look alike and use the same techniques. The answer is to have everyone seeking the same thing: to glorify God by being an indigenous expression of church life where they are.

Churches Should Be Spiritual

Growth is a spiritual work, not a mechanistic formula. John Mark Terry explained, "We have the best materials, media, and methods, but we lack spiritual power. Christians of the apostolic era had none of our advantages; they didn't even have the New Testament. Still, they turned the Roman Empire upside down. What impact does your church have in your community?"[4]

Too often, research-based books offer constructive insights and principles, leading some to conclude that church growth can be reduced to formulas, probabilities, and statistics. There's value in research because it shows what God has blessed and used in other churches. But imitating another church does not guarantee that God will use those same things to revitalize your church. In other words, don't expect to read this book and conclude, "If I do A and then B, C will automatically occur." There is no "plug and play" formula, and anyone who says there is wants to sell you a product and not help transform your church. Instead, read this book and others, listen to their advice, then seek the guidance of the Holy Spirit.

Because you are reading *Comeback Churches,* you obviously have a passion to see your church grow. Have you ever wondered why one church grows and another one struggles? On any given Sunday in "Anytown," America, a church may be thriving—growing spiritually and numerically. Just down the road, another church—maybe even from the same denomination—has not grown in years. The second church has begun the long, slow process of decline that may eventually lead to death, unless decisions are made to stop that slow, painful process.

You may observe this situation and say, "I thought church health and growth had to do with demographics or methods, but here are two churches in the same setting, with the same approach, yet only one is growing. Why?"

When was the last time you read a book about growing God's church that really dealt with spiritual issues? One reason a church may experience decline is because Jesus is displeased with the way the church has handled past challenges. Another is that the church may have been disobedient at a crucial point. Repentance may be a spiritual issue, but it's also a pressing need.

In the book of Revelation, Jesus evaluates seven churches. There is a pattern to these evaluations and a template for churches throughout history. If you look around your city today, you will most likely find a church that is facing challenges like the church at Ephesus. You could find several churches resembling Laodicea. You may find several that are enduring false teaching (Thyatira). Jesus, as Head of His church, evaluates us and calls us to repentance when we lose our proper focus (Rev. 2:5, 16, 21–22; 3:3, 19–20).

Consider, for instance, the evaluation of the church at Ephesus, Revelation 2:1–7. Jesus comes to His church, presents His credentials, then He begins to list all the strengths of the church:
- I know your works, your labor, and your endurance,
- and that you cannot tolerate evil.
- You have tested those who call themselves apostles and are not, and you have found them to be liars.
- You also possess endurance.

Then Jesus assesses the church's weakness and provides a clear path to renewal—"But I have this against you: you have abandoned the love [you had] at first. Remember then how far you have fallen; repent, and do the works you did at first" (Rev. 2:4–5). Jesus declares that if we acknowledge that weakness and zealously repent, committing ourselves to overcome it, He will give His personal blessing.

This leads us to an important spiritual principle for growth: **comeback leaders know that our Lord considers commitment to Him and His desires an *indispensable* ingredient to growing spiritually and numerically.**

Many spiritual problems and barriers exist, hindering a church's growth through evangelism. The following growth barriers cannot be overcome by accepting statistics or adhering to strategies:

1. Churches aren't concerned about God's glory, believing the church is just for them (Isa. 42:8; 48:11);
2. Pastors are more concerned about self-interests than about God and His people (Phil. 2:21);
3. God withdraws Himself from the church because of sin. He hardens hearts and gives the people over to sin (Isa. 63:15–19; Heb. 3:12–13);
4. People are unwilling to take hold of God (Isa. 64:7);
5. People do works for their own honor and not the glory of God (Matt. 5:16);
6. People think of prayer as being for themselves (Matt. 6:5);
7. People think of giving as being for their own honor (Matt. 6:2–4);
8. People think of fasting as being for themselves (Matt. 6:16–18; Isa. 58:3ff);
9. Traditional practices are done without a heart for God (Mal. 1:6ff);
10. People "do church," but do not teach the true gospel (Gal. 1:6–10);
11. People grieve the Spirit, resulting in weakness in the church (Eph. 4:29–32);
12. Sin is not dealt with, bringing weakness to the church (1 Cor. 5:5–7);
13. A lack of love for Christ devastates the church (1 Cor. 16:22; Rev. 2:4);
14. A lack of unity brings division (John 17:23; Col. 3:12–15);
15. A lack of love within the body creates strained relationships (John 13:35);
16. Wrong or heretical teachings lead people astray (Rev. 2:14);

17. Immorality in the church is condoned (Rev. 2:20);
18. Lukewarmness in the church becomes prevalent (Rev. 3:16);
19. Lack of biblical teaching in the church leaves people unequipped (2 Tim. 3:17; 4:2);
20. Lack of true and earnest prayer in the church leaves people powerless (Matt. 6:9ff; 2 Thess. 3:1);
21. Not teaching people what Christ commanded and how to do His commands causes them to be immature and unfocused (Matt. 28:18–20);
22. People try to substitute self-made religion (Col. 2:23);
23. Saints are not equipped in the body (Eph. 4:12); and
24. Saints are not doing the work of service in the body (Eph. 4:12);
25. People are not growing spiritually (Eph. 4:12–16);
26. People must grow spiritually for their work and witness to grow (Mark 16:15);
27. People must be careful not to deny God by their actions despite their profession (Titus 1:16);
28. People must speak in a way that opponents of the gospel have nothing bad to say about them (Titus 2:8);
29. People must live in accordance with sound teaching from God our Savior, not just give lip service to it (Titus 2:12); and
30. Pride in a church will always bring it down (1 Pet. 5:5; Prov. 6:17).[5]

Spiritual factors are the most important focus of the congregation. Spiritual churches are led by spiritual leaders, encouraged and equipped by godly pastors. Yet, many pastors struggle to balance ministry demands and spiritual focus. While the best pastors minister out of their spiritual "overflow," many struggle in their spiritual commitments. H. B. London writes in his excellent book *Refresh, Renew, Revive,*

"Weary and worn" is a phrase we often hear from pastors at Focus on the Family. I don't think our colleagues are complaining, I just think they're stressed to the max and need to find a place where they can lean back against a shade tree and relax. One pastor wrote us recently, "I grow weary. . . . I wrestle with my own needs—how to continue fresh in spiritual growth, how to nurture family life, how to be faithful and accountable in my personal life." He probably could have continued with a longer list of things that help to create challenges in every aspect of his ministry. We all could.[6]

Let's face it, ministry is struggle! It always has been and always will be. While God may not have called us to suffer as He called Paul to do in 2 Corinthians 11:24–27, we still feel what he reveals in verses 28–29, "Not to mention other things, there is the daily pressure on me: my care for all the churches. Who is weak, and I am not weak? Who is made to stumble, and I do not burn with indignation?" (2 Cor. 11:28–29).

Your leadership is absolutely essential in guiding your church to be a comeback church. Love for the church and a desire to bring people to Jesus will reinforce and renew your leadership (Matt. 28:18–20). It will not be easy, but "times of refreshing" come from the Lord!

Barna is correct when he writes, "After fifteen years of diligent digging into the world around me, I have reached several conclusions about the future of the Christian church in America. The central conclusion is that the American church is dying due to lack of strong spiritual leadership. In this time of unprecedented opportunity and plentiful resources, the church is actually losing influence. The primary reason is the lack of leadership. Nothing is more important than leadership."[7]

Conclusion

As a pastor or church leader, you are and will always be—under the headship of Jesus—the key to the church. You are the primary shaper of your church's values, beliefs, strategy, and direction. You set the direction for your people. God calls you to focus on both quality and quantity; not just "how many" but also "how well."

So, please don't read the next chapter and try to apply its principles. Instead, pray and get right with the Lord first. Then, read and pray some more about how to lead your church. Then, pray with your church about how they can be more faithful in reaching people for Jesus, whom they love with all their heart.

All of us are busy. Life isn't slowing down, it's speeding up, and our Daytimers reflect the fact. *Yet that is precisely why we need to take time to pray.* It is said that Martin Luther declared he had so much to do, he could not get through it without spending at least three or four hours on his knees before God each morning. Unlike him, we are tempted to think that, when life slows down, then we'll take time to pray. Jean Fleming almost stepped into that trap. Fleming wrote, "I find myself thinking, *When life settles down I'll . . .* But I should have learned by now that life never settles down for long. Whatever I want to accomplish, I must do with life unsettled."[8]

Church leaders get entirely too busy, and prayer is often what is neglected. We are so busy in the work of the Lord we have little time for the Lord of the work. Oswald Chambers puts it all in perspective when he writes, "Remember, no one has time to pray; we have to take time from other things that are valuable in order to understand how necessary prayer is. The things that act like thorns and stings in our personal lives will go away instantly when we pray; we won't feel the smart anymore, because we have God's point of view about them. Prayer means that we get into union with God's view of other people."[9]

One of the most important conclusions we've drawn from our study of comeback churches is that they first had a spiritual experience that redirected and reenergized their lives, beginning with their leader. This spiritual experience gave them a vision of what could—and surely would—be. The vision provided a compelling focus, helping them develop practical and powerful plans. Spiritual empowerment from their ongoing time with God allowed them to persevere in implementing their plans.

God was at work in their church! They had an unwavering sense that what God had called them to do would be accomplished (Phil. 1:6). As the people saw the leader's passion and spiritual fervor, they began to want that in their lives. They sought opportunities to serve, to grow, and to share with others.

The church changed from the inside out. And when it did, the community took notice that something special was happening.

Many churches never experience a comeback because they want the community to change while they remain the same. But comeback churches are different. They realize that no one remains the same when they've experienced a fresh touch from God. Our prayer is that you'll experience God's fresh and mighty touch in your life, your church, and your community.

Suggestions for Further Study

Frost, Michael and Alan Hirsch. *The Shaping of Things to Come: Innovation and Mission for the 21ˢᵗ Century Church* (Peabody, MA: Hendrickson Publishers, 2003).

Gruder, Darrell L., ed. *The Missional Church: A Vision for the Sending of the Church in North America* (Grand Rapids: William B. Eerdmans Publishing Company, 1998).

Mims, Gene. *The Kingdom-Focused Church* (Nashville: Broadman & Holman Publishers, 2003).

Stetzer, Ed and David Putnam. *Breaking the Missional Code: Your Church Can Be a Missionary in Your Community* (Nashville: B & H Publishing Group, 2006).

Why Consider Becoming a Comeback Church?

Harold stood up, paused for a moment, and began to speak softly. "We don't want our church to die. We'll do what it takes." That was when I (Ed) first knew the church could make it. This well-respected, elderly deacon and pillar of the church spoke from his heart. He really meant it, and he was speaking for the church. They were ready to make the big changes that were necessary to rescue their church from decline and eventual death.

Like many churches, this church had its heyday in the 1950s and 60s. Decline had been slow but steady. A church that once served hundreds (and had the building to prove it) presently averaged thirty-five on a Sunday morning. Now, they wanted to reach young families—a difficult task since their median age was in the sixties.

Over time, most churches plateau, and most eventually decline. Typically, they start strong or experience periods of growth, but then they stagnate. Patterns and traditions that once seemed special eventually lose their meaning. Churches that were once outwardly focused eventually become worried about the wrong things. They become more concerned about a well-used policy manual than a well-used baptistry.

In the 1980s, Ross Perot spoke about the national budget deficit as "the crazy aunt living in the basement that nobody wanted to talk about." We have our own "crazy aunt"—hundreds of thousands of dead or dying churches. Like that "crazy aunt," we love her. We want to treat her with dignity. But, ultimately, we think she is hopeless and best ignored.

According to *Leadership Journal,* 340,000 churches are in need of church revitalization.[1] Many of us know the statistics, but few of us care enough to engage these churches. Churches need to change in order to reach their communities, and denominations need to help them. Not every church needs the radical transformation that Harold's church required, but most need a transformation. In the months following Harold's heartfelt commitment and challenge, his church changed its worship style (from traditional to blended/contemporary), its constitution (formerly requiring a churchwide vote for any expenditure over $100), and its outreach strategy (from none to active involvement).

The natural question is, "Who wants a stagnant church?" And the obvious answer is, "Nobody!" Yet, the real truth is that most churches will not make the adjustments and changes necessary to move from stagnation and decline to revitalization and growth. There are many reasons why, and they cannot all be explained here. However, churches with a low baptismal ratio need to initiate and experience change. Doing the same things the same way will not revitalize them. The chart below may help illustrate the need for change and the degree of change required.

	A church needs ...	If it is ...
Less ↑	Refocusing	stagnant in size. (It needs to have a clearer focus on evangelism and outreach.)
	Reenergizing	declining in size. (It needs to deal with some internal issues and begin to reach its community again.)
Change	Restructuring	a church that has experienced substantial decline. (It needs large internal changes and a new outreach strategy).
↓ **More**	Restarting	near death. (A church with a long history of decline that will close if current trends continue. It needs to restart with new leadership or an entirely new church.)

Revitalizing a stagnant church is not easy. If it were, 70 to 80 percent of North American churches would not be stagnant or declining, and 3,500 to 4,000 U.S. churches would not close each year.

Dead and dying churches should concern us all. Today, millions of Christians attend churches that demonstrate little concern for the lost around them. Billions of dollars of church property sit idle and unused. Revitalization is not just about evangelism; it's also a stewardship issue. God has provided many stagnant churches with people, resources, and buildings. God has also given them a calling. He desires them to be more than museums of past glory days.

Many pastors are reading this right now and saying, "That's us! What can we do?" Realize that making a transition requires making change. No one would argue that doing the same things the same old, anemic ways would ever produce different results, although most of the time that is what we see. Yet, many are unable or are afraid to face change. This book can help you think biblically and strategically about how to make needed comeback changes. It starts with recognizing the problem.

How Churches Get Stuck: A Look at the "Dirty Baker's Dozen"

Many are probably familiar with the classic war movie *The Dirty Dozen*. The movie told the story of a group of misfit soldiers who were given the opportunity to prove their worth once again by agreeing to conduct an especially dangerous military mission. The "Dirty Baker's Dozen" in this case illustrates how churches get stuck in plateau and decline. We believe that even some of these misfit churches can get back on mission, experience revitalization, and start growing again. Also, we thought of thirteen types of churches, hence the "baker's dozen." Do any of the following describe your church?

Institutionalized Church. Many churches have regressed into a state of merely functioning as an institution. An institutionalized church focuses on and is more committed to the forms and programs of ministry. It no longer sees the purpose for which the church was created, nor what the church is striving to produce.

In an institutionalized church, the good has become the enemy of the best, and activity has choked out productivity. Please take note that an institutionalized church is not necessarily small. Some of the larger churches in America are perfectly plateaued for this very reason.

Voluntary Association Church. Some churches have become what Lyle Schaller calls "The Voluntary Association Church."[2] The VAC has unwittingly modeled its organization after a democratic government rather than New Testament principles. It is a church of the people, by the people, but most importantly *for* the people. Its purpose is to make sure it retains as many people as possible and keeps any new people in their place. In order for this to become a reality, the board of the church is a balanced set of people who represent opposing factions in the church. Whenever one group seeks to make a positive change in the church in one direction, the opposing factions begin to whine, complain, and gossip. It's a perfect democracy modeled after our government—which most would say does not always work so well. The board then meets in emergency session, and the point is raised that three or four people might leave if the positive change becomes a reality. Then compromises are made and deals are cut so that the church retains the "status quo." Of course, someone has explained that "status quo" is simply Latin for "the mess we're in." Due to an overwhelming need to keep everyone happy, the Volunteer Association Church ends up bound, at the mercy of a rotating vocal minority, and ineffective. This type of church will not change until they change their value system.

Unintentional Church. Many churches mean well, they have good intentions, but do not act on those intentions to reach their community. They may even be willing, but ultimately, they never "do" what they "hope." Unintentional churches do not embrace an intentional process for making disciples of all nations (Matt. 28:18–20). The churches naively believe that as long as they include the ingredients for making disciples—worship, nurture, teaching, outreach—disciples will be produced.

"Us Four and No More" Church. Some churches have adopted an "us four and no more" mentality. They have determined that if they get any larger, they will lose their sweet fellowship. They do not intentionally reject "new" people, but their present relationships are so intimate that any new attendee of the church cannot break into the group. They want a family feel, which means a group small enough to relate like family. Like residents in the suburbs, they don't want anymore people to crowd in once they are there.

"We Can't Compete" Church. Many "stuck" churches have simply given up. Like a family-owned store next to a new Wal-Mart, they have given up on making a difference. They have decided that they cannot "compete," and they stop trying. Unfortunately, they have bought into the idea that the unchurched are only interested in program-rich megachurches. The data here shows that churches of all sizes can turn around and reach the unchurched.

"Decently and in Order" Church. These churches have a high regard for processes but lack passion. They run everything by the book; unfortunately, it's not the Bible. As long as matters great and small meet the approval of various committees and are discussed in minute detail at business meetings, all is well. Unfortunately, they've forgotten—if they ever knew—that the business of the church was given by our Lord in the Great Commission and the Great Commandment.

"Square Peg in a Round Hole" Church. In this congregation, people are enlisted for leadership and service, not by their gifts or passions, but by other criteria. You might hear, "We've got to fill this position. Who can you think of that we've not already talked to?" Someone else may suggest, "He's here all the time. Let's make him an elder." Bankers automatically go on the finance committee, though they have the gift of evangelism or mercy. People are all in their place, but it might not be the right place to help their church reach those around them. The organization stifles the church's impact.

"Time-Warp" Church. Somehow these folks have preserved, not just the tenets of the faith, but the positions, practices, and appearances of years gone by. They may still have an "Intermediate" or "Junior" department. They expect others to adapt and accept what they've grown comfortable with doing, and they give no thought at all to change. The church doesn't seem to attract

people like it did before, but "If it's good enough for me and my family, it should be good enough for them." This church was probably once very effective, but the community has experienced a major transition, leaving the church perplexed, wondering what it should do.

"Tidy" Church. The members take pride in their church. They've worked hard to get it and keep it in its present condition. The buildings, furnishings, and equipment are well kept. The materials are meticulously organized. Everything operates smoothly until noisy youth or messy children begin to come. As outreach efforts continue to draw more exuberant kids and their families, a greater sense of unrest develops. The new growth is suddenly viewed as a threat, leading to efforts to contain it and to prevent further disruptions or damage.

"My Way or the Highway" Church. A number of the members in this church know how things ought to be, and are vocal—maybe even vociferous—in expressing it. They like a certain kind of music. Maybe guitars are out; anthems are in. Or, choir robes are more appropriate than "street clothes" for worship. Comments such as the following abound: "I don't like to stand when we sing." "It's always too hot (or too cold) in here." "I liked it better when we had the announcements in the middle of the service." "The attendance board has always been on that wall." "This is our room and we're not about to move." No matter the issue, these people won't be satisfied unless it's done their way. This is the stereotypical church wherein the senior adults are given the new van to use on their apple orchard trips while the student ministry is asked to drive the old van because "those teenagers are so messy." Young families get the message that their children are unwelcome.

"Chaplaincy" Church. The church hired its minister and expects the "chaplain" to be busy about meeting needs and making the church grow. It's not uncommon to hear a statement like "Preacher, you need to visit Mrs. Gray. She hasn't been feeling well." The members identify the needs and the prospects and expect their pastor to respond. After all, they haven't been to seminary, and that's what he's being paid to do. Despite the fact that the church's ministry impact is limited to the staff's time and abilities,

the church body remains committed to an employer/employee model. They want a hired "chaplain," not a leader.

The "Company" Church. This church is more focused on what is handed down from the denomination than how to reach its community. One after another, the denominational calendar and programs come and the local church seeks to apply them (not realizing that most denominational departments crank out programs like a Ford in the 1970s—too many and not well thought out). So, while denominational departments produce competing materials without communicating with each other, the "Company Church" faithfully seeks to staff every one—while pretty much ignoring its community.

"Play It Safe" Church. Here, there's little faith that God will provide. Rather than enabling ministry and evangelism, it hinders them. The church wants to protect what it has. As much money as possible is placed in a certificate of deposit. But no plan is made to use it to reach others for Christ. It's a safety net that's guarded carefully. Members have little incentive to give. This leads the treasurer and finance committee to conclude that they were wise to protect the "nest egg."

You could probably think of many more, but they all have in common one thing. They have lost the passion for making disciples and the focus of God's glory in His church. Yet, identification is easy. Change is hard.

How Do You Change It?

My (Ed) dad used to tell me, "If it was easy, everybody would be doing it!" He was right. Since 3,500 to 4,000 churches close each year,[3] it is obvious that most churches won't make the turnaround. There are probably two main reasons for this. First, most churches will not admit how bad it is. Second, most churches will not make the needed changes.

This book is about those churches that have done what it takes to make a turnaround. They have faced their bad situation and have made the needed changes. Though once in decline (and not just for a short time), they are now growing again—and growing through evangelism. These churches turned around, and they represent a handful of the churches from each denominational group that are growing. On average, only about 1 percent of the churches in participating denominations qualified for the study. But these are the ones we want to know about. We want your church to join the list of churches reaching those who are without Christ. You want your church to be a comeback church too, or you would not have picked up this book! Our desire is to show you the principles from God's Word and from the experience of others that you can implement in your situation to become another comeback church. This book is about how to make these changes.

Do We Really Need a "Comeback"?

For years, various writers and researchers have reported that the North American church is anemic and lethargic at best. Many believe that Jesus' commentary about Laodicea fits the church in America today, "I know your deeds, that you are neither cold nor hot. I wish you were either one or the other!" (Rev. 3:15 NIV). As early as the mid-1960s, some mainline denominations were apparently in trouble. Peter Wagner stated, "In the ten-year period from 1965 to 1975 the Episcopal church lost 17 percent of its membership or 575,000 persons. The United Presbyterians lost 12 percent or 375,000 members. The United Methodists lost 10 percent or 1,100,000 members, and so on."[4]

|||||||||||||||||||||||||||||||||||||||||||||||||||||||
You can download a PowerPoint with these statistics at www.comebackchurches.com

In more recent years, more and more evangelical churches have shown signs of plateau and decline. In his book *Vision America*, Aubrey Malphurs asserted that much of the perceived church growth in the 1970s, 1980s, and 1990s was actually due primarily to the redistribution of believers, not genuine church growth. He stated, "The problems of the church in the 1980s carry over into the 1990s. The church as a whole continues to experience decline and the unchurched increase."[5]

State of the Church in North America Today

How serious is the challenge facing the church today? Aren't the activities of worship, fellowship, preaching, and outreach making disciples and changing the lives of people? Let's look at some of those who were courageous enough to participate in this study.

Denominational Examples

Here are a few examples to help us see the situation. They are not intended to be compared (not all the denominations count exactly the same) and they are certainly not for bragging purposes. But they do illustrate that evangelicals are in decline in North America, and something needs to change! We could include all the denominations, but these should illustrate.

Assemblies of God: The Assemblies of God is often listed as a fast-growing denomination, but they, too, have many declining churches. For the reporting years 2004 and 2005, 36 percent of the Assemblies of God churches that opened prior to 2001 experienced growth (10.1% or more) in Sunday a.m. worship attendance compared with almost 41 percent of their churches experiencing a decline (-10.1% or more). Just over 22 percent remained steady during the same time period.[6] That means about two-thirds of Assemblies of God churches have plateaued or declined during that time period.

Nazarene: Since 1995, the Nazarenes had 1,551 existing churches grow by 10 percent or more and 2,620 decline or close during that same time period. Staying close to the same, they had 3,889 churches plateau over the past ten years.[7] About 80 percent of Nazarene churches are plateaued or declining since 1995.

Southern Baptists: Although about 70 percent of SBC churches are plateaued or declining, the plateaued number does not tell the whole story for Southern Baptists or any of the other denominations studied. Most recently, the Leavell Center at New Orleans Baptist Theological Seminary did a study revealing that only 11 percent of Southern Baptist churches were experiencing healthy growth. The Leavell Center used the following criteria to define healthy churches:

1. The church experienced 10 percent total membership growth over five years.
2. The church baptized at least one person during the two years of the study.

3. These churches needed thirty-five or fewer members each year to baptize one new convert (a member-to-baptism ratio of thirty-five or less in the final year of the study).

4. For the final year of the study, the percentage of growth that was conversion growth must be at least 25 percent.[8]

Moreover, the number of baptisms in the Southern Baptist Convention (SBC) has been relatively flat for the last fifty years.[9]

The Growing Numbers of Unchurched

In 2002, George Barna's research indicated that 95 to 100 million Americans of all ages were unchurched[10] (approximately one third of the population), an estimate that was based upon a very generous definition of "unchurched."[11] In another study, the Barna Group explained, "Since 1991, the adult population in the United States has grown by 15%. During that same period the number of adults who do not attend church has nearly doubled, rising from 39 million to 75 million—a 92% increase!"[12] Overall, Barna's research has not indicated that churches in North America were healthy and growing.

When using a different methodology, we see numbers that are of even greater concern. According to "Special Report: The American Church in Crisis" in *Outreach Magazine,* "Less than 20% of Americans regularly attend church—half of what the pollsters report. While Gallup polls and other statisticians have turned in the same percentage—about 40% of the population—of average weekend church attendees for the past 70 years, a different sort of research paints quite a disparate picture of how many Americans attend a local church on any given Sunday."[13]

According to Dave Olson, a researcher with the Evangelical Covenant Church, who was cited in the previous article, "church attendance from head counts is less than half of the 40% the pollsters report. Numbers from actual counts of people in orthodox Christian churches (Catholic, mainline, and evangelical) show that in 2004, 17.7% of the population attended a Christian church on any given weekend." Another scholarly study backs up his study, stating "that the actual number of people worshipping each week is closer to Olson's 17.7% figure—52 million people instead of the pollster-reported 132 million (40%)."[14]

Of course, one reason for the conflicting data is the difference between how people want to be perceived versus what they actually do. People claim that they do more "good things" than they really do. Regardless, the point is that change is needed.

Of those churches that are "growing," most of the growth is from transfer growth and not the result of making an impact among the unchurched. Transfer growth occurs when a church receives members from another Christian church who "transfer" their church membership. This type of growth may increase the rolls of a local church, but it does not enlarge the kingdom of God.

The current twenty-first-century context in the United States presents a constant challenge to churches. George Hunter wrote way back in 1978, "In the USA, only about 20 percent of the nation's 360,000 churches are growing, and 19 of the 20 are growing mostly by biological growth . . . or transfer growth."[15] I (Ed) recently asked him for an updated statistic hoping it was better, but it was not. Hunter explained, "Now, *less* than 1 in 20 would be growing substantially by conversion growth."[16]

Stagnant or Stuck?

The statistics are true, and there's no denying them. But they prompt important questions: *Why can't established churches stay focused and effective? How can established churches reignite their passion for outreach and refocus on their purpose?* It isn't easy. If it were easy, 70 percent of North American churches wouldn't be stagnant or shrinking, stuck on a plateau or sliding into decline.

Based upon the results of the comeback surveys, it is apparent that churches desiring a comeback will need to *make changes* in order to start growing again. Whether those changes occur through rekindling Jesus' mission for the church, mobilizing the laity, focusing on leadership development, engaging in more strategic prayer efforts, increasing evangelistic emphases, or making other needed changes, business as usual will continue to produce the same slow or no-growth environment that plagues the large majority of churches.

We believe that a stagnant, plateaued, or declining church needs to do several things to change that pattern. We heard from many different leaders that they led their church on this kind of similar journey. The steps are simple to identify but difficult to apply. The church will need to have an honest evaluation of their current condition, get the church working together for a common solution, and determine what to do together.

Evaluate Your Church's Current Condition

As you read this book, be honest. Take off any blinders and take a long look at your church. Is it where you want it to be? Take a hard look at the way things really are. Step out of slow or no growth denial. The first step in getting unstuck is to acknowledge that your church is stuck in the muck of stagnation or decline.

For tools and instruments to help you evaluate your church's current condition, go to www.comeback churches.com.

We are often surprised that few are willing to look clearly at their own situation and conduct an honest appraisal. We probably shouldn't be. Most of us struggle with being honest about ourselves or our churches. But the first step of church revitalization is to be like the "men of Issachar" who understood the times and knew what Israel should do (1 Chron. 12:32).

The enemy of God would love nothing more than to have biblical churches be ineffective, defeated, declining, and doing nothing about it. Let's remember that we are in a spiritual battle raging for the hearts and souls of people! That's why it is imperative that we follow our Lord's desires in the battle: "Be sober! Be on the alert! Your adversary the Devil is prowling around like a roaring lion, looking for anyone he can devour. Resist him, firm in the faith, knowing that the same sufferings are being experienced by your brothers in the world" (1 Pet. 5:8–9).

Think honestly for just a moment: do the names of several people who have come to Christ through your church in the last year immediately spring to mind? Is the community in which

God has placed your church "brighter" and "saltier" because of your church's influence? How many people living within driving distance of your church have received a clear presentation of the gospel? We exhort you to evaluate the true effectiveness of your church and "Come back to your senses as you ought, and stop sinning; for there are some who are ignorant of God—I say this to your shame" (1 Cor. 15:34 NIV).

Being a good leader means being a godly person of influence. Comeback leaders influence their churches to strive for something more than the present stagnation. Erwin McManus puts it this way: "Manipulation is the use of influence to control others for personal gain. It is the dark side of influence. . . . While manipulation is inherently evil, influence is the best way to lead and move others toward what is good."[17] Comeback leaders use honest church evaluation and godly influence to motivate their congregations to change.

Involve Many People in the Church

Pastor Aaron Blache of First Church of the Nazarene, Hartford, Connecticut, led in the revitalization of five churches. When asked about challenges, he had this to say: "People don't want to work when a church is struggling. They let the pastor do the work then; when he is successful, they want to take over."[18] Blache has resisted this by getting people involved through the utilization of their gifts. Church members "bought into" the change because they were serving together.

Most of the churches in North America need a new approach, a new philosophy, and a new passion. Yet, most won't make the change. Most of those that try will not succeed. Why? Because too many pastors will see the need for change but will be unable to convince their churches to make the changes that are necessary.

Most pastors reading this believe that the church exists, at least in part, to fulfill the Great Commission, "Go, therefore, and make disciples of all nations, baptizing them in the name of the Father and of the Son and of the Holy Spirit, teaching them to observe everything I have commanded you. And remember, I am with you always, to the end of the age" (Matt. 28:19–20). But the average person in a church believes that the church exists to meet his or her needs and the needs of the family. Even though most people coming to a church for the first time cannot articulate this verse, they are probably thinking something similar to what James and John said to Jesus, "Then James and John, the sons of Zebedee, came to him. 'Teacher,' they said, '*we want you to do for us whatever we ask*'" (Mark 10:35 NIV, emphasis added). Each week people show up telling the church, many times, "We want you to do for us whatever we ask." Usually that means solving all issues of relational strife within families, meeting each individual's specific needs, having great youth and children's ministries, teaching deep, powerful truths from God's Word in fifteen minutes or less that answer all their questions about God, providing a vibrant, dynamic worship experience . . . and, of course, get it all done before the game begins at noon. It is an unwritten contract of sorts. No wonder it is hard to get the congregation to buy into a compelling vision.

Comeback leaders have recognized that the congregation has to be part of the turnaround. Your church may not be a congregational church. Not all the churches in our study would identify themselves as "congregational" in their church government. But, honestly, every church is. People vote every Sunday—with their feet and with their money. If a church makes too many changes without the consent and the participation of its people, the people in that church will very quickly conduct a church vote. People will "elect" to stop giving and, eventually, vote not to come anymore.

Churches wanting change must discuss, discuss, discuss. The church really needs to take a realistic look at its current effectiveness. This does not mean just the pastor and lay leaders. The entire church must embrace its current state before it can move forward. It needs to take an honest look at its current situation so that it can make an honest effort toward revitalization.

It won't be simple. There are systems issues that will need to be addressed. This might involve an outside consultant or denominational leader, some reading on the part of the congregation, and/or a self-study. Issues might include:
- The spiritual dynamic
- Congregational dysfunction

- Inadequate leadership
- Faulty or nonexistent processes
- Lack of vision
- Or many others

It is necessary, helpful, and biblical to lead the entire congregation to recognize the problem(s) and envision necessary changes. It is important to take the time to talk about everything and discuss possible solutions. The churches that made comebacks were those that understood together what it would take. Not everyone has to agree, but some must.

The Scriptures model such a process, as seen in the troubling situation in Acts 6:

> In those days, as the number of the disciples was multiplying, there arose a complaint by the Hellenistic Jews against the Hebraic Jews that their widows were being overlooked in the daily distribution. Then the Twelve summoned the whole company of the disciples and said, "It would not be right for us to give up preaching about God to wait on tables. Therefore, brothers, select from among you seven men of good reputation, full of the Spirit and wisdom, whom we can appoint to this duty. But we will devote ourselves to prayer and to the preaching ministry." The proposal pleased the whole company. So they chose Stephen, a man full of faith and the Holy Spirit, and Philip, Prochorus, Nicanor, Timon, Parmenas, and Nicolaus, a proselyte from Antioch. (Acts 6:1–5)

Notice the apostles brought everyone together and identified the challenge. A team was selected to deal with the challenge, and people were empowered for ministry. The challenge was a catalyst for growth instead of a cause for division. It unified instead of divided.

If your church is like most churches, one of your greatest obstacles to growth is not one of vision but of *visions*. Every person who attends or has attended your church has an idea of what the church should be or do. "Where there is no vision, the people are unrestrained" (Prov. 29:18a NASB). Through this book, we are not only going to show you *what* the marks of a comeback church are, we are also going to give you some practical tracks to run on in order to effectively apply these principles in your own situation. That leads to our third point:

Decide on a Course of Action

Change requires decision making, and decision making requires action. Most churches don't make turnarounds because they never get to the action. Discussion only begets more discussion. Together, and led by the pastor, the church must decide on a course of action. Choosing a course of action sounds easy, but it isn't. It may require a change of style, location, systems, leadership, or plan. It certainly will involve a new plan for evangelism. All great ideas eventually turn into hard work.

Make specific plans to enable new growth to take place. The majority of church members need to be involved in the change or it will soon produce resistance. An old proverb says, "Those who row the boat have little time to rock the boat."

In most cases, it will be hard. Opposition is natural, even after the church has decided on a new course of action. **Change sounds great until you start to experience it.** But, a course must be set, and then it must be navigated.

Conclusion

If you are willing to set sail on a new course of action, *Comeback Churches* will help you chart that course and navigate the waters of change. The 324 churches described here will help you to think about your own church and what it will take to turn it around.

To make such a change will not be easy; but not to make a change will result in disaster. The pain of the present must exceed the pain of change in order for you to succeed in applying these biblical principles to your own church. Our prayer is that the name and fame of Christ might become more widely known because you will choose to chart a course for change and lead a comeback church. Why? Because the church matters for at least these reasons (and for many more):

    1. The church is the only institution that our Lord promised to build and to bless (Matt. 16:18).

2. The church is the gathering place of true worshippers (Phil. 3:3).

3. The church is the most precious assembly on earth since Christ purchased it with His own blood (Acts 20:28; 1 Cor. 6:19; Eph. 5:25; Col. 1:20; 1 Pet. 1:18; Rev. 1:5).

4. The church is the earthly expression of the heavenly reality (Matt. 6:10; 18:18).

5. The church will ultimately triumph both universally and locally (Matt. 16:18; Phil. 1:6).

6. The church is the realm of spiritual fellowship (Heb. 10:22–25; 1 John 1:3, 6–7).

7. The church is the proclaimer and protector of divine truth (1 Tim. 3:15; Titus 2:1, 15).

8. The church is the chief place for spiritual edification and growth (Acts 20:32; Eph. 4:11–16; 2 Tim. 3:16–17; 1 Pet. 2:1–2; 2 Pet. 3:18).

9. The church is the launching pad for world evangelization (Mark 16:15; Titus 2:11).

10. The church is the environment where strong spiritual leadership develops and matures (2 Tim. 2:2).[19]

Suggestions for Further Study

Lewis, Robert, Wayne Cordeiro, and Warren Bird. *Culture Shift: Transforming Your Church from the Inside Out* (San Francisco: Jossey-Bass, 2005).

McManus, Erwin Raphael. *Seizing Your Divine Moment: Dare to Live a Life of Adventure* (Nashville: Nelson Books, 2002).

Rainer, Thom, and Eric Geiger. *Simple Church: Returning to God's Process for Making Disciples* (Nashville: B & H Publishers, 2006).

Roberts, Wes and Glenn Marshall. *Reclaiming God's Original Intent for the Church* (Colorado Springs: NavPress, 2004).

Rising with Leadership

New Hope Community Church, an Assembly of God church in Marlborough, Massachusetts, had experienced great pain in its recent history. Emotional healing was needed, and it was Pastor Woods's job to lead the congregation to that point. He explained, "Everything I did was bathed in much prayer. Instead of preaching against the people's shortcomings, I listened to their needs and preached accordingly. . . . I sent cards with Scriptures of encouragement as well as giving encouraging phone calls weekly. [And] . . . I never joined in the attacks against the former pastor." Pastor Woods said that he immediately established an atmosphere of leadership and of expectation by letting the people know "just exactly what I expected of them and what they should expect of me. Whenever they didn't live up to those expectations, I called them on it, and I told them to do the same to me. We didn't all change immediately, but over time, people knew I meant business."

Let's face it—"everything rises and falls on leadership" is a cliché. We hate clichés, but we can't help pointing out that they often reflect reality. Leadership was rated as the number one factor by the churches that experienced revitalization. Leadership and vision are major keys to any type of turnaround in churches.

We wanted to put "spiritual" factors first, thinking it would better reflect a God-centeredness in our approach. But, we let the data set the agenda, and godly leadership was at the top.

On the surface, leadership seems to be more of a secular emphasis or reality than a spiritual endeavor. However, the Bible often reflects the fact that God calls people and uses them to fulfill His purposes. There is no denying that leaders like Moses, Joshua,

David, Nehemiah, Gideon, Jesus, Peter, Paul, Deborah, Priscilla, and many others in the Bible were leaders. So, maybe leadership is truly as much of a spiritual factor as renewed belief, servant-hood, and strategic prayer. Good biblical leadership requires being a devoted Christ follower.

Leaders Matter

Leaders matter for church revitalization. *Leadership Journal* studied 761 respondents from thirty-one churches to analyze the factors leading to church revitalization. They found five key factors, the first of which was helping the church get honest about its condition. They said that, "Turnaround leaders distinguish between obvious symptoms and underlying problems. The first step is helping the congregation admit there is a problem, and find the underlying (foundational) causes."[1]

It took leadership to help these churches see the real issues involved. An analogy of an infant might help illustrate:

An infant is learning to crawl. She begins by push-ing herself backward around the house. Backing herself around, she gets lodged beneath the furniture. There she thrashes about—crying and banging her little head against the sides and undersides of the pieces. She is stuck and hates it. So she does the only thing she can think of to get herself out—she pushes even harder, which only worsens her problem. She's more stuck than ever.

If this infant could talk, she would blame the furni-ture for her troubles. She, after all, is doing everything she can think of. The problem couldn't be hers. But of course, the problem is hers, even though she can't see it. While it's true she's doing everything she can think of, the problem is precisely that she can't see how she's the problem. Having the problem she has, nothing she can think of will be a solution.

Self-deception is like this. It blinds us to the true cause of problems, and once blind, all the "solutions" we can think of will actually make matters worse. That's why self-deception is so central to leadership—because leadership is about making matters better. To the extent we are self-deceived, our leadership is undermined at every turn—and not because of the furniture.[2]

Leaders help churches see that their real problems are spiritual.

At the same time, we rejoiced to find that Three Faith Factors surfaced next (see the next chapter). Yet, it required leadership to create an atmosphere for revitalization in these comeback churches.

By leadership, we do not mean just the pastor. But it does start with the pastor. Pastors have to be leaders and have to develop others to lead. Both are essential, and we found that leadership was the number-one factor associated with turnarounds.

Pastor Maurice "Mo" Seneca of the First Assembly of God in Des Allemands, Louisiana[3] played football in high school and college. He saw leaders and followers in action and has seen the principles at work. Leaders have to lead . . . and they have to motivate others to lead.

Seneca explained that leadership expert John Maxwell was a key influence in his life. He stated, "*The Twenty-One Irrefutable Laws of Leadership* helped mold me into the leader I am today. I am more informed and try to put everything I learn into practice. I mentor leaders to deal with problems that I don't need to deal with, which lightens my load tremendously."[4] Referring to Maxwell, Pastor Seneca said, "Management is doing things right. Leadership is doing the right things." He then said, "I'd much rather do the right things."[5]

"I had to wake up!" That's what Pastor Cere of Angleton Foursquare in Texas finally realized. If his church was going to realize its growth potential, he would definitely need to climb out on the limb of leadership. That is the challenge that many pastors and other church leaders face—am I willing to become all that I need to be as a leader where God has placed me? Am I willing to take the risk and learn to become a more effective leader?

In some circles, the term "leadership" has frightening connotations. Many people do not want to be identified with the term and its perceived responsibilities. They want to have a position of leadership without possessing a desire to become a real leader. In reality, leadership can be an overwhelming responsibility and it needs to be approached with a great deal of humility and seriousness. God makes a profound statement about leadership in 1 Timothy—"It is a trustworthy statement: if any man aspires to the office of overseer, it is a fine work he desires to do" (3:1 NASB).

So while aspiring to leadership can certainly be a joyful and worthy ambition, leadership requires action in order to rise above the level of mediocrity and casual existence. It requires growth, change, work, and courage. In a recent interview, church and leadership expert Lyle Schaller asserted, "The final thing leaders will need is courage . . . the willingness to tell the truth, to say what is not politely or politically acceptable. . . . The most common expression of the courage to tell the truth is to say, 'It ain't workin'.'"[6] Many of the comeback church leaders had to be willing to say, "It ain't workin'" and chart a new course, cast a new vision, and call God's people to sail toward a new destination.

To better understand the vital importance of leadership, it is important to define the term. Many simply define leadership as influence, and active leadership certainly results in that. Others say that leadership is doing the right things in an effective manner, while others define it in terms of being able to manage the chaos of a rapidly changing world. Leadership is all of those things and more, but primarily, leadership involves how we interact with ourselves, God, family, friends, coworkers, partners in ministry, and the world around us.

Leadership—What Is It?

Comeback churches were always led by strong leaders. Christian or biblical leadership can be defined as:

1. A person
2. involved in a process
3. of influencing and developing a group of people
4. in order to accomplish a purpose
5. by means of supernatural power.[7]

When asked, "Was your church's comeback affected by strong leadership?" the large majority of comeback leaders said that it was. We wanted to know more specifics. "If strong leadership had a major effect, please describe the leadership factors that affected the comeback (such as being more proactive, sharing ministry, more intentional planning, change in attitude toward growth, specific training, style change, etc.)." Comeback leaders offered many responses, including:

- Without strong leadership [a church] cannot move.
- Declaring a vision of what God could do—in the past [there was] no big dream.
- Leaders became proactive in getting people to share ministry.
- Leaders caught and carried the vision; attitude change caused others to seek growth.
- "No-nonsense" approach to leadership; leaders are proactive and excited about ministry; made ministry enjoyable.
- Leaders emphasizing evangelism; preaching about and challenging members to evangelize.
- Leaders share ministry; empower people; challenge them to try new things to achieve growth.
- Pastor trained leaders; leaders are gifted at getting people to understand vision.
- Individual leaders set specific goals for each ministry; casting and maintaining vision.
- Leaders catching vision and transferring to members.
- Leaders are concerned for lost; want to be involved and want to get others involved.
- Pastor exercised biblical principles of leadership—asked some board members to step down.
- Leaders take action to make sure people are involved.
- Leader training; planning; casting and maintaining vision.

In analyzing these and other responses from comeback leaders, several issues rose to the surface—being proactive and intentional, sharing ministry, changing attitudes toward growth, and activating a shared vision.

Proactive Leadership

Comeback leaders took the initiative for change. Pastor Stephen Sinclair of River City Wesleyan Church in Bangor, Maine, had revitalization experiences in three smaller churches (each older than seventy-five years) and two church plants. He says there are different things that are unique to each. "In younger churches, it is easier to establish an effective key leadership team that really buys into the vision. . . . However, discipleship is harder because not many people were churched before. In the older churches you initially have to deal with people always saying, 'we've never done it this way.' The major keys have been strong pastoral leadership and effective lifestyle and outreach evangelism. Every church I've been a part of has seen the need for change in order to become healthy and grow."[8] Pastor Sinclair understood that leading a church out of a rut requires proactive and intentional leadership.

Many comeback leaders stated that a key issue in effective, revitalizing leadership was proactive leadership that utilized intentional planning. These leaders refused to be passive. They were willing to make changes. In addition, the comeback process involved setting goals. These leaders understood the old proverb—"When you aim at nothing, you will hit it every time." Establishing tangible growth goals was a key in getting other leaders involved in the revitalization process in these comeback churches.

One thing we've learned in ministry: It's hard to continue reaching new people with the gospel. It's hard to keep a vision before the people. Believers get busy. Churches lose focus. But evangelism must remain a priority or transformation will not occur. Comeback leaders have learned intentional ways to make a difference—and we have suggested a few below.

Challenge Excuses

Let's start with wrong attitudes, such as this one: We don't need more believers; we need better believers. To some, this sounds so right. It's a plea to spend more time on discipleship than evangelism. But discipleship and evangelism go hand in hand, and mature believers know this by studying Jesus' last words. Anyone's last words are important, especially those of our Lord Jesus Christ. The Great Commission—to make both more *and* better disciples—is unquestionably the most important directive given to the church. No other command gets as much emphasis in Scripture, being stated no less than five times (Matt. 28:18–20; Mark 16:15; Luke 24:46–49; John 20:21; Acts 1:8). Our mission is to make more *and* better followers of Jesus Christ *simultaneously.* A disciple who grows spiritually will have a growing desire to be a witness and reach out to those who are lost.

Pray Matthew 9:37–38 Regularly and Passionately

This is simple, but are we really doing it? Jesus told His disciples: "The harvest is plentiful but the workers are few. Ask the Lord of the harvest, therefore, to send out workers into his harvest field" (NIV). In other words, "Hey folks, there are souls out there to be harvested and brought into the Kingdom. There's just one little problem. We don't have enough people willing to get out there in the harvest field and work."

What does Jesus identify as the simple solution to this huge problem? *Prayer.* Ask the Lord to address this need. And really, *ask* is not a strong enough word here. It's more like beg, plead, or petition. It means to beg in such a way that you bind yourself to the request. What are we to beg for? That God will raise up and call out people to go into the fields of humanity to seek and to save those who are separated from God. We will spend more time on prayer in the next chapter, but teaching people to pray leads them to see the needs.

See the Harvest

Jesus said something similar about the harvest in John 4:35, "Don't you say, 'There are still four more months, then comes the harvest'? Listen [to what] I'm telling you: Open your eyes and look at the fields, for they are ready for harvest." In his book *Cultivating a Life for God,* Neil Cole reflects on Jesus' statements about the harvest this way:

- If we can't see them, we won't love them (Matt. 9:36).
- If we can't love them, we won't pray for them (Matt. 9:36–38).

- If we can't pray for them, we won't win them
  (Matt. 10:1).
- If we can't win them, we won't send them
  (Matt. 10:2–5).

We have to see them in the harvest fields. Why? Because in seeing them, we can have compassion for them. Do we really take the time to grasp what it means for people to be lost, separated from God, spiritually condemned, bound to sin, and without hope? Maybe the first thing we need to pray about is for God to help us *see* the huge field of people waiting to be harvested and to give us an incredible love for those people. Then, we'll be ready to pray for them, win them, and send them back into the harvest field.

Before people begin to see their opportunities to be witnesses, they have to *really see* the people standing around them in the harvest field—not with physical eyes but with spiritual eyes. Then, we will truly grasp what it means for people to be lost, separated from God, spiritually condemned, bound to sin, and without hope.

When we see them and have compassion for them, we also begin to realize that people are open and responsive to the gospel. They are *ripe* for the harvest. Multiple studies have demonstrated that people are open to Christ and to His church if invited. Regrettably, too few of us have our eyes truly open to what God wants to accomplish.

Model Evangelistic Passion

Comeback churches care about the things God cares about. They display that "lost people matter to God" by the way they live, pray, and witness. This challenges and encourages others around them to live the same way.

In *Building a Contagious Church* (Zondervan, 2000), Mark Mittelberg shares one reason Willow Creek is an evangelistic church. Pastor Bill Hybels consistently models it in his own life. "Bill made a decision to participate in sailboat racing with a completely non-Christian crew. Recently Bill informed our congregation that the fourth person from his racing team circle made a commitment to Christ after one of our holiday outreach services. Then, during our summer baptism service we all watched Bill baptize Dave in our pond. This kind of experience obviously will keep Bill motivated, but it also inspires the rest of us."

Maybe boating isn't your thing. Maybe your interest is hunting, fishing, crafting, cars, scrapbooking, or something else. Use it to spend time with lost people and help them come to know Christ too. Then, tell your church about it. What you do and what you talk about shows people what you truly value.

Sharing Ministry

Comeback leaders shared the ministry. Being an effective leader involved the process of getting the people connected in the ministry of the church. Repeatedly, comeback leaders mentioned shared ministry as a key to effective leadership. They emphasized the importance of intentionally training and empowering God's people to fulfill their ministry purpose in serving the body of Christ and reaching out to the lost. Comeback leaders worked to develop and promote an atmosphere of teamwork.

Eugene McBride, executive pastor for Lakeshore Assembly of God[9] in Rockwall, Texas, explained how they transitioned to shared ministry. McBride explained, "We hired a secretary with experience, so no training was necessary. We also hired a custodian with experience. The pastor trained key leaders and let them lead some meetings that were really unnecessary for him to attend."[10] We heard stories like that from many of the respondents. Pastors adjusted their schedules to spend more time developing leaders and spurring an attitudinal change toward growth. Sharing ministry meant that leaders were willing to change both attitudes and responsibilities.

Leaders and Attitudes

Comeback leaders made choices about those in whom they invested their time and how they invested their time. They reordered their priorities to spend time with other leaders and created a change in those leaders' attitudes toward growth.

It takes strong, committed leadership to change people's attitudes, which result in comeback congregations. Negative attitudes such as slow or no-growth thinking, or small church mind-sets had to be confronted by comeback leaders. Pastors of comeback churches accomplished this by removing growth barriers, overcoming self-defeating attitudes, casting a God-sized vision, and raising expectations.

Leaders and Responsibilities

Comeback leaders quickly gave away nonministry tasks. Two areas surfaced in relation to nonministry tasks: building maintenance and administrative duties. How did the churches and pastors transition from previous ways of handling these responsibilities? What specific tasks were removed? Did the pastors have difficulty letting go of these responsibilities? Did they intentionally train up people to lead in these areas?

Delegation was a consistent theme from comeback pastors. Bob Biehl has written, "In determining your leadership competence, your ability to delegate effectively is far more important than your innate intelligence."[11] Pastor Tony Haefs of Gillionville Baptist Church[12] in Augusta, Georgia, saw that clearly. He was able to delegate administration—a time-consuming task—freeing him to concentrate on reaching the lost. His church hired a secretary who took over all administrative duties (phone calls, scheduling, paperwork, etc.). Pastor Haefs is not a natural administrator, so he gladly gave up these duties. Since the secretary had secular experience, no training was necessary.[13]

Data revealed that a number of pastors changed their weekly schedules as their churches grew. We looked at these changes by asking two questions: "What led you to change?" and "How specifically did you change your habits and time management?"

As lay leaders came forward, Vernon Johnson, pastor of Trion Heights Baptist Church in Trion, Georgia, made dramatic changes in his schedule. Pastor Johnson said, "I went from counseling, reconciling relationships, and putting a lot of my time into studying the Word to less study time and more focus on lay leader training." The men's, women's, children's and youth ministries are all lay led now. The deacons have taken over visitation and coordinating building projects at the church and members' homes.[14]

Less study time can be a concern. We are not advocating abandoning the study of God's Word, but some respondents said they had focused a disproportionate amount of time on study, consuming too much of their ministry. Conversely, as part of the changes made, at least 40 percent (the largest response in the category) said they spent *more* time in sermon preparation, not less. These leaders freed themselves up for more study, more leadership training, and more evangelism.

John Shamblin, pastor of Briarwood Church[15] in Cordova, Tennessee, said his church's growth effected the change. "The addition of the music, youth, education and children's pastors required leadership training, staff management, and group prayer times. The growth required more outreach and visitation. Personal prayer time and sermon preparation time also had to be scheduled differently."[16]

You can't change a church without changing your schedule. But priorities reflect in calendars as much as they do in the mission statement. Comeback church leaders are willing to pay the price to make schedule change happen.

Intentional Planning

Comeback leaders intentionally used their time and the time of others differently. When we asked, "What areas received a greater priority or emphasis of time for the pastor (sermon preparation, personal evangelism, prayer, training members, etc.) and how?" we found that they refocused their time in two key ways.

Many planned to spend additional time focusing more on study and message preparation. Even though time demands and responsibilities increase as growth takes place, many of the comeback pastors still made sermon preparation a priority. This meant that some responsibilities were given away to others.

"My schedule changes came about as a result of our growth," said Brian Moss, pastor of Oak Ridge Baptist Church in Salisbury, Maryland.[17] As the church grew, more people became involved in leadership, requiring more meetings during the week for service planning. Pastor Moss also met with his staff an hour and a half before the Sunday morning service for prayer. Making time for personal prayer and concentrated sermon preparation times was difficult, but vitally important to continued personal and corporate growth.

Comeback leaders intentionally planned to spend more

time doing "people stuff." They spent more time doing visitation, staff management, mentoring, leadership training, and counseling. They invested in leaders and in the lost. (Let us suggest that you should make this adjustment to your schedule now. Begin to make minor changes that will allow you as the leader to begin showing the fruit of such changes to the people of your church.)

Pastor Harry Austin of the First Assembly of God in Millerton, Oklahoma, made schedule changes in order to meet the growing demands of people's needs. "The schedule change was partially because of the growth. I had to make time for concentrated prayer for the needs of my people. I also had to create more time for hospital and new prospect visitation."[18]

As growth occurred, many comeback churches were also in a position to hire new staff members, which meant the need to manage more people. The growth meant more people to visit in the hospital and new prospects to visit. These comeback leaders saw the need to train lay leaders for a higher level of ministry involvement and commitment, which ultimately relieved time constraints and responsibilities on comeback pastors.

Often, leadership is more about what you can get done through others than what you can do yourself. Comeback leaders began to understand this principle and found ways to train others to use their time, talents, and treasures to fulfill ministry needs.

There was no indication that comeback leaders manipulated or "guilted" people into doing things. They promoted a vision for growth, trained people, and multiplied ministry among the people. This allowed the pastors to utilize their time differently.

Vision

Comeback leaders agreed that having a clear and compelling vision was foundational in the transformation of their churches. Casting the vision with other leaders and with the congregation was an integral part of their leadership. Through vision casting, a sense of unity developed as other leaders embraced a new sense of urgency about church growth and reaching the lost. Comeback congregations shared vision, unity, and ministry, at least in part, because of strong, effective leadership.

Pastors face the "vision challenge" every day. They must cast a vision so that people can respond. People only "get on board" when they see the boat. God uses this vision to help us commit our time, talent, and treasure to the cause. Anytime we call people to commit to a strategy, we must cast vision. It is essential in church revitalization.

Why We Need Vision

Goals, mission statements, or commitments to biblical purposes do not necessarily indicate that a church has vision. Vision is not adhering to statements—it is recognizing and committing to something bigger than you. Comeback leaders guide their churches to such vision. The vision is not for some abstract idea of "church growth," but, instead, it is a vision for making disciples.

People will follow vision because they are interested in committing to something worthwhile. Yet, so often our churches do not call people to life-changing visions and are surprised that the commitment level is so low. We need to cast and promote big visions that people will commit to and follow with enthusiasm. These visions need to be ones that matter. As Andy Stanley has explained: "There is always a moral element to vision. Vision carries with it a sense of conviction. Anyone with a vision will tell you this is not merely something that *could* be done. This is something that *should* be done. This is something that must happen. It is this element that catapults men and women out of the realm of passive concern and into action. It is the moral element that gives a vision a sense of urgency."[19]

What Vision Is

Vision has a variety of meanings in the Old and New Testaments. Vision comes from faith and allows a church to be or to do something beyond its current abilities to impact the Kingdom. It is a vision of faith, the "evidence of things hoped for, the substance of things not seen" (Heb. 11:1 NIV). Though these things cannot be seen physically, they must be seen mentally and spiritually if people are to commit themselves to the task.

We commonly ask children a vision question: "What do you want to be when you grow up?" We encourage them to have a picture of the future. We hope that our children will have a great "picture" that will begin to influence the order of their lives.

Pastors often sense that God has given them a great picture of the future. That, too, can be a vision (though it is too often a dream or just a wish). The challenge is to lead God's people to share in seeking that desired future place. The vision might be to reach specific people at a given time. Fulfillment of the vision might include a specific event, task, or program. Whatever God's vision for a particular church, that vision must reactivate the church's heart for the community.

When to Share Vision

When it comes to church revitalization, the works of author and businessman W. Clement Stone are helpful. While speaking of business, his remarks are equally applicable to the church: "I think there is something, more important than believing: Action! The world is full of dreamers, there aren't enough who will move ahead and begin to take concrete steps to actualize their vision."

Andy Stanley observes, "All God ordained visions are shared visions. Nobody goes it alone. But God generally raises up a point person to paint a compelling verbal picture. A picture that captures the hearts and imaginations of those whom God is calling to embrace the task at hand."

Many pastors have a clear understanding and direction regarding a vision. They find it frustrating that church members seem less enthusiastic about that vision. The visionary leader faces the challenge of convincing followers to own the vision. Vision is not vision unless it is shared; it is merely a dream. Comeback leaders led their churches to achieve a "Comeback Vision."

A vision must be credible. Since the vision caster is probably you, the church must trust you and its other leaders. The congregation's experience with its leadership helps them have the confidence necessary to follow the leaders' direction. As a leader, you have a "credibility tank." Every

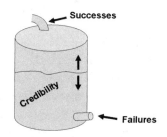

time you have a success, you add to that tank. As you add to the credibility tank, you make it possible to cast an even larger vision. On the other hand, each time you fail, your tank is drained. Then you have to restore that credibility before pressing on to a new task. Build your credibility by casting a progressively larger vision. Begin with small victories. Celebrate what God has done through your people. Whenever possible, throw a party at church to help your people see that growth is occurring and lives are being transformed. Then move to bigger victories!

Paint the Picture

Visions are God sized. Although vision usually comes from God through a single leader, God chooses to involve His people in the fulfillment of the vision. "Since vision is more than just a set of propositions, value statements, or truths, it requires a mental image."[20] This is an image in the "mind's eye." When people are committed to biblical Christianity and have a clear image of how to advance that cause, the mental image can be a powerful motivator.

Comeback leaders are able to explain, both in speech and in writing, what a better future looks like. They convince people that things are not acceptable as they are, and then describe a better future to pursue. That vision and imagery make a dramatic difference.

Persuade the Persuadable

A God-anointed "Comeback Vision" always requires an appeal that is persuasive and practical. This appeal makes it possible for others to get on board and follow the vision. A good vision persuades those who are open that there's something greater. At some point, you will have to recognize that not everyone will be persuaded. So, find those key leaders who will be persuaded and move forward with them.

Persuasion starts with a good plan that makes sense to others. It can and should be challenging, but if the plan seems unachievable, people won't commit themselves to fulfilling the vision. If the pastor says, "Let's double the church this month" but presents no viable plan, strategy, or preparation, people will ignore the suggestion. If, on the other hand, the pastor says, "Let's double our attendance this month by having a Friend Day. Imagine doubling our attendance on one day and seeking to keep 25 percent of the gains. We will do this by . . . ." Then people are more likely to commit themselves because it's a challenging, but achievable, goal.

Explain the Risks; Count the Costs

Any good vision caster knows that painting only the good parts of the picture soon leads to disappointment. Church members get discouraged when the pastor keeps saying how "great" things will be and ignores the work and sacrifice required to make a turnaround. On the other hand, when people see the big picture and see the challenges that it will take to overcome, they are inspired to greatness. They know that change will occur in their revitalized church. But it will be worth the efforts and sacrifices to see the God-sized vision fulfilled.

Don't understate the cost of commitment. The Bible never teaches that Christian ministry will be easy, but it does say it's worthwhile. "So, my dear brothers and sisters, be strong and immovable. Always work enthusiastically for the Lord, for you know that nothing you do for the Lord is ever useless" (1 Cor. 15:58 NLT). The comeback churches we describe are filled with people who made the change—and it cost them some things which they valued. It is important for us to help people see that the pain of change is worth it for the pleasure of vitality.

Keep the Vision before the People

Once developed and cast, the vision for outreach must be shared again and again. Here are ways to keep that vision *consistently* before the church:
- Share brief testimonies of witnessing experiences.
- Highlight components of the church's evangelism strategy.
- Pray Matthew 9:37–38.
- Invite new believers to share their testimonies.
- Provide reminders of the church's outreach goals.

The pastor could meet monthly with key leaders. Updating and recasting the evangelism vision would be a central feature of the meeting along with planning the following month's weekly strategies for keeping the vision in front of the congregation. This keeps everyone focused and united. Some see the repetition as risky, redundant, or boring, but congregations benefit from regular reminders of who they are and the evangelistic purpose to which God has called them. Vision is contagious. Once it's in the heart of a church and its people, it spreads like a wildfire on a drought-stricken prairie.

Ultimately, vision alone won't grow a church. Comeback leaders are frequently visionaries, though they might not consider themselves to be. They help others see what does not exist. Then, they lead others to work toward making it a reality. Once that vision is successful, they lead them to the next level of ministry and service.

Developing Leaders

Comeback leaders multiplied themselves. It was not just important to be leaders themselves; these comeback leaders had to develop other leaders. Perhaps one of the most vibrant examples of revitalization leadership was found at Cumberland Community Church in Cumberland, Maryland. Pastor Ron Yost stated, "We make all of our leaders go through the Saddleback Leadership Seminar. We constantly talk in our meetings about what it means to be a leader. In addition to being a member, our leaders must go through a spiritual gifts test and a spiritual maturity class."[21]

Pastor Yost also described a bigger picture of comeback leadership. Bedford Baptist Church, which was started in 1958, was a dying church in Cumberland, about to close its doors. But the church asked Pastor Yost to preach one Sunday. Afterward, the church asked him to be their interim pastor. He refused, citing the deadness in the church. But he offered the Bedford church family the option of joining a group that was starting Cumberland Community Church. The Bedford Church accepted. Their building was closed three months for renovations, after which it became the new home of Cumberland Community Church. Yost provided pastoral leadership and people followed.

If leadership development matters, we need to know what it is. According to Malphurs and Mancini, it is "the intentional process of helping established and emerging leaders at every level of ministry to assess and develop their Christian character and to acquire, reinforce, and refine their ministry knowledge and skills."[22] Comeback leaders were not just leaders—they were developers and leaders of leaders.

Lead, Follow, or Get Out of the Way

There are many "religious" voices proclaiming that pastors should not lead. If that is their attitude, they are not leading comeback churches. Comeback pastors are leaders. Pastor Mark Canipe used to believe that people did not want pastors to lead. After a year and a half into his pastorate at Heights Baptist Church in Beech Island, South Carolina, he read about Joshua assuming leadership responsibility after Moses' death (Deut. 34 and Josh. 1). This led him to conclude that people did want to be led. Consequently, starting with the deacons, the pastor made changes in his leadership style. If Canipe perceived the Lord telling him to do something, he followed God's direction. But he also listened to the counsel of the deacons. If the deaconate believed some actions should wait, Canipe was willing to wait. Patience is always a virtue when it comes to enacting change in an established church. Be mindful that the church did not plateau overnight and it will not "rev up" for growth overnight either.

Over time, the deacons began to discern a change in their pastor's approach to leadership, and the Lord began to bless his efforts to do new things. This different approach by the pastor led to attitudinal changes among the deacons, and then the congregation. In addition, the church provided finances and worship leaders for the Saturday night service of its church plant.[23]

Find Resources to Develop Leaders

Pastor Richard Jueckstock of the Willard Christian Alliance Church in Willard, Ohio, emphasized the priority of developing leaders, "One leader has worked to mentor and develop other small-group leaders; another trains evangelism teams. Some key leaders have decided they are going to be true disciples of Christ and have really studied the Scriptures. Also, we have studied *Growing Healthy Churches,* a Christian and Missionary Alliance leadership training program."[24] Leaders of leaders find ways to multiply themselves.

It is sad but true that many people who are "take charge leaders" do not know how to replicate themselves. Leaders who cannot reproduce can lead a squad, but never an army. Replicating leaders found leadership resources to help them intentionally develop leaders for the purpose of evangelistic growth.

Living Leadership

When asked about leadership, 279 responded (86.1%) out of 324 total surveys. We posed the question: "If strong leadership had a major or vital effect, please describe the leadership factors that affected the comeback (e.g., being more proactive, sharing ministry, more intentional planning, change in attitude toward growth, specific training, style change, etc.)." Twelve pages of responses were compiled from these 279 respondents.

In the responses, nine words stood out. The word mentioned most often was "attitude" (in 34.8%, or 97, of the 279 responses). "Growth" was another key word (in 33.3%, or 93, of the responses). "Vision" was mentioned 88 times (31.5% of responses). Comeback leaders also cited "change" 81 times (29% of responses); "unity" 51 times (18.3% of responses); "proactive" 49 times (17.6% of responses); "training" 47 times (16.8% of responses); "sharing" 46 times (16.5% of responses); and "intentional planning" 27 times (9.7% of responses).

John Boquist, pastor of Cardinal Baptist Church in Ruther Glen, Virginia, referred to the *The Twenty-One Irrefutable Laws of Leadership,* explaining, "The two points most influential to me and Cardinal are 'The Law of the Buy-In' and 'The Law of the Lid.' People aren't going to buy into the vision until they can buy into you. The Law of the Lid affirms that God has designed you to do something. The question is what are you doing with what God has given you? Like it has been said, everything rises and falls on leadership."[25]

Conclusion

Comeback leaders found that revitalization starts with godly leadership, beginning with the pastor and touching every leader in the church. The pastor must be able to communicate the vision. It does not end with leadership. Godly leaders are just gifts from God to bring people to godly action.

Suggestions for Further Study

Allender, Dan B. *Leading with a Limp: Turning Your Struggles into Strengths* (Colorado Springs: WaterBrook Press, 2006).

Biehl, Bobb. *30 Days to Confident Leadership* (Nashville: Broadman & Holman Publishers, 1998).

Blackaby, Henry T. and Richard Blackaby. *Spiritual Leadership* (Nashville: Broadman & Holman Publishers, 2001).

Burke, H. Dale. *How to Lead & Still Have a Life: The 8 Principles of Less Is More Leadership* (Eugene, OR: Harvest House Publishers, 2004).

Malphurs, Aubrey and Will Mancini. *Building Leaders: Blueprints for Developing Leadership at Every Level of Your Church* (Grand Rapids: Baker Books, 2004).

Maxwell, John C. *The 21 Irrefutable Laws of Leadership: Follow Them and People Will Follow You* (Nashville: Thomas Nelson Publishers, 1998).

Sanders, J. Oswald. *Spiritual Leadership: Principles of Excellence for Every Believer* (Chicago: Moody Press, 2nd Revision, 1994).

Stanley, Andy. *The Next Generation Leader: 5 Essentials for Those Who Will Shape the Future* (Sisters, OR: Multnomah Publishers, 2003).

———. *Visioneering: God's Blueprint for Developing and Maintaining Personal Vision* (Sisters, OR: Multnomah, 2005).

3

Three Faith Factors

Pastor Brian of Visalia Foursquare Church in California saw several barriers to church growth the first Sunday he began his pastorate. The first indication was an usher chewing a big wad of tobacco as he greeted people. Now, isn't that just what every member, attender, or visitor wants to experience as they arrive for church?

The second indication came after the service started when another usher stood at the front of the church, in full view of the congregation, and counted the number of attendees. Often, people already feel like a number or statistic without being "pointed out" as one in a church service. Pastor Brian knew some things would have to change. The church was focused on the wrong particulars and needed to begin focusing on spiritual dynamics.

Too often, churches are interested in the wrong issues. The Church Growth Movement has declined because people became tired of its perceived emphasis on endless lists of nickels, noses, and numbers. Our hope is that this book is different. Intuitively, we have believed that it is God that changes churches. A recent study in *Leadership Journal* also showed that spiritual factors are of foremost concern. It explained, "Spiritual initiatives are vital, especially prayer, fasting, forgiveness and reconciliation."[1] Our study found similar factors.

Comeback leaders know that change takes place as the church is renewed spiritually. The motto of the Welsh Revival was, "Mend a church, save the world." That's what we want to see happen beginning with our own churches.

A comeback requires at least three elements. First, there is spiritual energy in the lives of individual believers and the church family as a whole, brought about by revival. Second, the church is restructured around its missional purpose. Third, there's a long-term commitment to change. Comeback churches implement these elements in an ongoing process of personal and corporate repentance and revitalization, keeping their focus on mission.

Faith is the indispensable, foundational ingredient for true growth in the church, both spiritually and numerically. Without faith, it is impossible to please God (Heb. 11:6) and to reach people for His kingdom (Col. 1:28–29). Vibrant faith leads us to set personal and congregational goals to accomplish God's purpose in our lives. The graph below shows the results of the first set of spiritual factors we rated in the survey—intentional, specific growth goals, more strategic prayer effort, reconciling interpersonal relationships, a renewed attitude for servanthood, and a renewed belief in Jesus Christ and the mission of the church. While each factor is important, three stood out. We believe these **Three Faith Factors** help a church regain a missional focus and are always necessary to lead a comeback church:

1. **Renewed belief in Jesus Christ and the mission of the church,**
2. **Renewed attitude for servanthood, and**
3. **More strategic prayer effort.**

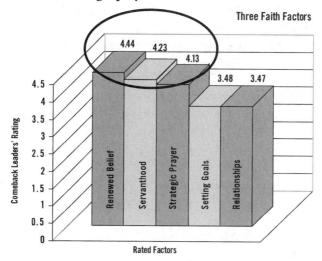

1. Renewed Belief in Jesus Christ and the Mission of the Church

These elements show why the largest number of church leaders rated a renewed belief in Jesus Christ and the mission of His church as the top factor in their church's comeback. With this renewed belief, staying the course through continued change had the most lasting impact. As one pastor stated, "That's what brings a focus and determines your actions and how you spend money. Find out what God is calling you to do—and do it."

You will see us use the word "missional" in this book. Churches must be missional in order to be biblical and effective. But what does that mean? Let us review a bit (and you might want to look at chap. 0 again).

Missional is an important word that is "popping up" in various contexts. Yet its meaning is simple. The word "missionary" is used as a noun. Missional is the adjectival use of the word "missionary." If someone is your adversary (a noun), then they are your enemy. If you have an adversarial (an adjective) neighbor, then they are acting like your enemy.

Thus, missional leaders and churches are ones that are thinking and acting like missionaries. They understand their culture, lead biblically faithful and culturally relevant churches, and think in missionary ways about their contexts. The end result may be traditional, contemporary, emerging, ethnic, or some other approach. You will find them all represented in this book. What they have in common is not their style, but their mission. These churches came back to a biblical focus. They started to exercise faith in Jesus Christ and think and act like missionaries.

Think about it for a moment. Just as we'd need to learn the language, culture, context, and accepted avenues through which we could communicate the gospel overseas, we need to adapt our church to the changing culture in which God has placed us. Even though we may know the same language, we may not be speaking in ways that people can hear, understand, and believe. We never change or compromise the gospel (1 Cor. 4:6), but we communicate it clearly and with a sense of urgency to our changing culture.

Comeback pastors underscored the impact of renewed belief in Jesus Christ and the mission of the church with comments such as:

- We had a renewed vision of who Jesus Christ really is.
- We had a new outlook on the harvest; the Lord is willing to increase the fold where shepherds are looking for the sheep. We started looking outward.
- Renewed belief—realizing the daily relevance of Christ and how the mission lines up with that.
- Renewed belief in Jesus—specifically, their everyday lives.
- Renewed belief in Christ and an attitude of servant-hood—focus was on the lordship of Christ and a model of the incarnational Christ.
- Renewed belief—built values around the people's involvement in the mission of the church.
- Renewed belief—greater desire to fulfill a kingdom purpose; new vision.
- Renewed belief—refocused from the foundation of Scripture upon the mission of the church.
- Renewed belief—created a culture that endorses mission.
- Renewed belief—the people realized that the mission was theirs to carry out at any cost.
- Renewed belief in mission—accepted personal responsibility for encouraging lost to come to church.
- Renewed belief—instilling in people the idea that everyone is a minister.
- Renewed belief/mission—taking time to refocus on Christ and His mission.
- Renewed belief/mission—people needed to know that Jesus was real; they began to carry out the mission and growth happened.
- Renewed belief/mission—the church regained a sense of direction based on Christ's mission.
- Renewed belief—keeping the mission and vision in front of the people was the key to growth.
- Renewed belief—people saw how Christ commanded them to live and began doing so; they saw the pastor lead by example.

- Renewed belief—finding that their mission was to evangelize their community.
- Renewed belief—people fell in love with Jesus again.
- Renewed belief/mission—becoming more outward focused.
- Renewed belief—daily renewal in hearts of people.
- Renewed belief—emphasis placed on our reason for existing.
- Mission/belief—emphasis on the people's role in God's plan.
- Renewed belief—refocusing on purpose of Christian life.

Comeback Churches Got Back on Mission

Summit Church in Durham, North Carolina, formerly named Homestead Heights Baptist Church, was an older church that fit the description of many Baptist churches in the area. Under Pastor J. D. Greear, the church experienced significant revitalization. It had always been a large church, but as the Durham community changed around it, coupled with some internal issues, the church rapidly declined in attendance (averaging in the 600s through the 1990s). J. D. began as the youth pastor at this church, but a few years ago they called him as pastor, commissioning him to lead the church in a fresh direction.

Changing the church's name to Summit, they did much more than change their marquee. They became intentionally missional in how they operated. The church recently sold its large, historic building to start meeting in a high school. This approach seems backward to many traditional churches, but Summit Church considers it a great opportunity to become mobile and find a location that better suits their mission. Their once-dwindling attendance now tops 1,600 and is still growing. It's a great turnaround story. But such remarkable stories are, unfortunately, rare. For Summit, their mission determined their meeting place, how they did worship, and their strategies.

Over and over, we heard stories of renewed belief in Christ and renewed passion for the mission of the church. These are inseparable. Loving Christ and not loving the church is like telling a friend that you love him, but you couldn't care less about his wife. Both the groom (Jesus) and the bride (the church) are essential. God put His glory on display in the Garden of Eden (Gen. 2), on Mount Sinai (Exod. 20), in the tabernacle (Exod. 40:34–38), in the temple (1 Kings 8:10–11), and in Jesus Christ when He came to earth (John 1:1–14). Before our Lord Jesus died on the cross, was buried and rose again, He said that He would come back with "great glory" (Matt. 24:29–31). Where is His glory on display now? In the church! "Now to Him who is able to do above and beyond all that we ask or think—according to the power that works in you—*to Him be glory in the church and in Christ Jesus to all generations, forever and ever. Amen*" (Eph. 3:20–21, emphasis added). Churches get renewed when God is glorified anew in them.

Renewal is a pretty common word in church revitalization circles. But it means different things to different people. For the comeback leaders in our survey, it means that they know Jesus more fully, and love the church and its mission more passionately.

Growing Deeply in Love with Jesus

Comeback leaders helped people know and experience the reality of Jesus Christ in their lives. People who experienced the reality of Jesus on a daily basis motivated their churches to overcome a slow or no-growth mentality. In many cases, they overcame a survival or small-church mind-set. They found that true belief translates into action. Comeback respondents affirmed the relationship between belief and behavior. As people were renewed in their beliefs, their actions changed. Follow-up interviews provided further insights about how an atmosphere of renewed belief developed in some of these comeback churches.

According to Pastor Dave Banfield of Bethel Baptist Church, a Baptist General Conference church in Mankato, Minnesota, developing an atmosphere of renewed belief involved "a gradual, consistent teaching of Scripture combined with a day-by-day lifestyle of spiritual maturity. Strategic discipleship classes have helped us grow. Also, our ALPHA and DivorceCare ministries, along with ministry to internationals and college students at Minnesota State University, allow our people to see what non-Christians really think. This has helped them reestablish their belief in the mission Christ has for the church."[2]

Richard Culpepper, pastor of Harvest Church in Covington, Georgia, preached about what Jesus intended His church to be. Culpepper discipled men, and his wife discipled women. They used Pastor Ken Adams' (www.crossroadsnewnan.org) *Impact Discipleship* (www.impactdiscipleship.com) material. They specifically addressed what Jesus did in His ministry and how that applies to the church today. Subsequently, that first group of members agreed to serve in lay leadership roles and two became staff members.[3] These leaders led people to grow more deeply in love with Jesus, having a passion for Jesus, His church, and its mission.

Growing Deeply in Love with the Community

Comeback leaders helped churches grow in love with the community through their preaching, teaching, and praying. They specifically asked the Lord of the harvest to open their eyes to the needs He is calling their church to meet (John 4:34–36). A Saturday morning prayer meeting was the first project for Pastor Stephen Willis of the Lynchburg Church of the Nazarene in Lynchburg, Virginia. Next came a prayer lab—an entire Sunday morning service of music and prayer for the community. This occurred twice a year. They also conducted twenty-four-hour prayer vigils twice a year, churchwide prayer chains, and Pastor Willis preached one series a year specifically on prayer. The staff meets for prayer four mornings a week.[4] As the church and staff prayed for the community, they developed a heart for the community.

Too many pastors love someone else's community. They long to minister to the nice, happy, and affluent families in the suburb, thinking that they have fewer problems. I (Ed) was recently in Mississippi where, in an open field surrounded by farms, a young man told me about his church. The church had been there more than a hundred years, and all the families were local farmers. This young pastor was quite enthusiastic when he announced that he was going to revitalize that church using the strategies of Erwin McManus.

Now, we love Erwin McManus. We read all his stuff and think he is great. But I encouraged this young pastor to rethink his strategy because the trendy-L.A.-nightclub-meeting-church might not be the best model to revitalize a First Church of rural Mississippi. The problem was that the pastor had not yet grown to love his people. In order to lead a church of farmers to reach farmers, you have to love farmers. In order to love the farmers, you have to pray for them, and get to know them, their needs, and their concerns.

Growing Deeply in Love with the Lost

Comeback leaders helped their churches grow to love the lost. This statement is somewhat harsh, but it does reflect reality: "Most churches love their traditions more than they love the lost." Many of the leaders surveyed indicated that making the comeback required an attitudinal change among the people of the church. As Pastor Harold of Precision Valley Baptist Church in Vermont stated, "Many churches in the Northeast have given up hope of growing."[5] Through intentional prayer and persistent efforts, that pastor helped lead the congregation to care about and reach those without Christ.

Too many churches never answer the hard questions: When is the last time I have led someone to Christ? What has been our attendance trend over the past five years? How many visitors have we had in the past year and the year before that? When is the last time this church baptized someone from outside the existing church family? Knowing the answers to these kinds of questions can help your church grasp whether or not it is truly growing.

Comeback leaders turned their churches outward. Pastor Jeff LeBert of the New Hope Church of the Nazarene in Rogers, Arkansas, said, "I really preached on the purpose of the church using Ephesians 3."[6] The church organized a community carnival called "Family Fest" in which they had games and activities for kids, and music and door prizes for adults. Anyone who came had to register for the door prizes, giving the church a prospect list. "However," says LeBert, "they knew up front they would receive an information packet from the church." The church did excellent follow-up on the prospects. All this led to new attitudes. A love for the lost often leads to changes in programs, priorities, and finances.

Most Christians don't like lost people. We wish it were not so, but it is. Lost people don't think like us; they often don't vote like us; they influence our kids; they don't know our inside references to Dobson, *Left Behind,* and Dave Ramsey. They are not "our" people. Let's face it: people outside of Christ can be messy! Most of the time there is at least one or more divorces, meaning blended families. Their credit card debt is so high that they cannot be financial givers to the church. Their kids can be unruly, putting marks on the clean walls of the church building and running around unrestrained. They do not often know the unspoken "cues" in "our church"—when we stand; how we act; what version of the Bible we read from; that when the pastor asks a question from the front, usually we are not expected to call out an answer; and so forth. Comeback churches made the hard decision that they will love the lost as much as Jesus did.

We know that Jesus came to seek and save people who are lost—He told us that in Luke's Gospel. He told three stories in Luke 15 that demonstrate how passionate He is about this. And the question for us is: Are we really willing to love those pagans, those heathens, those lost people who are often not very lovable? Actually, the issue probably comes down to the fact that we often want God to "clean them" before we "catch them." The need to reach them in whatever condition we find them often requires us to make changes in the way we do things. We have to find ways to love lost people the way they are, and that is hard work.

Think about what Jesus did when He picked Zacchaeus out of that crowd in Luke 19. Old Zack was not exactly the most popular guy around town. Jesus not only spoke to him, He also asked to visit his house. You can almost hear the collective gasp. How could Jesus go over to the house of someone like Zacchaeus, much less talk to him? As the Scripture says, "All the people saw this and began to mutter, 'He has gone to be the guest of a sinner'" (NIV). Are we making anyone mutter about the lost people that are being reached in our churches? If so, rejoice! You are in good company! "A student is not above his teacher, but everyone who is fully trained will be like his teacher" (Luke 6:40 NIV).

2. Renewed Attitude for Servanthood

Comeback leaders led their churches to develop the same passion, having a heart for service. They emphasized the impact of a renewed attitude for servanthood within their churches with responses such as:

- Emphasis on Christ and servanthood; stagnant country church that did not want to change; new emphasis revealed Jesus' desire; community is experiencing growth.
- Renewed belief in Christ and attitude of servanthood; focus on lordship of Christ and model of incarnational Christ.
- Began community center at church; service increased.
- Increased emphasis placed on service in small groups.
- Elderly congregation waiting to be served; attitude changed to servanthood.
- Church had become inward focused and didn't reflect makeup of community.
- Refocus on being engaged in service to community.
- Emphasis on service with outward focused attitude; renewed belief/mission—how do we effectively reach our community?
- Every member must be involved in some ministry.
- Began a school and other things to better the community.
- Getting people to understand it's not about them.
- An expectation for each member; a core emphasis.

Southside Baptist Church in San Antonio, Texas, was down to nine members in 1998 when Al Byrom came to be the bivocational pastor. "The church had no mission, vision, or excitement for ministry. I came in, under the Lord's leading, and empowered the people to *do* ministry. I led by example. I have a 'no-nonsense' approach to leadership. My leaders now are proactive and excited about ministry because it is more enjoyable."[7] By 2004, the church's morning worship attendance was 744. Byrom modeled and led the church to serve.

As you begin to love your community, you'll likely discover some community needs that aren't being met. By starting a particular ministry you'll not only help your community, but you'll build relationships with unreached people who have those particular needs. Some churches have found that DivorceCare, Celebrate Recovery, parenting classes, and other programs become important points of connection for their outreach strategy.

That requires a church with a different kind of attitude; a church that realizes its reason for existing is about more than itself and its preferences; a church that develops the attitude of Christ and engages in acts of service. William Temple, the former Archbishop of Canterbury once said, "The Church is the only organization organized primarily for the benefit of its non-members."

John Brokopp of Fairlawn Community Church in Cogan Station, Pennsylvania, told us the story of Bill. Bill was seventy years old. Though he had been in church all his life, he never served in any way. Pastor John saw something in Bill that others didn't. He began to pray that Bill would gain a servant's heart. He took Bill under his wing, and they prayed and studied Scripture together. Through this, Pastor John found out that Bill had received little discipleship in his life. Never forget that the length of time someone is in the church has very little to do with how mature they really are spiritually!

As Pastor John began encouraging Bill to learn Scripture and to take part in some form of service, he saw Bill develop a new confidence. Now, two years later, Bill is an elder in the church. He comes to the church early to pray with other men, and he makes sure everything is in place for the services. Pastor John said, "I think we have to stand beside people and give them the confidence to do things. We have to give them the power to do the work of the church, then we must stand back and cheer them on as they carry out those tasks."[8] When people begin to grow and serve, their churches begin to grow.

Vibrant faith and strategic prayer, which connect with the power of God, have often resulted in practical acts of Christian grace and love. When believers obey the Scriptures and truly forgive others who have offended them, unbelievers are influenced to receive Christ. When churches lovingly serve the communities around them, the unchurched very often are motivated to come to Christ.

Attitudes of Service—Overcoming Preferences with a Servant's Heart

Comeback churches led people to care more about their communities than their preferences. Churches will split over preferences—without either side caring about the lost. Comeback churches have decided that the "sin of preferences" leads to the "sin of a dying church." This is particularly true when the culture around a church changes quickly.

Most American churches today are well suited for ministry in a different era. All churches are culturally relevant; the question is whether they are relevant to a culture that currently exists in their community or to one that disappeared generations ago.

Internationally known church consultant Lyle Schaller frequently asks the same question when beginning to consult with a church. Lyle asks, "What year is it here?" Every church is living in some era. The issue is whether it aligns with the reality of the era where the gospel needs to be proclaimed.

Silver Dollar City is an amusement park in Branson, Missouri, and a cultural phenomenon to behold. Inside the park is a log cabin chapel. It's a fun place to sing and stomp. The songs are from an era long gone. It is a great place to see how people worshipped in that era. Yet, if it weren't for the amusement park behind us, you might forget that this, like much of Silver Dollar City, is preserved culture, not today's culture. It is not a presentation of the gospel that would be readily accepted in Harlem or Havana. For too many, their churches are museums of past cultures no longer relevant in the world today.

Randy Pope recently preached at the Presbyterian Church in America's (PCA) annual meeting in 2006. No other way to say it—those Presbyterians can be a pretty serious and formal bunch. We have heard one of their leading members refer to Presbyterians as the "Frozen Chosen."[9] Randy Pope's topic was on whether the PCA would be a "missional" denomination. All evangelicals would benefit from listening to his address, and you can find it at http://www.pcaga.com/. His point was excellent—every church should be contemporary (though he was not talking about music). He explained, "If the PCA is to be missionally effective, it must become contemporary to its culture and repent of any traditional idolatries." One blogger wrote in his live commentary, "He just made the room very silent." Such a statement would make many churches fall silent. How sad!

Before you conclude that his point contradicts earlier statements, a word of explanation is important. Pope means that every church should function in such a way that it can live in and reach people in contemporary culture, and he's right! Comeback churches accept this truth and act on it. It's not just about music. Being contemporary to your culture will mean different styles in different communities. If we choose not to serve our community as it exists, what's the alternative? We are then making a choice to function by our own preferences and the internal cultures which we create. Sadly, churches that serve their preferences and church culture do not reach the unchurched and will not experience comebacks. It takes a servant spirit to not focus on your preferences.

Having This Attitude

Scripture teaches us to "make [our] own attitude that of Christ Jesus" (Phil. 2:5). Paul goes into detail about not putting ourselves first:

> Do nothing out of selfish ambition or vain conceit, but in humility consider others better than yourselves. Each of you should look not only to your own interests, but also to the interests of others. Your attitude should be the same as that of Christ Jesus: Who, being in very nature God, did not consider equality with God something to be grasped, but made himself nothing, taking the very nature of a servant, being made in human likeness. And being found in appearance as a man, he humbled himself and became obedient to death—even death on a cross! Therefore God exalted him to the highest place and gave him the name that is above every name, that at the name of Jesus every knee should bow, in heaven and on earth and under the earth, and every tongue confess that Jesus Christ is Lord, to the glory of God the Father. (Phil. 2:3–11 NIV)

When we put others before ourselves as Jesus did, *and* we are known for caring about the lost like Jesus did, comeback churches result.

These can be hard changes to make. Many are convinced that the need for better believers is greater than the need for more believers. This can sound so spiritual and so right. After all it is important for believers to grow. However, Jesus' directives leave no question regarding the mission that we have been given—to share the good news. As stated previously, no other command gets as much emphasis in Scripture!

Sometimes we try to separate the tasks of evangelism and discipleship, even though they go hand-in-hand. But true disciples are going to be witnesses. Making more believers is not antithetical to making better believers. This spiritual dynamic is not an either/or proposition; it is a both/and proposition. Our mission is to make *more* and *better* followers of Jesus Christ simultaneously. A disciple who is growing spiritually will evidence a growing desire to be a witness and reach out to those who are lost.

So, comeback churches don't focus exclusively on their own spiritual maturity or demand their preferences. Instead, they make themselves servants of all for the glory of God. It sounds strangely similar to 1 Corinthians 9:19–23:

> For although I am free from all people, I have made myself a slave to all, in order to win more people. To the Jews I became like a Jew, to win Jews; to those under the law, like one under the law—though I myself am not under the law—to win those under the law. To those who are outside the law, like one outside the law—not being outside God's law, but under the law of Christ—to win those outside the law. To the weak I became weak, in order to win the weak. I have become all things to all people, so that I may by all means save some. Now I do all this because of the gospel, that I may become a partner in its benefits.

Actions of Service

Comeback leaders model and promote acts of service. When they started Coastal Community Church in Virginia Beach, Virginia,

Pastor Hank Brooks and his team went door-to-door passing out light bulbs. As a team they moved through the neighborhood, handing out the light bulbs to people and offering to change burned-out bulbs. At one house, a man was in the basement when his bulb burned out. Just then the doorbell rang. The team shared with him, and he attended their first service. The team shared God's love in a practical way and God transformed that encounter into a supernatural one! People know that a serving church is a different kind of church.

A significant number of comeback leaders identified a renewed attitude for servanthood as a major factor in their comeback congregations. They led their churches to overcome their traditional preferences, adjust their attitudes to become more like Jesus Christ, and then act like servants in their communities.

3. Strategic Prayer Efforts

Comeback churches are praying churches. Comeback leaders also underscored the impact of strategic prayer efforts as a key to renewal when they mentioned:

- Prayer—revitalizing prayer; prayer works; Bible tells me so.
- Preaching and outreach; praying fervently.
- Prayer and fasting; Jesus said to pray and fast.
- Prayer; different attitude in praying; started praying for God's leadership; being awakened.
- Got serious about corporate effort and praying for the lost.
- Prayer; dead church that became alive again as a result of specific prayer emphasis events.
- Prayer—increased emphasis on prayer which in turn affected everything; started specific prayer ministry.
- Prayer—seven prayer meetings during week, age-graded (one children, one youth, five adults); body has seen spiritual warfare overcome with prayer.
- Prayer—Wednesday night, Sunday morning, Tuesday morning prayer times; fifty outside prayer warriors (friends of church).
- Prayer—every time people have prayed seriously, growth has happened.

- Prayer—Saturday night prayer service, all night prayer vigils.
- Prayer—Monday night prayer meeting spurred lifestyle of prayer for many members.
- Prayer—three twenty-one-day periods of fasting and prayer.
- Prayer—church was declining; people began to fast and pray.
- Prayer—emphasized in preaching and acted out weekly.
- Prayer—group of people praying weekly.
- Prayer teams; this is the key to the church's growth.

The Bible teaches a central truth about prayer: Prayer changes things, including us, our churches, and our communities. In 1 Thessalonians 5:17, the Bible exhorts us, "Pray constantly." John Ortberg says, "*Prayer is learned behavior. Nobody is born an expert at it. No one ever masters prayer.*"[10] An increased emphasis on prayer was a major factor of importance to these comeback churches.

In our study, strategic prayer rated 4.13 on a scale of 1 to 5, as a component of vibrant faith. Prayer was also mentioned as an important aspect of time management for comeback leaders. Prayer became a higher priority among many comeback leaders who changed the way they spent their time. In addition, prayer was mentioned as important in the responses regarding influential people in comeback congregations. Comeback leaders indicated that they made many changes in their prayer patterns during their comebacks.

Praying as a Leader

Comeback leaders lead their churches to pray for things that matter. Pastor Paul Grigsby of North Malvern Assembly of God in Malvern, Arkansas, has had revitalization experience in five churches. North Malvern is his first senior pastorate. He knew that it would be a challenge to get commitment among his people. Grigsby instituted seasons of fasting and prayer which turned into a churchwide focus at least once a month.[11]

Historically, revivals have taken place when God's people prayed fervently and earnestly, and when they obeyed God's Word profoundly. Not only do churches and missionary leaders need to seek earnestly the power and presence of God in their lives, but they also need to pray strategically to utilize God's power in places where God is multiplying disciples and churches. Iain Murray in *Revival and Revivalism* says, "What happens in revivals is not to be seen as something miraculously *different from the regular experience of the church.* The difference lies in degree not kind. In an outpouring of the Spirit, spiritual influence is more wide spread, convictions are deeper and feelings more intense. But all this is only a highlighting of normal Christianity."[12]

The Holy Spirit's presence and power is released through intentional prayer. The book of Acts provided several examples of early believers coming together to pray for boldness (Acts 1:14–2:41; 2:42–47; 4:23–31; 6:3–7). In his work *The Book of Church Growth,* Thom Rainer explained, "Prayer is the power behind the principles. There simply is no more important principle in church growth than prayer. The prayers of the early church unleashed the power of God to add thousands to the church. It happened then. It is happening in some churches today. And it can happen in your church."[13] After praying, those early believers were empowered by the Spirit, and people were saved.

The same pattern could be followed today. Praying for boldness and for a movement of God's Spirit within the community and in the lives of those who are lost is part of an effective outreach strategy. It's clear that comeback leaders, by praying strategically and fervently for themselves, their church families, and their communities, set the tone so that churches can experience revitalization.

Praying as a Church

Comeback leaders led their churches to pray. Several comeback leaders described how they developed strategic prayer emphases in their churches. According to Roger Lipe, pastor of First Baptist Church in Woodlawn, Illinois, the Word of God and renewed prayers were keys to renewal. They gave a new emphasis to prayer during the Wednesday evening services. Pastor Roger read Scriptures dealing with prayer and led the church family to focus on praying for the needs of the church. His attitude toward change and belief in the power of prayer caused others to believe. This church was $109,000 in debt in July 2001, but was completely debt-free by November 2002! Giving continues to increase, and the once-dead church is alive and ministering effectively to the community around them.[14]

Praying for the Community

Comeback leaders and churches pray for their communities and then act on those prayers. At the Sumter Wise Drive Church of the Nazarene in Sumter, South Carolina, Pastor William Watts and the members have helped grow the church through an increase in evangelistic zeal.[15] Pastor Watts emphasized the importance of the weekly prayer meetings, and that prayer has led to a deeper passion for the community. Prayer for salvation, healing, and other needs continues to be emphasized. Outreach events, including the REACH program,[16] as well as a weekly visitation program are strongly promoted. The REACH evangelism training is conducted by lay people who had already been through the program. Prayer for the community leads to actions that reach out to the community.

Other Factors

There were two factors that did not rise to the level of "Three Faith Factors" but were mentioned by many respondents. We have included them below.

Goal Setting

Comeback leaders made plans. Many comeback leaders saw that goal setting made a difference. For some, it was the primary difference.

Growth did not occur without intentionality. When responding to questions about vibrant faith, 13 percent of comeback leaders selected "setting goals" as *most* important. Vibrant faith and a desire to grow result in making plans, defining strategies, and setting goals for growth. Consequently, most comeback leaders perceived that defining growth goals had a great impact upon church revitalizations.

In his book *Coaching Ministry Teams,* Kenn Gangel affirms the need for setting growth goals in ministry: "Which is the most significant characteristic of administrative leadership? Credibility? Courage? Critical thinking? In my view *purpose* leads the list—the ability to set and achieve goals . . . *leadership means helping groups of people achieve goals.*"[17] Proverbs 20:18 contains this precept, "Finalize plans through counsel, and wage war with sound guidance." Churches are in a spiritual battle and need to seek God's counsel, then make plans to grow. Part of that process is goal setting. Having a desire to grow and planning for growth are essential elements in applying biblical faith that results in church growth.

Comeback leaders affirmed that planning for growth was an essential part of the church growth process. As outlined by McGavran years ago, the efforts of comeback leaders confirmed three basic steps that should be taken in setting church growth goals:

1. The first step in setting goals is to emphasize that evangelism is a thoroughly biblical activity. . . .

2. The second step is to chart past growth. . . .

3. The third step is to make faith projections. . . .
Faith projections are made in prayer and with a confident assumption of the continued presence of the Holy Spirit. Faith projections are what we feel God wants to do through us. As responsible stewards of his grace we ask if what we believe is in accordance with his will.[18]

These practical steps will help make an outward focus a reality. Wanting to grow is not enough. Planning for growth involves making bold plans based upon God's leadership, trusting Him, and working hard to accomplish those goals.

According to the comeback leaders, making no plans for growth results in little or no growth every time. Timidity is not God's desire for us. Many of these leaders boldly identified and made necessary changes and set growth goals. Leading the church in the process of embracing new outreach goals is extremely important, because the difference between leadership and martyrdom is about three steps! If the pastor gets too far out in front of the people without their ownership, the results can be disastrous. Of course, this three-step process can be used for any ministry in the church.

Valuing Relationships and Reconciliation

Many comeback leaders saw the value of reconciling relationships. A number of comeback leaders saw relationships as key to revitalization, with 14 percent mentioning "reconciliation" or "relationships." Some identified this as the most significant aspect of vibrant faith and revitalization. In many instances, these leaders had to help wounded congregations heal from church splits or tumultuous experiences with previous pastors. In those situations, people have to forgive others who have offended them before the church can move forward and grow effectively.

A spirit of unforgiveness can permeate a congregation, can be sensed by newcomers, and will hinder growth. Of course, unforgiveness is nothing new in the history of the church. One of Satan's most-used tools to stifle the spread of the gospel is unforgiveness among believers. "When you forgive this man, I forgive him, too. And when I forgive whatever needs to be forgiven, I do so with Christ's authority for your benefit, *so that Satan will not outsmart us. For we are familiar with his evil schemes*" (2 Cor. 2:10–11 NLT, emphasis added).

Some comeback leaders indicated that they directly addressed reconciliation issues and allowed wounded congregations time to heal before moving forward with growth plans. Paul's instructions to believers in the New Testament still hold true: "accepting one another and forgiving one another if anyone has a complaint against another. Just as the Lord has forgiven you, so also you must [forgive]. Above all, [put on] love—the perfect bond of unity" (Col. 3:13–14). Comeback leaders understand that healthy relationships among the people in their congregations have an impact on church renewal.

Faith Factors Matter

Faith factors are a significant factor in revitalization. *Leadership Journal*'s revitalization study also indicated the importance of spiritual factors. They explained, "Spiritual initiatives are vital, especially prayer, fasting, forgiveness and reconciliation."[19] We found it to be true.

If the percentages hold true across North American churches, what churches believe about the person of Jesus and about God's mission for the church really matters. Creating a renewed focus on Jesus is vital to making a comeback. Believers need to experience the reality of Jesus Christ in their everyday lives. In order to create an atmosphere of renewed belief, comeback leaders find ways to translate that belief into practical activity through strategic prayer and servanthood.

Comeback leaders know that church transformation is a spiritual business. Only God can move a church from sickness to health. Mac Brunson and Ergun Caner, in their helpful book *Why Churches Die,* explain that spiritual sicknesses have spiritual answers:

> One continuing theme among the churches that have staved off the infection of spiritual ailments is a central belief that they are curable. They firmly believe that no disease is terminal, no matter how bleak the prognosis may be. They have a resilience that is commendable, because they do not allow the pessimistic prognoses to keep them from attempting recovery.
>
> Second, these churches also have an aggressive method of "spiritual therapy" to deal with these issues. In virtually every case, the pastor took the lead in dealing with these illnesses. In virtually every case, he had leaders who backed him when he took a stand. . . .
>
> Finally, every church that has survived one of these lethal outbreaks viewed every spiritual malady as a form of leukemia. That is to say, they viewed every problem as a spiritual ailment rather than just a personality conflict or a confrontation between leaders. By viewing each problem as a spiritual one, they enabled the church to see it for what it really was—a leukemia or a cancer of the blood.[20]

Brunson and Caner saw the answer that sick churches need— the blood of Christ. Through the cross, spiritual solutions come.

Before we can be a genuine comeback church, we must first change our spiritual values. If we love the people Jesus loves and value those He values (the lost), it brings fresh spiritual energy because we are missional in our approach. That leads us to change our behavior through prayer, reconciliation, and repentance. This, in turn, leads us to structure our church for mission, not maintenance.

Suggestions for Further Study

Brunson, Mac and Ergun Caner. *Why Churches Die: Diagnosing Lethal Poisons in the Body of Christ* (Nashville: B & H Publishing Group, 2005).

Cole, Neil. *Cultivating a Life for God: Multiplying Disciples through Life Transformation Groups* (St. Charles, IL: ChurchSmart Resources, 1999).

Gangel, Kenn. *Coaching Ministry Teams: Leadership and Management in Christian Organizations* (Nashville: Word Publishing, 2000).

Ortberg, John. *The Life You've Always Wanted: Spiritual Disciplines for Ordinary People* (Grand Rapids: Zondervan, 2002).

Warren, Rick. *The Purpose-Driven Life: What on Earth Am I Here For?* (Grand Rapids: Zondervan, 2002).

C
H
A
P
T
E
R

4

Worship and Preaching Matters

Scott Brooks, pastor of Wadsworth Alliance Church in Ohio, believes that God should get all the glory for the changes that have taken place at Wadsworth—but that worship and preaching made a big difference. In an e-mail, he discussed several truths about worship that we think are important enough to include his lengthy explanation:

> The atmosphere of our church when I arrived was very similar to the Titanic. People were jumping ship left and right, yet there was a crew that were manning the pumps still convinced the ship could be saved. They were a people that had been sternly preached to and reminded about their deficiencies and what a sorry lot they were. Fellowship was almost non-existent. The church was completely empty 5 minutes after the service; that's how acidic the environment was. I sensed God was calling me to bring healing and encouragement. I preached through Nehemiah and compared the church to Israel. She had been beaten and captured and demoralized but God had a remnant left, a remnant to rebuild a nation with. My preaching those first 6 months was filled with encour- agement. I tried to find every strength and accomplish- ment worth affirming in that church and let them know Sunday in and Sunday out that I saw it, and if I saw it God was certainly seeing it. In that first year the church didn't need to hear about how messed up they were, they

needed to know their pastor loved them and that God had not quit on them. To this day people talk about how they feel loved in our church. They sense that I'm not there to beat people up but to invite them into a life of love and obedience. Now, the last person doesn't leave until 30-40 minutes after the service.

A. B. Simpson once said, "Popular music is the heart of the people." Popular music today is full of energy. It uses sound amplification and it is typically a rock band set up (acoustic, electric, and bass guitars, piano, Hammond B-3 organ, vocals, and drums). If new Christians come in and hear a style of music they have already been listening to, their worship experience will already be familiar even though they have to learn new words. Having said that, every service we remain tied to our ancient faith through at least one hymn. We don't dare lose the rich heritage of our faith. The mandate I was given by the leadership of the church was "Do whatever you have to do to bring life back to our worship services." One of the things the church agreed to before I came was the style of music would change, and I gave a year's worth of service plans from my previous church so there would be no surprises.

For over 20 years, hardly any investment was made in the elements that facilitate worship. Our church had 30-year-old sound equipment and technology that at one time was considered state of the art. They agreed to invest in a complete overhaul and spend the money necessary to do it. What paved the way for the investment was the older generation not just permitting, but actually leading the charge to make the investment. They were the ones saying, "It is time for the next generation to lead and spread their wings. This investment will help bring a new generation of Christians back to our church." Their leadership and influence is what made this happen. Their humility and desire to place others' worship style preferences above their own broke my heart. They lost much in their desire to see this church turn around. Everyone knew their financial giving was sustaining the church, and rather than stop giving because they were diminishing they kept giving and kept encouraging the leadership to make the right moves. We spent $18,000 on a new sound system, including a 24-channel board of which at first we only used ½ the channels. We got a $2,500 drum set even though we did not have a drummer and we placed it on the stage to communicate a message of where we were going. We purchased a new computer, and after 2 years purchased an $8,000 video projector to replace the old one. Just recently, less than four years later we just had a new 48-channel sound board donated to the church because we have run out of room on the 24-channel board. We started with a team of 8 people. Now we are a team of 24 people and growing. . . .

After four years we have doubled in size averaging 16% growth. Trust me that growth isn't because of the formula. God is doing it. This church has tasted death and there is a desperation that is in our DNA. We don't want to forget the feel and sense of death because it reminds us, "Except for the grace of God, there go we."

It seems obvious—worship matters to comeback churches. Later in this chapter we will see that preaching does as well. Most growing churches we know have dynamic worship and excellent preaching. It is not just adding evangelism programs that makes a difference (though that did happen in many cases), but it's also the way you worship and the way you preach that impacts whether or not the church can be a comeback church.

Worship Matters

Comeback churches valued worship. Almost all comeback churches identified their mood of worship as celebrative and orderly (96% and 95%, respectively) with a significant emphasis on being informal and contemporary (81% and 69%, respectively). To illustrate, Kevin Hamm led Valley View Church in Louisville, Kentucky, from a declining church of 300 to a vibrant congregation of more than 2,000 (he recently moved to a new church in Alabama).

The church baptized 221 his last year there—a far cry from seven years before when they used buckets to catch the leaks in the sanctuary because they could not afford to fix the roof. Pastor Hamm explained the turnaround this way: "We worked from the premise that worship is the front door of the church. So we spent the whole year looking at our worship service without expending energy trying to draw in visitors. After that first year, we had our worship settled and we started to reach out to the community." Let's face it, most people's first exposure to your church is Sunday morning. The preaching and worship must be excellent and life impacting for first-time visitors to become newcomers and then members.

Churches often rediscovered their passion for God and His mission by examining their worship. Unfortunately, some think that "jazzing up" the worship is a quick fix. It is not. The solution lies in seeking God's heart while finding worship that helps others to connect with God. In many cases, the worship of the church was once meaningful but has since lost its cultural relevance. "The key to effective worship in the healthiest settings is engaging people's hearts, minds, souls, and strength. To be engaged in worship involves varying styles and forms, but is focused on actively drawing in and involving God's people."[1]

Worship cannot end the refocusing process, but it is a good beginning. When we create a God-centered and culturally appropriate worship service, it helps us begin the process of seeking God for other changes that need to take place.

Jesus taught us that worshippers of God must worship in truth only, right? Not so fast. Some of us forget the other part of His statement in the Gospel of John. Jesus asserted that true worshippers will worship in *spirit and* in truth. What does that mean? At the very least, it means that worship will involve the whole person—mentally, emotionally, physically, and spiritually.

In Psalm 100:1–2, we are exhorted, "Shout for joy to the LORD, all the earth. Worship the LORD with gladness; come before him with joyful songs" (NIV). Does this characterize what takes place in our churches? What about Psalm 150? Other Scriptures urge believers to do things like clap their hands and lift up their hands in praise and worship to God—not to mention the first and greatest commandment that exhorts believers to express their love for God with all their heart, soul, mind, and strength (Matt. 22:37–39).

Another dimension of worship is how it can influence unbelievers, which is further reason this discussion of worship is vital. While it is true that only believers can truly worship, their worship can impact unbelievers. Unbelievers who see true worshippers focused on God, experiencing His presence in genuine praise and worship, will be drawn to the true and living God. When unbelievers come to our worship, God uses it to touch their hearts and change their lives. Our goal is described in 1 Corinthians 14:25, "As they listen, their secret thoughts will be exposed, and they will fall to their knees and worship God, declaring, 'God is truly here among you'" (NLT). Worship focuses on God and His character, involves the whole person, and draws unbelievers to the one, true, and living God.

Worship Style

Comeback churches came in all different kinds of styles. Second Evangelical Free Church in Brooklyn, New York, made the transition from very traditional to very contemporary worship—and it was not an easy transition. The decision was made based on one factor—they believed that contemporary music would reach more people in the community. Worship change has been central to their revitalization.

However, not all comeback churches were contemporary. Many were blended. Harvest Baptist Church in Covington, Georgia, explained, "In our blended service the worship is horizontal and vertical. We decided to transition from traditional to blended because we wanted to reach a greater audience of people. There are some great theological principles in the old hymns. But there are some great new songs that people need to hear and sing to God. The blended worship gives us the best of both worlds."[2]

There were also traditional churches that experienced revitalization. Fairmount Wesleyan in Indiana explained that their traditional service still has a freedom to it. "The worship leader may add a song if he feels led. Songs, announcements, prayer, etc., may not always be in the same order. We always have a casual and celebratory atmosphere. This is a farming community, and most people wear jeans or casual clothes."[3]

We didn't ask respondents to name their worship *style* for obvious reasons—mostly because the words have come to mean different things to different people. Many people today think Contemporary is good and Traditional is bad. We don't agree. We think that contextual is best—worship that glorifies God and fits the context. The reason that many think traditional is bad has little to do with tradition itself. The concern is that the tradition has to do with a certain era—one in which we no longer live. To some, a contemporary church might be a full rock band. For others, it's a few pepped-up hymns. So, we decided to go a different direction.

Comeback churches were substantially more contemporary than traditional. We wanted to know how comeback churches worship. So, we asked about mood, instrumentation, and types of songs. The result: comeback churches tend to use instruments and moods, indicating that they are on the more contemporary side.

Survey respondents reported that the more traditional instruments—piano and organ—were used in 71 percent and 30 percent of comeback churches, respectively. The less traditional instruments—guitar, drums, and keyboard—were used by 71 percent, 62 percent, and 61 percent of comeback churches, respectively.

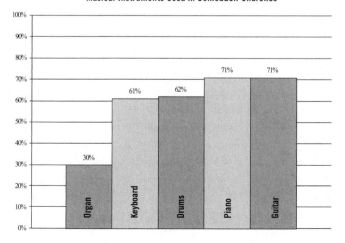

Musical Instruments Used in Comeback Churches

Music selections suggested an overall trend toward a more contemporary approach, as well. Praise choruses, hymns, and contemporary Christian music were utilized in 90 percent, 75 percent, and 59 percent of comeback churches, respectively.

Musical Selections in Comeback Churches

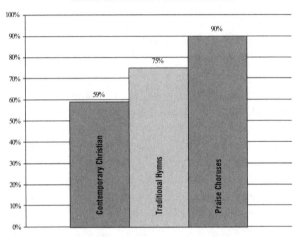

Asking about worship style or moods brought to light the most significant finding about worship. The top two responses indicated that comeback churches utilized a balance between celebrative (96%) and orderly (95%). While comeback leaders described their primary worship mood as celebrative, it did not mean the worship experience was without structure. Worship was done in an orderly fashion. The next three highest responses in this category were informal (84%), contemporary (69%), and expressive (62%). Analyzing these responses collectively pointed to a definite trend that comeback churches are more contemporary and less formal, especially when combining information about instrumentation and music selections with these results.

Follow-up interviews with a couple of comeback pastors illustrated how some comeback churches combined these elements—often in different ways. Eastside Baptist Church in Richmond, Kentucky, had services that were orderly, celebrative, and informal in nature. Pastor Virgil Grant explained, "Orderly means the services are planned out. Celebrative applies to the fact that the

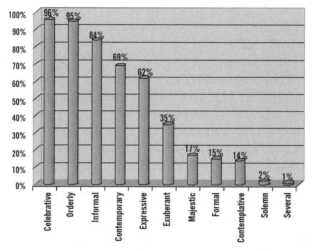

music is a blend of hymns and choruses, and there is clapping, raising of hands and greeting. Informal applies to the casual or business casual dress. The services are similar to the style of Hillsong's, mixed with hymns."[4]

Pastor Steven Fletcher described the services at Fairmount Wesleyan Church in Fairmount, Indiana: "Orderly applies to the structured pattern of the service. It is not a restrictive feel. Celebrative applies to the exuberant clapping and the greeting of one another. Informal applies to dress [and] atmosphere."[5]

Johnny Agnew of the Mt. Zion Community Church in Baldwyn, Mississippi, described his services as "exuberant." Pastor Agnew also said, "Orderly applies to the planned services. Celebrative applies to the blended services, clapping, raising hands, shouting during music and preaching (think typical African American service). Informal applies to structured service that is directed by the Holy Spirit."[6]

The Contemporary Factor

Comeback churches were more contemporary than traditional. Although we are not advocating that every church be contemporary, and many of the churches in our study were not, it would be inappropriate not to recognize the influence of contemporary worship. The vast majority of American churches are not contemporary; the majority in this study would seem to be, and that should make us take notice. One study by Ellison Research found that churches are embracing contemporary methodologies to make them more effective at reaching the lost. According to Ellison Research: "Churches moving toward more contemporary worship styles are outpacing those moving to more traditional styles by an 11-to-1 margin. . . . Fifty-one percent of the Protestant ministers who participated in the survey said their church's worship style has become more contemporary in the last five years. Just 5 percent said their style has become more traditional recently, while 44 percent said their worship style has not changed."[7]

However, this does not mean contemporary worship will be effective everywhere. Many emerging churches are embracing more liturgical forms of worship, while some other churches are finding that Southern Gospel music helps them to relate in their context. As you start the journey toward evangelistic effectiveness, be willing for God to stretch you in new ways, and be open to whatever music style God would use. If your community can be reached in a blended traditional service, then learn from other churches and do it well. If it's contemporary and your church is really willing to do what it takes, then talk about making that shift.

Changing Worship without Changing Churches

Few pastors survive a worship change, but many comeback churches made changes in worship. Making worship changes was in the top ten transformational changes made by comeback churches. (This will be discussed further in chap. 11.) Your church might need to make some changes in worship as well. If changing worship is in your future, it is difficult and challenging. Here's the process I (Ed) have used to help churches experience different styles of worship. If you're a pastor, you might try to lead your church through a similar process. As a layperson, you could help your pastor form a team committed to seeing your church grow spiritually and numerically. Start the revitalization process by examining the worship of growing churches.

Visit the Fastest Growing Churches in the Area

On three occasions I (Ed) asked the members of stagnant churches to go visit the area's fastest growing churches. You might wonder what the fastest growing churches have to do with your worship. The answer is simple. If your church is stagnant or in decline and you visit one that is growing rapidly, we promise that their worship will not look or feel the same as yours.

When we sent out our worship "spies," almost every member returned wanting some aspect of what they saw! Pastors and church leaders can tell the story all day, but a live picture is worth a thousand words. (Note: Maybe your committee members won't have to miss worshipping at your church since many growing churches have early services. But make sure their early service is consistent with the main service.)

Offer some guidance on what to look for when they attend. At the end of this chapter you will find the same sheet I gave to the visiting teams to evaluate the worship (you can download it at www.comebackchurches.com). My favorite part of church revitalization is to hear the reports of longtime church members who, after visiting other churches, come back saying, "The Church has changed, and nobody told us." (Those exact words were really spoken at one church.)

Invariably, they come back with several observations:

- Churches that are growing by reaching people through evangelism generally look very different from those in need of revitalization. For example, almost all growing churches have an outreach strategy; almost all declining churches do not.

- Growing churches have certain things in common but generally only with each other and not with the stagnant churches. People often report that changing to be more like these churches may be easier than they initially thought. For example, most growing churches have an intentional plan for welcoming guests; most declining churches do not.

- Growing churches rarely fit the stereotype the visitors from my churches expected: sold out to worldliness and marketing. The result is that committee members usually overcome their previously held objections to the methods used by growing churches.

One note of consideration: pick churches from your denomination and screen them. You will want churches that are theologically sound and focused on Word-based preaching and that are reaching people in a way that your church is not. In my experience, the best examples are churches:

- With more than 100 in attendance (or scaled appropriately to your area);
- That have grown at least 20 percent in each of the past three years; and
- That are not known for any major negative issues. (Of course, just growing gets you a negative reputation with some people!)

Be careful not to pick churches that simply fit your agenda. Instead, pick the five that are growing the fastest, so that your church members trust the process. If you rule out a church because of its preaching or views, tell your people why.

Think of this as an exercise in reconnaissance, like the spies in the book of Numbers, but in this case, they're identifying the challenges as well as what God is doing in healthy, growing churches. It's a great assignment and adventure for missional laypeople who are dedicated to revitalizing their church.

Experience Different Kinds of Worship

I (Ed) then led the same three churches through what I call "A Worship Experience and Experiment." Many churches with which I have consulted have done the same thing, usually after they visit other churches for ideas. For four weeks, the church experiences different types of music styles and formats. Here's a basic progression:

- *Week 1:* Traditional. Worship using only hymns, with a doxology and closing with a benediction.
- *Week 2:* Blended Traditional. Worship using hymns and slow choruses.
- *Week 3:* Blended Contemporary. Worship using a contemporized hymn, some fast choruses where people clap

along, and some slower worship choruses. Introduce other elements such as nametags, communication cards, and offering at the end of the service. In two cases, we also wore more casual clothing.

- *Week 4:* Contemporary. Worship using a group of contemporary upbeat songs that people clap to and slower songs that people focus on.

Of course, these are only our descriptions. Traditional and contemporary look different from community to community and from person to person. (At one church, a deacon wanted to know when we did the banjos and fiddles—a worship expression that was new to me!) That's why you visit other churches before planning your own worship experiment.

The services went well because we did them with equal enthusiasm. We did traditional well (most traditional churches don't actually do them that well). When we began to introduce some blended elements, we made sure the new parts were done with excellence.

The blended contemporary service is a hard threshold for most traditional churches, but we made sure that everyone agreed to participate in all the expressions. So, people nervously clapped along and sang to words which we projected on the borrowed data projector. They sang and participated because it was their project.

The contemporary service is probably the most difficult—musicians had to be brought in to help—and the farthest from the church's experience. Attending a contemporary church service taught those three congregations three things. First, it wasn't so bad. Second, churches could do it and still love God. Third, it probably wasn't for them.

I remember vividly what happened at one of these three churches. It was the town center First Church (First Baptist Church of Emerson, Georgia) and had been around for more than one hundred years, but had recently experienced a split, with most of the younger families leaving with the younger pastor. I (Ed) came and encouraged them as their interim pastor. When they asked me to help their church grow again, I suggested we look first at worship. Soon, we began the process described above.

The funniest part (it won't sound that way at first, but he turned out to be fine) was when the chairman of deacons—Scott—had a mild heart attack during the contemporary worship service. There was some commotion in the back, but the band kept playing and the service went on because no one could see all that was happening. He was wheeled out to the hospital while making one request, "Please tell the band it wasn't because of the music!"

Scott and I joke about that day, but not about the result. The church soon voted to adopt a blended contemporary style of worship, with Scott's support. That decision changed the church, and one of the results was that Scott's son and daughter-in-law returned to church. And not just them. The church has doubled in size since that worship change.

Many churches are discovering the value that other biblically discerning expressions can bring. They are learning that their worship can be biblically sound, God centered, deeply spiritual, and culturally relevant. Yours can too.

Bring Home and Discuss

What's next? Have a family meeting with the whole church, so everyone has ownership of the process. You can't change a church suddenly and without the church's permission. (Well, you can, but you will probably end up worse off or at another church.) Instead, involve them in the process. After they visit other churches, ask them:

- What are these churches doing, and why is it working?
- What is our church doing, and why is it not working?
- What can we learn?
- What can we try?

In the case of the three churches I led through this process, we brought all of them to a vote on which worship style they should adopt. They had seen the worship of growing churches in the area. They had seen different kinds of worship in their own facility. I then asked them to vote on three things (in writing on a sheet of paper to be turned in), with discussion between each.

The discussion was carefully orchestrated. Each time someone would criticize a style, I would ask if that was a preference or a conviction? Would other people feel the same way? What about the people we want to reach?

Then, we passed out ballots:

All three churches voted to change their worship. All three experienced substantial growth when they did.

Lest you hear only examples of churches that turned contemporary, it might be helpful to consider that I (Ed) actually had the privilege of starting a blended service at a contemporary church. We had started a church in Erie, Pennsylvania, and things were growing well, but many people in our community, including the unchurched, found our church to be too contemporary. Yet, we were reaching the community well—just not *all* of the community. We decided to start a blended church and reached a whole new segment of the community. There are some churches that have found traditional to be an effective approach in their community. But, that is the exception, and we want to be honest—most comeback churches were moving in a more contemporary direction.

What was your favorite worship style?
- Traditional
- Blended Traditional
- Blended Contemporary
- Contemporary

What do you think would reach the most people in our community?
- Traditional
- Blended Traditional
- Blended Contemporary
- Contemporary

What style should we adopt at our church?
- Traditional
- Blended Traditional
- Blended Contemporary
- Contemporary

Other Worship Changes

Churches also made other changes that were important to their worship. These changes were generally part of their turn-around process.

Changed Facilities

For some churches, the comeback process involved new facility designs and uses for worship. Rocky Mountain Ministries in Pocatello, Idaho, gave their facilities a complete face-lift. "We remodeled our entire worship center to be seeker-friendly," said Pastor Scott Sampson. "We took out the stained glass windows, removed the crosses from outside, moved from pews to chairs, upgraded our sound system, and added a coffeehouse at the front of the main facility. All this contributed to our growth, because we had several people come who said they had seen our building for years, but were uncomfortable coming in."[8]

Changed Staff

A number of these comeback churches reported that they changed worship leadership. Regarding pastoral or staff changes (other than senior pastor) two areas stood out: "youth" was mentioned in 37 percent of responses and "worship/music" was mentioned in 25.4 percent of responses.

Lynchburg Church of the Nazarene's Stephen Willis talked about the revamping of their entire staff. "The first thing we did after I came here was bring on an energetic worship leader. Other staff members followed, such as a children's, youth, and senior adults pastor, and an office administrator."[9]

We heard these stories regularly. Keith Thompson of High Pointe Baptist Church said, "We changed our entire staff. First, we added a worship leader. Then, we brought on a children's pastor, youth pastor, myself [missions], and a secretary."[10] The Eastridge Community Church in Duluth, Minnesota, added a worship leader, counselor, small groups pastor, and a secretary.[11]

A new worship leader was among the three most commonly added staff positions (between youth and children's ministers, see chap. 10). The churches were affected because with a new staff comes a new and fresh vision for the future. This new vision and direction from the Lord sparked excitement in the lives of the church members, who in turn conveyed this excitement to people in their everyday lives. True worshippers worship God in spirit and in truth. That not only invigorates them, it also influences the church's ability to connect with lost people.

Preaching's Impact

Comeback churches practiced biblical preaching. Another key component of worship involves communicating the Word of God in a biblically faithful, practical, and relevant way.

Preaching . . . For many, that word has negative connotations. Many people remember arguing with their mother and yelling, "Don't preach at me!" Lots of people are saying the same thing in regard to churches. The question remains, how can we communicate biblical truth through preaching in a culture that does not want to be "preached at"? God still uses preaching; "For since, in God's wisdom, the world did not know God through wisdom, God was pleased to save those who believe through the foolishness of the message preached" (1 Cor. 1:21).

For some conferences and books, the answer has been to streamline, simplify, and spice up sermons. Some have streamlined and made messages shorter and pithier so the message is more applicable and helpful. Others have focused on the practical and positive, creating a simple message easily communicated. Many have spiced up the message with videos, drama, and testimonies. These are not necessarily bad things, but they can be if they become the focus of the message and not a tool for preaching the text. If we want streamlined, simple, and spiced up truth, then we can watch Wayne Dyer on PBS. Comeback churches are passionate about the Word of God and their preaching reflects that. They also use diverse tools and methods to communicate it.

Preaching is always a hot topic. People regularly go to seminars, read books, and listen to podcasts to learn how to do it better. Rightly so. Turning a church around requires good preaching. That's no secret.

There does not seem to be only one approach, although the slight majority of comeback pastors used a verse-by-verse style of preaching. The leaders were given five options from which to choose—verse by verse, topical, thematic, narrative, and/or other. Each person was allowed to choose one or more of the options, but required to make the overall percentage add up to one hundred. While the verse-by-verse style was used 53 percent of the time, the other four styles combined were used 47 percent of the time. All the percentages are shown on the next page.

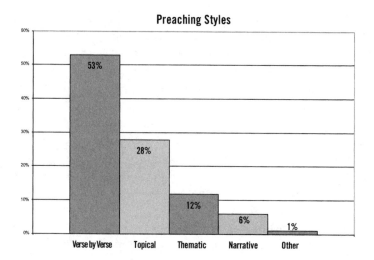

Very few of the comeback leaders (only 15%) preached exclusively using one approach.

At Silver Creek Church of the Nazarene in Owasso, Oklahoma, Pastor Larry Brinkley said his journey took him through two or three different preaching styles. Pastor Brinkley tried both narrative and inductive styles, and he felt that the thematic style was best. He chose themes based on the church calendar and important topics of the day, which seemed the best format for his congregation.[12]

Pastor Chip Garrison of the New Hope Family Church of the Nazarene in Sioux Falls, South Dakota, stated, "Topical preaching requires a thesis and a 'take-home principle.'"[13] Because themes and topics seemed to reach his congregation, New Hope's services—from class themes to songs to messages—often were set around a central concept. Garrison made a final observation, "We haven't figured it all out, but we're transforming lives. It [the key to growth] is relevant ministry that connects with people on a heart level."[14]

Biblical Preaching

Comeback leaders know that preaching is more than just persuasive speech. Everybody seems to be an expert on preaching, because everyone who listens to a sermon has an idea of whether they like it or not. False boundaries abound when it comes to preaching. Many will say that there is only one biblical form of preaching, but they miss the point. There are many ways to communicate through preaching, but all of them require a biblical foundation and an appropriate form from which to communicate.

Comeback leaders know that biblical preaching must include *something* to make it a biblical message rather than a speech. The Bible does compel us to "proclaim the message" (2 Tim. 4:2). New methods of preaching have emerged, but they must still be evaluated in light of this biblical command. The Bible gives clear direction about preaching: "Proclaim the message; persist in it whether convenient or not; rebuke, correct, and encourage with great patience and teaching. For the time will come when they will not tolerate sound doctrine, but according to their own desires, will accumulate teachers for themselves because they have an itch to hear something new" (2 Tim. 4:2–3).

If the Word is preached faithfully and fervently, it will accomplish God's objectives. "All Scripture is inspired by God and is useful to *teach* us what is true and to *make us realize what is wrong* in our lives. It *corrects* us when we are wrong and *teaches us to do what is right*. God uses it to *prepare* and *equip* his people to do every good work" (2 Tim. 3:16–17 NLT, emphasis added). Whether a sermon is verse-by-verse, thematic, or another style, as long as Scripture sets the agenda and the text is faithfully and passionately delivered, it's effective preaching.

The agenda of a truly biblical message is always set by the words of the Bible and nothing else. Real expositional preaching begins with an examination of God's Word. When we did our surveys, we based them on four common types of preaching: verse-by-verse, thematic, narrative, and topical.

1. *Preaching verse-by-verse* involves the systematic reading and explanation of a passage of the Bible. Often, this type of preaching results in a series of messages based upon a single book of the Bible. While this style breaks down the meaning of each passage piece by piece, it also defines the meaning of each passage within the context

of the entire biblical book being addressed. It is a great way to faithfully present the whole counsel of God.

2. *Thematic preaching* is an excellent method to utilize when preaching on doctrinal subjects or biblical themes. Preachers can combine the teaching of a number of Bible passages in order to address various everyday topics. For example, a speaker could present three different passages (John 14:25–27; Eph. 2:14–18; Phil. 4:4–7) in a message series entitled "Experiencing Real Peace in a Chaotic World." The key is to be faithful to the meaning of the text, not just to use them to prove your point.

   Thematic expository preaching may also involve utilizing as many as ten or twelve Scripture passages in each sermon. Since the Bible provides teaching on various themes dispersed in different books of the Bible, this style of preaching exposes people to the broad spectrum of God's Word. This method helps new Christians or uninformed unbelievers learn about the general themes and consistency found throughout the Bible.

3. *Narrative preaching* utilizes biblical texts that tell a story. The story is the centerpiece of the message and is woven into the entire fabric of the sermon from beginning to end. When using this type of exposition, the preacher might relate a story from one of the Gospels such as when Jesus fed the five thousand (John 6). In sharing the story, the preacher seeks to draw the audience into the story as though they were part of it. Consequently, those listening grasp the full meaning of Jesus' words and teachings and how they apply to everyday life. Narrative preaching can be effective in the postmodern North American culture because personal stories communicate meaning in our culture.

4. *Topical preaching* usually examines one passage of Scripture and centers on one theme. Hence, it is topical.

On the other hand, it is expositional because it utilizes one biblical passage as the source of its content. In regard to the four styles of biblical preaching, this is the easiest to get off track. It can be difficult to be faithful to the biblical context, and it limits the preacher's ability to honestly let the Bible be the foundation of the message. While it is relevant at times, preachers should use this approach to exposition sparingly.

Our team found preaching to be one area that changed little during the church comeback. Churches changed their practice of the ordinances more frequently than they changed their preaching. Though preaching remained the same, it undergirded the entire change process. Other studies, particularly one from Thom Rainer, have indicated the importance of preaching for growing churches. Rainer explained, "The pastors from our study group of evangelistic churches spent five times more time in sermon preparation compared to the pastors in the nonevangelistic churches. We also found a strong relationship between assimilation and sermon preparation time."[15]

The churches in our study utilized more than one style of preaching. Many used three or four. But preaching was a key influence in their turnaround strategies.

Conclusion

Almost all comeback churches identified their mood of worship as celebrative and orderly with a significant emphasis on being informal, contemporary, and expressive. Worship that focuses on God and connects with a church's context is extremely important. In addition, a slight majority of the surveyed churches utilized a verse-by-verse style of preaching, and three other preaching styles were widely used as well. Being faithful to the biblical text is the key. Comeback churches definitely desire to be biblically faithful, but they also seek to be culturally relevant and practical.

Growing Church Worship Review Guide

Church Name: _____

Your Name: _____

(Please bring back a copy of their program/bulletin.)

Order of service at our church:

_____

_____

_____

_____

_____

_____

_____

_____

_____

_____

Order of service at this church:

_____

_____

_____

_____

_____

_____

_____

_____

_____

_____

- How many young adults and families did you see?
  (circle one)   few   about 1/2   most of the people

- How many middle-aged adults and families did you see?
  (circle one)   few   about 1/2   most of the people

- How many young senior adults did you see?
  (circle one)   few   about 1/2   most of the people

- How was the greeting handled, particularly to visitors? How about announcements?

- What was the nursery like? (Please be sure to visit.) Were there children in the service? Did they have activities during the service or separate from the service?

- How did the service "flow"? How long did it last?

- How did the music flow? Where did people "see" the music? (on-screen? hymnbook? etc.)

- What was the music like? Was there a team of leaders or one person? A choir? How many hymns and how many choruses did they sing? How long did they sing? Did they clap? When?

- Did you like the service? Y____ N____   Why or why not?

- What else did you notice?

- What part(s) should our church consider?

Suggestions for Further Study

Gaines, Steve and Dean Merrill. *When God Comes to Church* (Nashville: B & H Publishing Group, 2007).

Macchia, Stephen A. *Becoming a Healthy Church: 10 Traits of a Vital Ministry* (Grand Rapids: Baker Books, 2002).

Murrow, David. *Why Men Hate Going to Church* (Nashville: Thomas Nelson Publishers, 2005).

Rainer, Thom S. *Surprising Insights from the Unchurched and Proven Ways to Reach Them* (Grand Rapids: Zondervan, 2001).

Towns, Elmer L., and Ed Stetzer. *Perimeters of Light: Biblical Boundaries for the Emerging Church* (Chicago: Moody Publishers, 2004).

Towns, Elmer. *Putting an End to Worship Wars* (Nashville: Broadman & Holman Publishers, 1997).

Intentional and Strategic Church Evangelism

When Peniel Baptist Church called Danny Williams as their new pastor, it was a stagnant church on the edge of Palatka, Florida. The church had about 125 in worship; a number that hadn't changed for many years. "It was a typical rural church that had never been able to make the changes it needed to grow," explained Danny. But over an eight-year comeback, the church grew to more than five hundred in two services. One year they baptized more than one hundred people.

How did such a dramatic change occur? Under Danny's leadership, Peniel Baptist Church began a process of reorganization—from Sunday school, to leader training, to prayer and outreach. Lay leaders embraced and increased the vision. They contacted every missing member (hundreds were on the rolls but had not attended for some time). They implemented a churchwide prayer ministry. Finally, they decided to get directly involved in church planting, helping start a church in Crescent Beach, Florida. The church experienced a dramatic upswing in growth and mission.

Today, Danny is leading another church through a similar process. First Baptist Church of Lyons, Georgia, averaged 150 in attendance when Danny became pastor but has added about 100 members in eighteen months. Churches can be revitalized. These churches are evidence, but they're not the only ones. Hundreds turn around every year, stop the decline, and grow both spiritually and numerically. According to our study, most of them develop and implement a more strategic and intentional process for evangelism. The principles for effective evangelism that we've learned and will share in this chapter and the next, if applied, will help your church immensely in its quest to be a comeback church.

Comeback churches think and live evangelism. But how can a church develop a comprehensive and effective evangelistic strategy? Realize that it is possible and churches are doing it every day. It's simple to understand but not easy to implement. Developing an effective evangelistic strategy requires a good plan and people who are willing to go "fishing" with more than one type of lure. A multipronged approach acknowledges that there is no "silver bullet" when it comes to reaching people with the gospel of Jesus Christ. The days of "Lone Ranger" evangelism are a thing of the past. Developing an effective evangelistic strategy requires stages, helping people move from the ranks of the inactive and unreached to being active followers of Jesus Christ.

In the next two chapters, we will talk about how to develop a comprehensive outreach process. In this chapter we will share seven principles for effective evangelism that we've gleaned from comeback churches and from our own ministry. The entire outreach process described in the next two chapters looks something like this:

Church Vision →
   Draw People →
      Welcoming Guests →
         Connecting Guests →
            Assimilating Members →
               Discipling Members

We've all seen outreach and evangelism done badly. Maybe a bad newspaper ad with a picture of the pastor holding a big leather Bible with light shining down from above, or a church sign announcing "Turn or Burn." They produce few results. And, besides repelling the unchurched, sometimes ineffective evangelism can discourage Christians who have invested themselves in what turns out to be a half-baked plan.

Building an Evangelistic Vision

Principle #1: The greatest motivation for evangelism is our own relationship with God, compelling us to love those He loves. Comeback pastors are able to cast a compelling vision for outreach that is shared by the leadership and then the congregation.

We have already dealt with this topic in the chapter on leadership, but it is worth mentioning again—people will not engage in evangelism until they have a vision to do so. Then they will "go and tell" and invite their friends to "come and see." Both are necessary.

Much of what we list below will be about "come and see" (bringing) approaches. That's because this book is about church evangelism and how churches became effective evangelistically. Our research showed that many of those churches grew because they cast a vision for people to bring their friends.

Think for just a moment about how you came to faith in the Lord Jesus Christ. If you are like 97 percent of other people, it was through an existing relationship—a friend, an associate, a relative, or a neighbor.[1] Using existing bridges of credibility and trust with unbelievers is the most effective way to reach those without Christ.

There are a dwindling number of people who are open to a "come and see by visiting my church" strategy. Such a strategy assumes that people have a certain respect for the church and an affinity for the gospel.

If a Buddhist asked you to attend "divine services" with him, you would be less likely to attend if you had no awareness of Buddha, other than something negative. You would think, "I have seen statues of a big guy sitting down, smiling, but I have no clue who he was or what he taught." Then you would begin to wonder, "What should I expect if I go with my Buddhist friend? Are they going to have me stand up and introduce myself? What about the kids? If they get restless during the 'divine service,' can we leave? Will this be incredibly boring to them—and me? I do not know how to find the place in the Buddhist Bible—or whatever they read—so do I not bring one? I don't want to look stupid because I can't find my way around the Buddhist Bible. What if they start chanting a bunch of songs I don't know; what do we do then? Do I have to give money? Can I just remain anonymous and listen to the 'priest' or whatever they call him? Let's sit in the back, drive separately from our friends who invited us just in case it gets weird or something, so we can leave quickly."

This scenario—only with Jesus and the church instead of Buddha and the "divine service"—is becoming more common with a growing percentage of the population in North America. They know little about the church and what they do know is usually informed by what they see on television, or by a negative experience they had with someone claiming to be "Christian." So, "come and see" has not produced good results, but it may still draw people (especially in the South and Midwest). Despite this, it will decrease in effectiveness as the culture continues to move away from its Christian background, heritage, and memory. The bottom line, then, is churches also need to train people to "go and tell." That leads us to the second principle:

Principle #2: In order to train people to "go and tell," we will need to teach them to live like Jesus—to live like a messenger of God in this world.

At His birth, Jesus became God incarnate. "The Word became flesh and took up residence among us. We observed His glory, the glory as the One and Only Son from the Father, full of grace and truth" (John 1:14). At our new birth (John 3:1–19), we become the incarnation of Christ in our communities. "Therefore if anyone is in Christ, there is a new creation; old things have passed away, and look, new things have come" (2 Cor. 5:17).

Because we are new in Christ, we live out the "new life" with integrity before others. Over the bridge of credibility and trust we have built with those in our sphere of influence, we can do much more than just "invite them to church." God uses us in the eternally rewarding ministry of reconciling men and women to God by "going and telling" as well. "All this is from God, who reconciled us to himself through Christ and gave us the ministry of reconciliation: that God was reconciling the world to himself in

Christ, not counting men's sins against them. And he has committed to us the message of reconciliation. We are therefore Christ's ambassadors, as though God were making his appeal through us. We implore you on Christ's behalf: Be reconciled to God" (2 Cor. 5:18–20 NIV).

Notice two important truths from these verses. First, we reconcile men and women to the One with whom they have a broken relationship. Salvation is by grace alone through faith alone in Jesus alone. We help people find reconciliation to God through both "go and tell" and "come and see" approaches. Second, we go as "ambassadors" not diplomats. Diplomats usually represent a country in an effort to negotiate a deal. Ambassadors represent a sovereign power with the message, "Thus says the King!" We represent the King of kings and Lord of lords, and the message we have is one of His willingness to reconcile with us! "God made him who had no sin to be sin for us, so that in Him we might become the righteousness of God" (2 Cor. 5:21 NIV).

The recurring pattern we found with comeback churches was that they cast a compelling vision for outreach. That led them to empower their people, not just to invite people to "come and see," but also trained them to "go and tell."

Becoming a Church of Open Arms

Principle #3: Organize for evangelism using multiple methods.

If evangelism best takes place in Christian community, we have to find a way for people to find their way to that community. Effective evangelistic churches find diverse ways to encourage people to visit and then stay. They don't do that simply by offering the greatest programs to attract people. Such programs often attract Christians, not unbelievers. Instead, they reach their communities through intentional outreach efforts.

Lighthouse Church in Costa Mesa, California, has evangelistic efforts that are mostly laypeople driven. Pastor Dale Fitch draws evangelistic knowledge from Dr. Joseph C. Aldrich's *Lifestyle Evangelism* and Erwin McManus' *Unstoppable Force*. He writes his own training materials based on that knowledge and his experiences.

He trains the laypeople to witness and minister to the homeless, and then they train other members to do the same. "We have to *be* the good news before we can *share* it."[2] Churches like Lighthouse Church have learned to *be, do, and tell the gospel.*

On many occasions, people shared with us that it was not just about "telling," but about "being" and "doing." They know that the gospel is not solely about proclamation but also about how we live. They model their commitment by living out the truths of the gospel in addition to sharing the gospel through their church's outreach efforts.

Principle #4: Comeback churches have learned that it takes a whole church to win a community, but it takes a leader to help them do so.

Pastor Jerry Harris of the First Assembly of God[3] in St. Charles, Missouri, said their evangelistic efforts have been motivated and led by their staff. Pastor Jerry is highly evangelistic in his personality and gifting. In fact, he has been a part of seven church plants since he began his ministry. First Assembly of God has used Outreach Marketing[4] with success, and the staff encourages their people to live a lifestyle of evangelism as well. The church members are encouraged to be, do, and tell the gospel to their friends, neighbors, and families. Pastor Jerry models outreach for the church and shares his stories with the church regularly. His defeats and successes in evangelism help motivate others to share their faith as well.

The church staff partners with the church family to help them bring their friends. They organize, promote, and conduct five major evangelistic events each year—Halloween outreach, Easter production, July 4th celebration, fall festival, and a children's Christmas musical.

The Easter production involves much of the worship arts ministry. Script, music, and choreography are all written by the worship pastor and others in that ministry. Of course, this coincides with a time of year that people are naturally thinking about the resurrection (hopefully) and are willing to accept an invitation to church.

The July 4th celebration includes a brunch for veterans and their families. This outreach event appeals especially to a particular segment of their community.

The children's Christmas musical includes children who may not necessarily be members or even attenders. The church opens the Christmas musical up to anyone who wants to be involved. This has allowed them to reach several unchurched families who came to see their kids at the Christmas musical. Some of those families have come to faith in Christ and some are still on the journey.[5]

Of course, major outreach events do not have to be limited to these five times of the year. If you are in a largely Hispanic population, perhaps a "Cinco de Mayo" celebration would attract and involve many people. If your church was near the Twin Towers, a special September 11th outreach might be effective. Be creative and sensitive to your community calendar!

Principle #5: Comeback churches know that the whole church has to embrace the mandate for evangelism. Everyone can be involved as a prayer, bringer, and/or teller, and should be trained and mobilized in one or more of these areas.

"At Willard Christian Alliance Church[6] in Willard, Ohio, they have used 'Growing Healthy Churches,' a Christian and Missionary Alliance leadership training program."[7]

The Christian and Missionary Alliance program is worth describing. According to their Canadian Pacific organization,[8] the program includes what every church needs to engage in its mission.

Our Ministry Mission: "To restore to the heart of the local church a passion for Great Commission and Great Commandment living!"

Our Strategy: "To help church leaders succeed in becoming Great Commission healthy through training, coaching and resource tools."

We Are Committed To:

. . . the fulfillment of the Great Commission among all age groups—believing that the training and mobilization of leadership is one of the most strategic ways to see this fulfilled.

. . . the autonomy of the local church—recognizing that every body of believers is unique in its potential and needs.

. . . training leadership within the local church in "discipling" strategies—working to make them more effective in reaching people for Jesus Christ.

. . . a philosophy of ministry that revolves around Great Commission and Great Commandment priorities—believing that Jesus not only gave us the message and the mandate, but also the method of ministry through His life.

. . . developing model ministries around the world which can serve as examples and training centers for other ministries.

. . . accomplishing the will of God concerning the Great Commission and giving all glory to Him.[9]

The genius of such programs is that they are tools for involvement. None of them are magical—they are simply helpful ways to get *everybody* doing *something*. Human nature causes many people to sit on the sidelines, but a well-orchestrated plan (like "Growing Healthy Churches") intentionally gets everyone involved and serving.

What the Numbers Mean to You

Principle #6: Comeback churches said that creating an environment in which spontaneous and planned evangelism can take place is a key. We hope so, since that is how we measured them.

Intentionally pursuing the lost and leading people to Christ was the major measuring stick we used in deciding which are "comeback churches" in America. In the last section of the survey, comeback leaders were asked about the top three factors that led to their church's revitalization. In the responses recorded to this question, eleven factors or words were prominent. The word mentioned most often was "prayer," occurring in 143, or 44.7 percent, of the 320 responses. We've dealt with strategic prayer earlier. Second, "evangelism/outreach" was highly valued in these churches.

Comeback leaders rated their perceptions of the impact that resulted from increased or changed evangelistic efforts upon their church's comeback. This question was designed to gauge whether or not the comeback leaders and their churches became more intentional in their evangelistic efforts, and generally, that proved to be the case.

Several observations came from those responses. Comeback churches became more intentional in their evangelistic efforts and they prepared for outreach with prayer and training. They did not just go *do* evangelism without preparation. These churches' evangelistic efforts occurred because they made intentional, strategic efforts to move outward. Responses indicated that many of these churches did not have a "Y'all come" ("come and see") philosophy; they developed a "Here we go!" ("go and tell") approach.

Responses also clearly indicated that comeback churches utilized different strategies and approaches that were appropriate to their particular setting. The most common factors were intentionality and moving outward.

Being intentional and moving outward cannot be overemphasized! The main reason a church does not grow—are you ready for this?—is that it doesn't *want* to grow. Most people who regularly attend smaller churches have their concerns about the "church getting too big." "Besides," someone will say, "if the church grows, my family and I will get lost in the numbers, and we won't have as much say in the future direction of the church," or similar self-centered pronouncements.

Do you have an unshakeable conviction—not just a belief—that God wants YOUR church to grow? Pastor Rick Warren teaches his church at every membership class that there are at least three reasons "Why Our Church Must Never Stop Growing"—even as they've reached 20,000. Those reasons are:

1. Because God loves people.

"The Lord . . . is patient, not wanting anyone to perish, but wants everyone to come to repentance" (2 Pet. 3:9). See also 2 Corinthians 5:14; Luke 15:3–10; and Matthew 9:12–13.

2. Because God commands us to reach out.

"Go out into the country . . . and urge anyone you find to come in, so that My house will be full" (Luke 14:23 TLB).

"In the same way that you gave me a mission in the world, I give them a mission in the world" (John 17:18 MSG).

"[Y]ou will be my witnesses . . ." (Acts 1:8).

3. Because growth is God's will.

"Under Christ's control, the whole Body is nourished . . . and grows as God wants it to grow" (Col. 2:19 GNB).

"Jesus said, '. . . *I* will build my church' (Matt. 16:18)."[10]

Making a decision to grow as a church begins with the leadership deciding to grow and modeling it—whether you think you are effective at it or not. People in comeback churches were intentionally trained and personally engaged in the church's outreach efforts.

Prayer was mentioned frequently as part of an effective strategy in the evangelistic efforts of comeback churches. Prayer is not "all we can do" when it comes to evangelism. Prayer is the best thing we can do! It is like launching long-range missiles into enemy territory.

Everyone in the church should be involved in three ways. Some will commit only to do one of the three—and that's a good place to start. But, eventually, all believers need to be engaged in all three.

First, they should be *pray-ers.* "First of all, then, I urge that petitions, prayers, intercessions, and thanksgivings be made for everyone, for kings and all those who are in authority, so that we may lead a tranquil and quiet life in all godliness and dignity. This is good, and it pleases God our Savior, who wants everyone to be saved and to come to the knowledge of the truth" (1 Tim. 2:1–4). Everyone can pray for the church's outreach to be effective, and pray, by name, for those the church is trying to reach, and pray for specific outreach events.

Second, they should be *bring-ers.* "Andrew, Simon Peter's brother, was one of the two who heard what John had said and who had followed Jesus. The first thing Andrew did was to find his brother Simon and tell him, 'We have found the Messiah' (that is, the Christ). And he brought him to Jesus. Jesus looked at him and said, 'You are Simon son of John. You will be called Cephas' (which, when translated, is Peter)" (John 1:40–42 NIV). Realistically, about half of the congregation will bring and include someone on a "bring a friend" day or some such outreach event.

Third, they should be *tell-ers.* "But you, keep your head in all situations, endure hardship, *do the work of an evangelist,* discharge all the duties of your ministry" (2 Tim. 4:5 NIV, emphasis added). God has put some "tell-ers" in your church already, but you need your church to be made up of tell-ers.

Pray-ers, bring-ers, and tell-ers should include all of us. When we fulfill our roles, true transformation occurs. Below are responses that comeback leaders gave us describing how they live this out in their context. Perhaps these include some ideas you can use:

- The people are good at working within the church. The goal is to get outside of church. This past summer we did a Community Carnival which led to our highest VBS attendance. We started an outreach team—their focus will be on outreach and getting outside of the church.
- We increased [our awareness of] the importance of evangelism training and actual community involvement—festival in the park, a citywide event where we gave away free meals, had a block party trailer, and had evangelism teams speaking to people.
- I led by example. We did outreach events and seed-planting efforts. We do a few events like the 4th of July parade and the Winnamucka Runnamucka—a motorcycle race. We made a simple card with the following message—"Life is short, death is sure; sin is the cause, Christ is the cure."
- We've become more intentional and committed to our evangelistic efforts; nothing else happens on outreach night.
- Assimilation process—Purpose Driven; intentional efforts on holidays; Wednesday night is strictly prayer for revival and community; we have become more intentional, focused, and specific.
- New staff emphasized training; intentional prayer led to acting out evangelism; planted new church in Estow, FL,

and sent three to four families to this plant and gained many more at the sending church.

- Outward-focused attitude toward evangelism; have people identify three unchurched friends to witness to each year; FAITH [see www.lifeway.com/faith]; almost every activity is evangelism focused; planted two churches in the U.S. and twenty-five in Mexico; launching satellite campus in January in Portland, Texas.
- Intentional prayer; attitude change; many churches in New England have given up hope of growing; pastor-instilled belief that growth was possible.
- Intentional prayer; outreach events; children's evangelism; lifestyle evangelism.

Mark Hoult, Gaylord Church of the Nazarene in Gaylord, Michigan, hit three areas frequently mentioned in our study. He explained the need to be sensitive to his congregation because he came on staff immediately following a split in the church. Pastor Hoult immediately set the church's priorities as (1) prayer, (2) leadership, and (3) evangelism. Most often these priorities were conveyed through his sermons. "The people of the church were so desperate for anything that would give them life and growth."[11] The church experienced transformation because they set the right priorities.

Our team asked, "If increased or changed evangelistic efforts had a major or vital effect, please describe how the efforts were increased and/or how they were changed (e.g., started new effort, assimilation process, started training program, revival, intentional prayer, style changes, attitude change, new service, satellite church, church plant, etc.)." The answers we received lead to our seventh principle.

Evangelistic Change and New Emphases

Principle #7: Comeback churches recognized, purposefully planned for, and utilized "doors of entry" to the church.

When most people in America think of "church," they think Sunday morning. Most do not enter the church for the first time through small groups or other means. However, comeback churches intentionally recognized, planned, and utilized "outreach events" or "doors of entry" to bring others to the Lord and into the church. This was by far the leading response. Some churches planned "doors of entry" like "Bring a Friend Day" for the last Sunday in October. That Sunday was the ending of "Daylight Savings Time," so people set their clocks back an hour. People who get an extra hour of sleep are more likely to accept an invitation to church on this day because you have just eliminated a common excuse for not attending, "It's too early." Be creative and think of other "doors of entry."

Of course, there are other effective ways to reach people. Methods used by comeback churches included (in order of frequency) the church evangelism program "F.A.I.T.H.," "preaching," "lifestyle/relational/friendship evangelism," and "training."

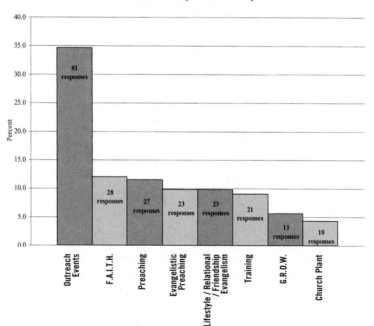

Effective Ways to Reach People

How Can You Lead Your Church to More Effective Evangelism Ministry?

People need plans, and vision helps them formulate those plans. Comeback leaders clarify the vision, provide direction, and help people accomplish God's purpose. How can you lead your church to accomplish God's vision for your congregation? We believe it takes intentionality and courageous faith. Here are some pointers from comeback churches that you can apply in your ministry context.

Start with Intentional Prayer

It is not just cliché—prayer is where it starts. We know it to be true from Scripture, but it also proved true in our study. It is how the early church received its power (Acts 4:23–32; Eph. 6:18–19, etc.). We can follow that same pattern today. Praying for boldness and for a movement of God's Spirit within the community plays a crucial role in any effective outreach strategy.

One way to approach this would be to canvas your surrounding community for prayer requests. Each person who requests prayer could be assigned one or more prayer partners. After prayer partners pray for the request, they can make another visit for an update on the initial prayer request and receive any new requests. This process builds relationships, provides opportunities to share the gospel, and taps into the power of prayer.

This is just one idea for prayer. For methodology, seek the Lord's counsel, and He'll reveal how you can most effectively reach your community for Christ. Perhaps drive around your area in a spirit of prayer and ask God to open your eyes to the needs that He is calling your church to meet with the relevant gospel message.

Help People Bring Friends

This is more than a clichéd "y'all bring someone." Connecting churches teach their members to "invest and invite." Members invest time, energy, and resources in building relationships with their unchurched friends and then invite them to consider the church and the Christ of the church. Having people bring friends to specific events helps them be more intentional about outreach.

I (Mike) and New Hope Community Church planned a Friend Day around our "Church-at-the-Park" on a specific Sunday. Our worship celebration at a local amusement park was an ideal setting for including visitors who might not be comfortable coming into a normal church setting—at least not yet. We invested weeks in preparation. Members and regular attenders were encouraged to follow a prayer strategy for inviting F.R.A.N.s (Friends, Relatives, Associates, and Neighbors). This simple prayer strategy helped members be more intentional about the guests they'd invite. New Hope Community Church used a public display every Sunday leading up to the event to track the number of people being invited. This resulted in the highest attendance day of the year and discovery of several prospects for the church.

Create a Special Ministry or Service

As you survey your community either formally or informally, you'll probably discover some community needs that aren't being met. By starting a particular ministry to meet one of those needs, you will not only help your community, but you will build relationships with unreached people who have those particular needs. Some churches have found that DivorceCare, Celebrate Recovery, parenting classes, and other programs become important points of connection for their outreach strategy.

Plan Outreach Events

The comeback leaders we spoke to frequently spoke of special events as being a key part of their turnaround. It seems that these events help church people have an "excuse" to reach out to others. When there is something special for their friends to "come and see," they are more likely to "go and tell."

Cast a Wider Net

Some churches find that advertising helps cast a wider net and reach people outside of existing relational networks. Many churches use direct mail, radio, newspaper, door-to-door surveys, and other methods to connect to a large number of people. The goal is to get the unchurched to visit the community of believers.

Once they're in that safe place, they can consider the "dangerous" claims of the gospel.

Of course, the most effective long-term strategy, providing the best results, is personal invitation. But advertising and mass media are an effective supplement to this, generating an initial boost of prospects. Word-of-mouth advertising is usually limited to an existing relational network. Mass advertising helps expand the horizons of communication. It creates new relational networks through which the gospel can naturally flow.

Many of these steps cause an expanded vision for outreach and provide opportunities for church members to invite friends. All of these things are tools to connect people and encourage them to "come." But it does not just involve getting people to "come." Part of an effective evangelism process is leading people who visit to become disciples and, eventually, leaders. That process includes welcoming guests, connecting people, assimilating new believers, and discipling members.

Welcome Guests with a Planned Process

Getting people to attend church requires hard work. Making them feel comfortable when they visit also requires a plan. Most churches have ushers, but ushers are for movie theaters and funeral homes. Churches need greeters—volunteers who intentionally welcome and encourage guests to connect with the church family.

For most churches, welcoming guests means an usher at the door to the worship center. That's expected! If you want to really connect with your guests, place greeters at four locations:

1. In the parking lot—so that they can make a great first impression. (Hint: On rainy days they can help with umbrellas.)
2. Outside the outer door—pointing people inside to a welcome center and the worship center.
3. At a welcome center—greeting guests and providing more information.
4. At the door to the worship center—handing out church programs and shaking hands. (Sorry we were so tough on the ushers, but this is where they enter the picture.)

Greeters provide a connection with the church that replaces older methods such as having guests wear special nametags, stand up for introductions, or even remain seated while members stand in "their honor." These methods are sometimes awkward for guests.

The last important element of welcoming guests happens immediately following the service. Guests evaluate the friendliness of their experience from the moment they arrive until the moment they leave. What happens after the service is just as critical as what happens when they arrive.

In many churches, as soon as the service ends, the regulars flock together and basically ignore guests. Train key leaders to employ the "3-Minute Rule"—for three minutes after the service, they should focus only on making sure that guests are properly welcomed. This could mean inviting them to grab a cup of coffee and exchanging small talk for a couple of minutes. Finish the conversation by saying, "It was great to meet you. Thanks for coming. I hope I see you again." In addition, you could have coffee greeters posted in the coffee area to be on the lookout for guests and make sure they feel welcome.

Churches need to develop a way of follow-up. That means keeping track of guests. Many churches use some type of communication card to accomplish this. When people visit, they're asked to fill in their name, address, and other personal information to the degree that they're comfortable. Within the next several days (best within 48 hours), contact guests by phone, letter, or both just to say "thank you for coming." Encourage them to return. Here is a simple process to follow for contacting guests:

- Sunday afternoon: Phone call from a layperson who's committed to outreach
- Tuesday: Letter from the pastor (mailed Monday)
- Thursday: Letter from a small-group leader (mailed Wednesday)
- Saturday: Call from the pastor inviting them to return

Once this system is established, you have a prospect database that you can utilize for special events. For example, when I (Ed) founded and pastored Millcreek Community Church, we planned a special event around Easter Sunday. We rented the theater of a local school, sent out mailers to the entire community, called previous guests from our prospect data base, and invited friends and family. Our average attendance at the time was 250, but about 750 came to our Easter service—many of them from our list of past guests. And, best of all, about 100 new people stayed around each Sunday thereafter.

Ministry and outreach is about connecting with people—for God so loved the world . . . that's people. He sent His Son, and His Son is sending us (John 20:21) to connect with and reach people. Developing a churchwide evangelistic strategy is about having the same vision that the Father, Son, and Holy Spirit have—to connect with, relate to, and love people.

When people experience the love of God within a genuine, caring, and biblical community of believers, they're more likely to connect not only with the church family, but also with the Lord of the church. This process requires faith, hard work, and a practical plan to partner with believers to reach their friends.

Conclusion

By now, its pretty obvious that it takes work to do outreach well. You will have to understand your community and then reach it. Lewis and Cordeiro remind us to ask, "What is your way of finding out the needs of people in your church and in your community? . . . *The more you know about your church and community, the more you'll be able to discern what God wants you to do next.*"[12]

Comeback churches have worked hard to reach out—and the dividends are eternal. Outreach involves much more than just getting people to come to Christ or visit your church. Many churches will expend more energy planning annual homecoming events than they do planning outreach. We should constantly help more people get to their heavenly home. If we are to see more churches make a turnaround, we need to be more intentional with church evangelism and discipleship. The end result will be transformed churches and transformed lives.

If we faithfully PLAN to sow the seeds of the gospel and actively PURSUE reaching others with the gospel of Christ, He will make sure that SPONTANEOUS GROWTH occurs as well.

Remember the promise of our Lord: "He also said, 'This is what the kingdom of God is like. A man scatters seed on the ground. Night and day, whether he sleeps or gets up, the seed sprouts and grows, though he does not know how. *All by itself* the soil produces grain—first the stalk, then the head, then the full kernel in the head. As soon as the grain is ripe, he puts the sickle to it, because the harvest has come'" (Mark 4:26–29 NIV, emphasis added).

Just as God has put laws at work in nature causing the ground to produce crops "all by itself," so He has put certain principles at work in the spiritual realm. "What, after all, is Apollos? And what is Paul? Only servants, through whom you came to believe—as the Lord has assigned to each his task. I planted the seed, Apollos watered it, but God made it grow. So neither he who plants nor he who waters is anything, but only God, who makes things grow" (1 Cor. 3:5–7 NIV). Let's sow the seed and watch God make it grow—"all by itself"—in our churches!

Suggestions for Further Study

Hybels, Bill, and Mark Mittelburg. *Becoming a Contagious Christian* (Grand Rapids: Zondervan, 1996).

Newman, Randy. *Questioning Evangelism: Engaging People's Hearts the Way Jesus Did* (Grand Rapids: Kregel Publications, 2004).

Mittelberg, Mark, with Bill Hybels. *Building a Contagious Church: Revolutionizing the Way We View and Do Evangelism* (Grand Rapids: Zondervan Publishing House, 2000).

Sjogren, Steve, Dave Ping, and Doug Pollack. *Irresistible Evangelism: Natural Ways to Open Others to Jesus* (Loveland, CO: Group Publishing, 2003).

www.outreach.com.

Connecting People to Spiritual Maturity

I (Ed) remember it like it was yesterday. We were reviewing our first year and planning for the future. We discovered that more than a thousand people had visited our church during that first year, but only a hundred had stayed; our "back door" was almost as large as our "front door." An honest review of our first year of ministry revealed to us that we not only had failed to close the back door, we seemed to have left it wide open, marked with a flashing emergency exit sign.

Our problem was not unique. Many churches have learned to attract guests but have a hard time leading them to become committed disciples. Why is it easier to generate visitors than to produce members? We decided some of our loss was related to style issues—perhaps visitors didn't like the music, the building, or our style of service. Yet, that was not the whole story. Many people who connected with the music, building, and style of service still weren't connecting with our church.

Having an excellent worship service is one thing. But, it is not enough. As Toler and Gilbert explain:

> Churches should be much more than Sunday morning "entertainment centers" for lukewarm saints. They should be "training centers" where people learn how to win the lost for Christ. They should be growing by adding souls to the Kingdom. But statistics show that only 20 percent of our churches are growing at all, and less than 5 percent are growing by conversion rather than

transfer. This appalling lack of tangible results must call us to our knees in prayer and then to our feet in action if the church is to fulfill the Great Commission that our Lord entrusted to us. Failure to employ effective ministry teams could be a major cause.[1]

At our church, we felt we were doing all the things we thought we should, but people were not moving from attendance to real discipleship. Evangelism that does not result in discipleship is flawed, and our church knew it. Change was needed and was soon implemented.

People Need Connection

Pastor Todd Lamphere explained to us in an e-mail:

For us at FBC Altamonte, so much of the growth has been with new or newly reconnected believers. Most of them desire membership, so our membership class teaches them the basic tenants of the faith through our core values. Additionally, through connecting them with our BodyLife class, new believers and new members are coached on how to have a daily time with God and discovery of their spiritual gift. New members and believers are encouraged to fulfill core value number six: Life change happens in small groups. It is in our Sunday school classes that we systematically teach God's Word. Our worship services are practical and relevant, so many of the connection with God issues (assurance of God's forgiveness, confidence that God hears our prayers, etc.), are covered in a life application format.[2]

Comeback churches used strategies that help people stay and grow. Getting people to come and visit is one thing, but getting them to stay is another. Neither is easy, but both are necessary. Comeback churches see evangelism as a journey, not a destination. They find ways to attract guests. And they develop a systematic way to welcome guests, utilizing greeters and making sure that guests feel as welcome when they leave as when they arrive.

With the right vision and a God-centered and culturally relevant worship service, church members will be encouraged and motivated to bring and welcome guests. But, we also need to help guests make relational connections within the church family. Connecting people can be difficult—and it takes true disciples to make the right connection. "The congregation needs to see that we genuinely live out our evangelistic mission, values, and strategy. If we want to build contagious churches, we as leaders must first become contagious Christians."[3]

Most worship services are not designed for true connection to take place. Dozens, hundreds, or thousands of people sitting with faces forward, looking at a stage is not the right environment for connection to occur. However, in our culture, most people visit the main worship service before visiting anywhere else. To connect people, you have to move them from the worship service to the small group or Sunday school.

Some churches use Sunday school while others use small groups that meet in homes. Whichever you use, it requires a strategy and small-group leaders must be an integral part of your connection strategy.

Guests in most churches give permission for a follow-up contact when they give you their names. When a person fills out a card today, they know someone will pass that information along. Nobody is fooled by the "Free Drawing for a Health Club Membership if you fill out this card!" They know if they fill out the card, someone from the club will contact them. So, this is true in the church as well. If someone fills out a guest card, they are giving the church permission to contact them.

Many churches get frustrated because their guests don't fill out a card, but it shouldn't cause concern. The guests are simply not ready to connect. Tricking them into giving their information (by taking it from the nursery sign-in or by having all the regular attendees stand) does nothing to build trust and confidence.

When a guest fills out a card, the first follow-up should include—at the very least—a letter and a call from the pastor or outreach leader. However, follow-up is not complete until the guest connects with a small-group leader. When guests have given their names, they expect a contact, and the most effective place for them to connect is the small group. So let a small-group leader make the next contact.

Comeback churches have found lots of ways to do this. Some use evangelistic visitation. In one plan—F.A.I.T.H.—churches take the names of permission-giving guests and visit them *with the purpose* of connecting them to the Sunday school class. Whatever system you use, the point is the same. People *must* connect with a smaller group if they are to "Velcro" to your church. If you want to connect guests, get them into a small group system so that relationships can be established.

|||||||||||||||||||||||||||||||||||||||||||||||||||||
It is helpful to think in terms of two different kinds of conversion: 1. conversion to community, and 2. conversion to Christ.
_____

Pastor Cere Muscarella from Angleton Foursquare Church in Texas e-mailed us and explained:

Small groups are essential to the church being the church. Meeting together, eating together, fellowshipping, sharing each other's needs . . . that's the church. . . . The small groups that we have today live on their own. We create community around enterprise. Outreach people meet with outreach people. Alpha people end up hanging out together, whether it's leadership or participants. People with transgenerational interests hang out with each other. People who work to inspire our kids end up hanging out. And it has created a culture in our congregation that works. The church has become a resource center for the groups, and the groups use the facilities here all the time. It has created excitement and the turnaround that we have been experiencing.[4]

People need to connect in community to consider the truth claims of the gospel. In a couple of my (Ed's) books, I have illustrated this as an evangelism journey. With few exceptions, people come to Christ in steps, and those steps usually involve conversation and community with believers. There really are two conversions—the first to community ("I like and trust these people and want to learn with them") and then to Christ ("I make a dangerous decision for Christ in a safe community of friends").

It is helpful to think of these as two different kinds of conversion—one earthly and one eternal. The *conversion to community* means that guests connect relationally with a community of

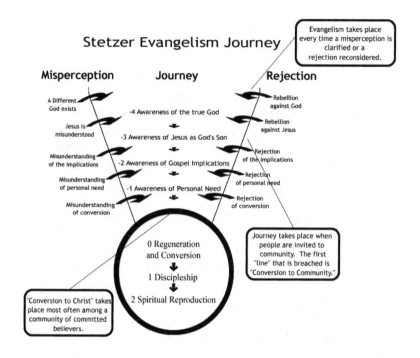

Stetzer Evangelism Journey

Evangelism takes place every time a misperception is clarified or a rejection reconsidered.

Misperception   **Journey**   **Rejection**

A Different God exists
Jesus is misunderstood
Misunderstanding of the implications
Misunderstanding of personal need
Misunderstanding of conversion

-4 Awareness of the true God
-3 Awareness of Jesus as God's Son
-2 Awareness of Gospel Implications
-1 Awareness of Personal Need

Rebellion against God
Rebellion against Jesus
Rejection of the implications
Rejection of personal need
Rejection of conversion

0 Regeneration and Conversion
1 Discipleship
2 Spiritual Reproduction

Journey takes place when people are invited to community. The first "line" that is breached is "Conversion to Community."

"Conversion to Christ" takes place most often among a community of committed believers.

believers because they feel "safe" in that environment. This involves several different points of contact. The funnel-shaped lines (representing community) stretch upward and have multiple points. At any of these points, a person can decide to begin a spiritual journey toward Christ because of his experience with community.

The circle in the diagram represents the church. Experiencing Christian community and becoming part of the church is not the same thing. Unbelievers can and should be encouraged to connect relationally with a community of believers. But that doesn't make them part of the church. When a person experiences the second type of conversion—the *conversion to Christ*—they become a part of the church eternal.

Each curved arrow represents a different kind of evangelistic encounter. For example, a person who has rejected and rebelled against Jesus can consider Jesus' identity and lordship in conversation with Christian friends. They may begin to believe that Jesus is God's unique Son and then accept the claims of Christ. Through their conversion to community, guests have the opportunity to work through their doubts or misperceptions, consider truth claims, and experience conversion to Christ.

The journey will not be the same for every individual, people group, worldview, or culture. The misconceptions and reasons for rejecting the gospel may differ, but each person who comes to Christ must make the journey along the center column. People who are connected in community are more likely to make the journey to connect with Christ.

People Need Community

As guests become members, they first make a commitment to Christ, and then commit to His church. People who move from attendance to membership must turn away from their sinful lifestyles and receive Jesus Christ. New believers often drop out because they are unstable in their faith, attached to their lifestyle, or deficient in their understanding of Scripture.

The task of the church is to introduce others to Christ, and we should recognize that people are especially receptive when their stability is shaken. Many people need help getting out of their current situations and making a stable connection. My friend Dan Morgan, former Saddleback assimilation pastor and now seminary professor, explains that people need relational, biblical, and functional stability. To assimilate new believers into the life of the church, current believers need stability in their own lives—and God uses the church family to help meet that need.

Relational Stability

William Hendricks argues that new Christians are likely to leave the church within the first six months if they don't develop at least seven significant relationships in the congregation during that time.

Unfortunately, many Christians make little effort to cultivate new friends because they feel comfortable with the friends they already have. Congregations need to accept new believers' immaturity and make it a priority to welcome and befriend them. If believers don't involve new converts in their circle of faith, these converts may never experience the biblical and functional stability that Christ offers.

Think of relationships in the church like building with Legos. If you have ever played Legos with your children, you know that only certain sizes "snap together." You could use three smaller sizes to snap onto a larger size, but once the blocks are filled, you cannot connect other pieces. There just are so many connections that can be made before you have to move on to another piece.

The same is true with relationships in a church. Because most members have already connected ("snapped together") with other members, the relationships are saturated to the point that there aren't anymore "blocks" to connect with new people. So visitors to the church are made to feel like they cannot connect until someone in the existing relationship either dies or leaves the church. The blocks are filled. This is why most churches have fewer than one hundred people. This is also why, if your church wants to grow, it is imperative that you constantly begin new small groups with new people. Find points of affinity and connect people together—even if the only connecting point initially is that they are all new to the church.

Biblical Stability

Churches that establish new believers in the faith must teach them several important matters: a mature understanding of God, assurance of God's forgiveness, certainty of their salvation, the purpose of the church, and confidence that God hears their prayers. New believers develop biblical stability in their lives when the church teaches and preaches that God's Word is powerful, authoritative, and true. This area of stability is the easiest of the three to develop—if the new believers are part of Bible study and worship.

Functional Stability

New believers long for "functional stability." If they still wrestle with drug abuse, sexual immorality, or other concerns, they will be unable to focus on issues of spiritual maturity. The church cannot expect new believers to demonstrate good spiritual habits immediately but must help them make a commitment to develop habits displayed by those who are mature in Christ. This may involve helping them get free of habits that hinder their spiritual growth. I have known very few adults who made commitments to Christ without a significant crisis. And that crisis does not automatically disappear after they become Christians.

People Need Commitment

Many comeback churches—53 percent—raised the requirements of church membership, challenging people to live out the privileges and responsibilities of the covenant community described in Scripture. Increasing membership requirements is not an easy process, but it is a sign of something significant.

When surveyed about membership requirements *before* the comeback, almost all respondents said that they required a statement of faith (94%). Almost as many (92%) indicated that they received people into membership based upon a transfer of letter. Some (78%) required baptism for membership. Other requirements included: new member class (28%), signed covenant (22%), tithe (21%), ministry involvement (9%), and small groups/Sunday school (2%).

Slightly less than half (47%) said their membership requirements stayed the same after the comeback. Only one respondent indicated that his church lowered its membership requirements. This significant discovery led us to explore further. How were membership requirements raised? Almost all the respondents mentioned that they had added a new member class (93.2%). Important to note was that 33.9 percent also added a signed covenant to their membership requirements.

Overall, the key finding was that the majority of comeback churches raised their requirements in regard to membership. All the rest (but one) maintained their existing membership requirements. Churches may need to raise expectations as part of developing an effective comeback strategy. The experience of one comeback church illustrates this point.

Rob Morris, pastor of Terrace Heights Baptist Church, in Yakima, Washington, said his vision included leading all church members to a deeper level spiritually. First, Pastor Morris communicated this vision to his deacons. Once they agreed, a plan was developed and shared with committees, then discussed in small groups and Sunday morning sermons. Finally, the plan was adopted at a church business meeting by a unanimous vote. "This church was dead and ready to close its doors. They were desperate for anything that might bring life. We know it is working because we have seen very few people leave or stop coming to the church."[5] Their membership requirements were changed to include the following: (1) a new members class and (2) a new members "boot camp," which is a one-year journey consisting of classes in spiritual foundations, spiritual formation, evangelism training, and spiritual equipping for ministry.

If your church doesn't have a membership class process, there are many places to look for help. Find existing membership materials from another church in your denomination, or in your area, and adapt them to fit your church's context. Also, you can look for materials and resources from Saddleback or Willow Creek or other well-known churches. You don't have to reinvent the wheel. Just find good materials and work with the church family to establish a membership process.

The pastor should lead the membership class, though other leaders can help. New people need to connect with the pastor and his vision. Invite each newcomer personally. Follow up within a week of the actual membership classes. Encourage the class attenders to review the materials and to consider the true nature of the commitment before them.

A membership class is a big step, particularly for a church that does not have one. But the formation of a membership class was a key to revitalization at two of the churches I (Ed) served. Both churches not only required the membership classes, but they made them retroactive. One church made a new category of "inactive member," since they were not ready to remove uninvolved people from the "rolls." We made sure that our members understood our vision and direction in providing the class. Many of our members wanted to be part of the class and it had a big, and very positive, impact on the church.

To encourage people to consider a membership class, many churches have an intermediate step—a brunch with the pastors to talk about the church and where it is headed. Many churches call this a "church chat." These are usually rather informal meetings after the church service with a handful of current members and a majority of new attendees. In a brief format, newcomers can learn about the pastors, the vision of the church, and the next step for membership. Make no mistake, membership matters!

Thom Rainer in his book *High Expectations* describes in great detail how churches with high membership requirements and expectations grow faster and are more evangelistically effective than those without high expectations. He states, "One of the key issues in closing the back door was the presence of a new member class as a required entry point for members. . . . Churches that *require* persons to enter membership through a new member class have a much higher retention rate than those that do not."[6]

Membership classes include: a clear presentation of what it means to become a Christian, the church's organizational structure, church ordinances (baptism and the Lord's Supper), the church's vision and mission, the church's significant historical events, and other appropriate topics. However, teaching about salvation is indispensable.

Most people seeking church membership do not understand the fundamentals of the Christian faith. They want to be "good," and church membership is a helpful part of being good. They want to be "right," and sense that membership is right. However, they need to be taught that none are "good" and none are "right." Only by experiencing the truths of the gospel can someone truly be good and be righteous. We take about one hour in every membership class to teach the truth of the gospel. This is about 25 to 30 percent of the total time necessary to complete an effective membership class.

People Need Discipling

Comeback churches do not just lead people to make decisions to accept Christ; they engage them in discipleship. When we connect people to Christ, involve them in a small group, and help them commit to membership, they make real, significant, and lasting relationship connections. Discipleship occurs organically.

Churches should ensure that each of their members receives biblical teaching on the key habits of discipleship: reading Scripture, prayer, small group, tithing, witnessing, and other disciplines. There are many things that people want to learn (end times, spiritual warfare, ad infinitum), but there are some things they need to learn—basic doctrines and habits of the Christian life. These are best done when a church has an intentional postmembership strategy to lead people to maturity. The most important thing is to lead our people, intentionally and systematically, to deeper maturity in Christ.

Some do it in a linear way (like Mike's church that uses Purpose Driven's baseball diamond). Some do it in a newcomer's class that covers a range of topics over several months. The church I (Ed) copastor uses a nonlinear model. I describe our process below, not because it is best, but because it includes elements that we believe every church needs in its discipleship strategy. In a nonlinear fashion, after taking the basic class (Lake Ridge Journey), members can choose to participate in Bible studies that fit their current needs of life.

- Practices of Spirituality (Prayer, Bible Study Methods, Spiritual Disciplines)
- Practices of Worship (Song, Meditation, Giving/Tithing)
- Practices of Missional Living (Evangelism)
- Practices of Service (Spiritual Gifts, Ministry Involvement)
- Practices of Community (Fellowship, Accountability)
- Practices of Simplicity (Simple Living, Family, Giving)

Comeback leaders learned and applied the principles of growth through discipleship. This, in turn, benefits the ones discipled, their church, and others whose lives they touch. Think of it this way. Life is a process. You have to crawl before you walk, and certainly before you run. You learn to say simple, one-syllable words before you utter a sentence. You don't do multivariable calculus until you've learned addition, subtraction, multiplication, and division (plus other concepts along the way). You can't lift heavy weights until you've strengthened your muscles by lifting smaller weights.

What do all these things have in common? Process and progression! We build on what we've learned or done previously. When we come to Christ, we're spiritually immature and certainly lack knowledge. God uses the process of discipleship to strengthen us, grow us, mature us, and make us into the image of His Son. All of the experiences, or ingredients, are there to accomplish His purpose in us. Look at the following two lists and you'll see a process. But more than the process, it's the purpose that's important.

For Cooks	**For Churches**
1. Use flour, salt, butter, and cocoa	1. Evangelize
2. Add sugar	2. Fellowship
3. Mix in two eggs	3. Teach and equip
4. Bake at 375 degrees	4. Worship
5. *Make a cake*	5. *Make disciples*

Each list has five actions, but only one fulfills the ultimate purpose. The other four are merely parts of the process; steps to accomplish that purpose. In God's Word, every other action is subordinate to the purpose of making fully functioning followers of Jesus Christ. We pray, we fellowship, we teach, we worship, we evangelize—for the purpose of making disciples. We do not make disciples for the purpose of praying, fellowshipping, equipping, evangelizing, etc.[7] Many churches get caught up in the process. They're mired down in minutia. They're too busy with programs and problems to look at possibilities and purpose. There's no intentionality.

Why is this significant? A church that is unintentional in the process of bringing new people *and* helping them become Christ followers is in decline for at least two reasons:

1. The leaders do not know *what* a disciple is. They don't have a clear, well-defined picture of the purpose God has for their church at this point in history, and what they are called of God to produce. If we went to a shoe factory and asked three employees what they're making, we should get the same answer. The same is true in the church. When we ask regular attenders in any church,

"What is this church producing?" there should be a consistent reply—"Disciples!"

2. The leaders do not know *how* to make disciples. They think that by just adding some "ingredients" a disciple will be produced. Such is not the case; there has to be an intentional process, based upon a clear purpose, to make a specific product (a disciple).

If you are still not convinced about the true state of your church, use the template of the comeback churches as a grid through which to evaluate your church. Or, for an honest evaluation of your church, why not have a mature, trusted, and truthful Christian (preferably from another town) visit your church as a first-time guest? Have him or her fill out an evaluation immediately following the visit that includes everything—the ease of finding the facility, the facility's appearance, finding the Sunday school room, the greeting, if the church felt "cliquish," the worship, the relational connectedness, and if they would attend your church regularly if they lived in your area. It is very easy for us to tell ourselves that we are "the most loving church in town," but are we really? This little exercise alone will give you a look at your church through a visitor's eyes. And that can be extremely helpful, especially if you have been in the same routine for very long.

Closing the Back Door

Pastor George Stevenson led a group of laymen at East Gate Church of the Nazarene in Roanoke, Virginia, to develop what is called the "Harvest Twelve" ministry. It includes the twelve most important ministries in their church. One hundred laymen signed up to be involved during a ministry fair. This effort has helped "close the back door." When combined with their CARE ministry, which reaches out to the shut-ins, nursing homes, and people who haven't visited church in awhile, these ministries help to successfully retain a majority of their members and attenders.[8] Comeback churches know that closing the back door helps them make a turnaround.

Often believers will bring a close friend or family member along with them in their own spiritual journey, inviting them to church, explaining the unfamiliar, and introducing the lost person to the Christian experience. In order to reach these community-conscious seekers, churches need to remember these things we gleaned from our own experience and from the comeback churches:

1. *Friendliness is not enough*—People are not looking for a friendly church, they are looking for friends. Many churches are not prepared to move visitors into relationships with others in the church.

2. *Christians and Christianity are peculiar*—Who we are and what we do is different. If we're doing it right, the "difference" will draw others to Christ. But, we can't expect the unchurched to put the puzzle together by themselves.

3. *Closing the back door takes planning*—In order to keep guests and new converts, churches need to work as hard as they would for a VBS, a large gathering, or a church outreach. All of these are only effective to the extent that guests become new believers and active members.

Closing the back door is not easy. It requires connected, stable church members, who stay for the long haul. Such church members need to develop in at least eight ways. These are adapted from *The Master Plan for Making Disciples* by Win and Charles Arn (Baker Books, 1998):

- Worship regularly
- Guide friends and family to follow Christ
- Identify with church goals
- Tithe regularly
- Identify seven new friends in the church
- Identify their own spiritual gifts
- Participate in at least one role or task in the church
- Participate in a small group

The goal is simple, but the task can be overwhelming. We have a sacred task—to care for those Christ sends our way. A church can do this by developing a complete outreach process: envision, invite, welcome, connect, assimilate, and disciple. This process not only opens the front door wide, it helps close the back door.

Conclusion

Many churches have found ways to attract the unchurched, but keeping them has been a bigger challenge. It can be done, but it takes work. Churches that are willing to intentionally connect people to Christ and other believers can become spiritual greenhouses—places where new believers can take root, grow and ultimately blossom in their relationship with Christ and His church. You and your new members really can fulfill that vision in your church!

Suggestions for Further Study

Lewis, Robert, with Bob Wilkins. *The Church of Irresistible Influence* (Grand Rapids: Zondervan, 2001).

McIntosh, Gary, and Glen Martin. *Finding Them, Keeping Them: Effective Strategies for Evangelism and Assimilation in the Local Church* (Nashville: Broadman & Holman Publishers, 1992).

Rainer, Thom S. *High Expectations: The Remarkable Secret for Keeping People in Your Church* (Nashville: Broadman & Holman Publishers, 1999).

Motivating and Mobilizing People Out of the Pews

At Hebron Baptist Church in Bush, Louisiana, Tim Payne, the church's minister of music and youth, said their deacons committed to serve at a crucial time in the church's history. "Visitation has been deacon and lay-driven in the absence of a full-time pastor. Initially forty people came each week to visit lost people and prospects, while the morning worship attendance was around one hundred. We're in a building program, and much of the work is being done by laypeople."[1] Now, Hebron is seeing the results. Attendance at the church is approaching 150 every Sunday—an increase of 50 percent from 2002.

The story of Hebron Baptist Church describes an important dynamic for many comeback churches. A transition took place in these churches that engaged more laypeople in meaningful ministry. One barrier that keeps some churches from growing is an inadequate structure for growth. When most of the ministry centers on the pastor, the church's growth potential is limited to the number of ministry areas the pastor can oversee. *For churches to be able to grow most effectively and reach their full potential, a change has to take place in the role of the pastor, and the people have to step up and use their spiritual gifts.*

Pastors should no longer see themselves as the only ministers of the church, realizing that God has placed a whole army of people around them with gifts, talents, skills, and abilities to mobilize and empower. The people need to become ministers as well. Christian Schwarz in his book *Natural Church Development* calls this "empowering leadership."

This process of motivating and mobilizing the people provides opportunities for them to discover and utilize their unique giftedness and serve in the power of the Holy Spirit. According to a *Leadership Journal* study on church revitalization, "Turnaround leaders pay careful attention to team building and timing, not just to vision." There is a tipping point when almost everyone in the congregation realizes that change is needed, but you can't rush this. Open and frequent communication, involving everyone, is a key factor.[2]

The rest of this chapter outlines the importance of, and methods for, changing the attitudes of the people in your church and getting them involved in ministry. Getting people involved in ministry rated third after leadership and vibrant faith as a strategic factor in comeback churches. But how did these comeback churches mobilize their people? What kinds of training materials did they use?

Getting People Involved in Ministry

Changing Attitudes Is Vital

Before people can be motivated, their hearts have to be changed. Attitudes were one of the top challenges these comeback churches faced in regard to being revitalized. What did pastors intentionally do to change attitudes or traditions?

Bluff Avenue Church in Fort Smith, Arkansas, used campaigns to spur their attitude change. "Several things led to our new attitude," said pastor Robert Berry. "Two major events were the *40 Days of Purpose* and *40 Days of Community* campaigns. Also, we make our services positive and inviting, which helped with visitors."[3] Two other contributions to the attitude change were [an evangelistic Sunday school program called] F.A.I.T.H. and a strong Vacation Bible School. The people bought into the vision of the church.

We heard many stories of changed attitudes, but in no case did these attitudes happen—leadership was exerted to change attitudes. Once attitudes were changed, people were soon motivated to serve.

Lay Ministry Is Vital

When asked, "Was your church's comeback affected by mobilizing the laity in a greater way?" comeback leaders responded that it was, rating this third (3.87) among the factors of vibrant faith, evangelistic efforts, mobilizing the laity, small groups, marketing, facilities' changes, and leadership. That tells us that lay ministry or mobilization is clearly important in effecting a comeback.

At Idaville Church of God in Indiana, the church had been focused on its building for many years. Pastor Raderstorf explained how he led the church to make a change, "We went through a six-week vision-casting workshop. We found out where we were as a church and where we needed to be." They established eight ministry teams that fit the needs of the church and community. "A new, fresh vision made the people excited because they knew what was going on."[4] Now, they continually equip their members for service through training and sermons geared toward service. They mobilized their people for ministry.

Comeback leaders were then asked, "If mobilizing the laity had a major or vital effect, please describe how the mobilization took place (starting a gift discovery process, increasing ministry expectations, renewal, evangelism training, increased prayer, etc.)." Over eleven pages of responses were recorded from 264 churches. Here is a sampling of their comments:

- Over three years of intentional study and training from pastor; work of ministry done from pew not pulpit; had never done any gift discovery; did study on motivational gifts; need to serve as gifted; only place people in area of giftedness.
- Primarily teaching SHAPE; people taking ownership of the church; they can be part of enacting change; phrase used—"nobody should have two jobs until everybody has at least one."
- Servanthood—increased ministry expectations and increased prayer.

- Emphasized unity in the church; taught biblical model of church evangelism training and gift discovery.
- Preached salvation and discipleship; encouraged from pulpit; increased prayer; programs don't work with our congregation.
- Discipleship program that trains people to get involved.
- Previous pastors created positions and threw people in to serve; this pastor took time to train, do gifts assessment, and place accordingly.
- Starting a discovery process; increasing ministry expectations; leaders cast vision for church and how members can get involved.
- Different venues for getting people involved (gifts inventory, volunteers, approaching, etc.).
- Increasing ministry expectations—challenged to get involved.
- Talking with people about gifts and talents and placing them accordingly.
- Emphasized high commitment; gifts assessment and placed accordingly.
- Preaching about service; changing mind-set of who should do ministry.
- Trained men to do ministry.
- Launched a team-oriented vision; implemented team strategy in everything.
- Challenging preaching; verbal encouragement; informal gifts assessment; people must attend six months before they can be involved in ministry.
- Involvement through small groups; NETWORK gifts assessment.
- Evangelism training; informal gifts assessment and ministry placement.

The word mentioned most often was "gifts" (136 times, or 51.5% of the total responses). More specifically, "gifts assessment" was mentioned 77 times (29.2% of responses). "Expectations" was recorded in 43 (16.3%) of the responses. Other key terms respondents gave for their revitalization included: "ministry expectation"

(38 times, or 14.4%); "training" (42 times, or 15.9%); "discovery" (32 times, or 12.1%); "prayer" (29 times, or 11%). In one or more ways—SHAPE,[5] PDC, 101–401, 40 Days—the Purpose Driven model was mentioned in 19 (7.2%) of responses. Finally, the word "challenge" appeared 15 times (5.7%) in responses.

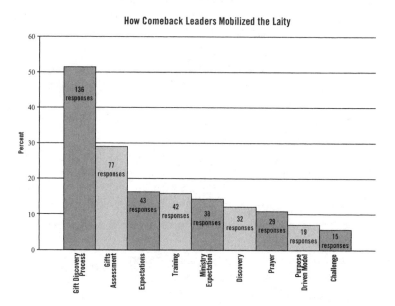

How Comeback Leaders Mobilized the Laity

Three Components of Effective Laypeople Mobilization

Create an Atmosphere of Expectation

Pastor Brian Salber explained how they created such an atmosphere at Visalia Foursquare Church in California:

> It was quite simple as a new leader to see the changes that needed to take place. From how we received the offering, to counting the attendance, to the order of worship, to the art work hanging in the church. It was a small church because it was run with a small church mentality. There was no rhyme or reason to how and why things were done. So we began to change all the major components of our Sunday Service. It was as though we

were getting ready for company to come over. . . . People began to get excited and started inviting their friends and growth was a natural outcome. It was some basic changes, a lot of prayer, and a little success. Our congregation finally felt like we had something to offer and we all anticipated growth. Since those early days we have grown out of our facility and moved to a larger one.[6]

In analyzing responses from comeback churches, three main issues rose to the surface—expectations, equipping, and empowerment. Over and over, comeback leaders stated that increasing expectations is a key to creating an atmosphere for mobilization of the laity. Church members are expected to be involved and to use their God-given gifts, talents, and skills.

Pastors and church members should recall God's job description for the pastor:

It was he who gave some to be apostles, some to be prophets, some to be evangelists, and some to be pastors and teachers, *to prepare God's people for works of service,* so that the body of Christ may be built up until we all reach unity in the faith and in the knowledge of the Son of God and become mature, attaining to the whole measure of the fullness of Christ. Then we will no longer be infants, tossed back and forth by the waves, and blown here and there by every wind of teaching and by the cunning and craftiness of men in their deceitful scheming. Instead, speaking the truth in love, we will in all things grow up into him who is the Head, that is, Christ. From him the whole body, joined and held together by every supporting ligament, grows and builds itself up in love, as each part does its work. (Eph. 4:11–16 NIV, emphasis added)

The word "prepare" refers to restoring something to its original state, setting a broken bone, or outfitting completely for a trip.[7] In the classical Greek language, the word is used for setting a bone during surgery.[8] The Great Physician is now making all the necessary adjustments so the church will not be "out of joint" as ". . . every supporting ligament grows and builds itself up in love, as each part does its work." Notice the verse does not say, "as each part watches the pastor do the work." God called pastors to help restore the church to its original state of bringing glory to God (Eph. 3:21). They do this by helping people heal from the broken places in their lives (the Puritans called themselves the "physicians of the soul"[9]) so that the church will be outfitted and equipped for every good work (Eph. 2:10). Comeback pastors lead their churches to fulfill this God-ordained mission of equipping and mobilizing the saints for "works of service."

In some churches, laypeople had to meet certain expectations before they could serve in ministry. At New Hope where I (Mike) pastor, people are expected to complete the membership class, be baptized, and sign a membership covenant. Other churches require people to complete a gift discovery process in order to serve in ministry. Chuck Lawless provided a helpful chart that compares the practices of churches that people "join" compared with those that have uncommitted members.[10]

CHURCHES THAT PEOPLE JOIN	
Churches that struggle with those who remain attenders and with members who are uncommitted—	Churches where people join and serve—
may have expectations but do not state them clearly or consistently	clarify expectations up front
often accept mediocrity	demand excellence
fail to build on the church's relational nature	emphasize and strengthen relationships
may have a membership class but fail to capitalize on its value	use a membership class to promote joining and serving
tend to emphasize only spiritual gifts (if anything) in ministry placement	have a strategic plan for leading members to see their overall spiritual makeup
recruit workers by broad announcements with little personal attention	recruit workers one-to-one
have a tendency not to think creatively about ministry opportunities, focusing only on positions already in place	provide entry-level positions for workers, even if they are new positions "outside the box"
take their workers for granted	affirm and celebrate their workers

There is an important balance here. Many comeback churches specifically described an atmosphere where unlimited expectations were not placed upon people. The congregation is expected to be involved, but their involvement is often to be limited to one or two specific ministries. The goal is to get as many people involved in ministry as possible, not overworking a small number of people. When the work of ministry is not fairly distributed, some people feel left out. Others get burned out because they're asked to do too many things. Either way—left out or burned out—they're still "out." That's not what the Lord wants, and it's not what we want!

In comeback churches, both pastor and people realize that the pastor cannot do everything that needs to be done in ministry. Sometimes people expect too much from their pastor. Sometimes the pastor does not expect enough from the people and is guilty of trying to do too many things himself. It's difficult to achieve a healthy balance between doing ministry as a good example of servanthood and doing ministry that laypeople should be doing. Pastors should examine their hearts and actions to determine whether they are really willing to give ministry responsibilities away to others.

As we mentioned earlier, the Second Evangelical Free Church in Brooklyn, New York, made a transition from very traditional to very contemporary worship. The transition process created a different level of expectations and ministry involvement. Pastor David Gehret said the transition "mobilized more people in media, choir/praise team, musicians and drama. We also started new small groups, which mobilized teachers and key laypeople who could contribute positively to the discussions."[11] The more people were involved, the more effective the process was.

In many comeback churches, the people were taught that they were responsible for the ministry of the church. Ephesians 4:11–13 was applied in church life. Comeback congregations were taught to be the body of Christ and encouraged to fulfill the ministries of the church. One comeback leader stated, "I made people aware that they are the church. Another big thing was making people feel empowered and also equipped." The people's involvement helped facilitate the turnaround.

Create an Atmosphere of Equipping

In his book *From Embers to a Flame: How God Can Revitalize Your Church,* Harry Reeder describes the importance of having a strategy and a process in place to multiply servant leaders. He asserts, "The work of revitalization cannot begin without one man to whom God has given a vision, but it also cannot continue unless there are other godly leaders constantly being raised up to carry out the ministry and carry on the vision. Leadership works, whether it is good or bad, so God will work through good leadership to bring your church from embers to a flame."[12]

Comeback churches utilize a strategy, or process, to identify and equip people for ministry as servant leaders. Part of that equipping strategy is the discovery of gifts. Whether informally or formally, comeback leaders engage the people in a process of discovering their gifts and passions, and place them in ministry accordingly. To facilitate the process, some use their own materials or processes. Others use resources such as Network,[13] the Discovery Class process from Saddleback, or the new online system from PLACE Ministries.[14]

Another model for equipping is the DESIGN system. Wayne Cordeiro describes this as the process used by his church in the book he authored, *Doing Church as a Team.* D.E.S.I.G.N stands for desire, experience, spiritual gift, individual style, growth phase, and natural abilities. He explains, "Add all of these components together, and you'll find your DESIGN. These ingredients will help you to find the shape and placement of your puzzle piece. Now all you need to add to this recipe is involvement!"[15]

The point is, whether it is the Network system of Willow Creek, the Discovery Class process of Saddleback, the DESIGN model of New Hope, PLACE Ministries, or something you create yourself, churches must help people discover their spiritual "equipment" and give them opportunities to use it. Explore the possibilities, select an option, and then lead your congregation to discover its ministry potential by equipping people to serve.

Effectively mobilizing lay ministers and equipping them for ministry involves more than a gift-discovery and placement process. Moving members into ministry requires a ministry placement strategy, face-to-face recruiting, entry-level ministry positions, and recognition and affirmation.

These components are described in Chuck Lawless's book *Membership Matters*. Face-to-face recruiting means asking people to serve in a ministry. Research identified a direct correlation between new people being challenged to serve and their subsequent involvement in ministry.

In order to create an equipping atmosphere, churches must make enough entry-level ministry positions available. Involve people in ushering, greeting, serving refreshments, parking, decorating, or computer and office support. These ministries can help people get involved quickly and easily, explore different ministries, and gauge ministry leadership potential. And don't sell new Christians short—they need to be involved in evangelism!

When a church adds recognition and affirmation, it has a good system for equipping people to serve. Encouraging and empowering people assists them in their spiritual development and kingdom impact. We'll talk more about this in the next section.

In *Membership Matters,* Chuck Lawless elaborates about churches' expectations and equipping ministry. "Though they saw room for improving their processes, the churches we studied expected attenders to join and then encouraged members to serve. One-to-one, they led members to discover their passions and gifts, gave them immediate opportunities to serve, and affirmed their commitment. In the end, faithful members most often found their place, knowing they were a part of something that really mattered."[16]

Create an Atmosphere of Empowerment

"Ministry in the Keys is very different. We don't need new buildings or big marketing plans to draw people here. They are already coming," said Pastor Keith La Fountain of the New Life Assembly of God in Marathon, Florida. "A lady who was more gifted in music was leading the children's ministry. We reluctantly replaced her— she was such a nice lady—with someone who has an elementary education degree. Now that we have her and are using new curriculum, we need more teachers. The children are telling their parents that they *want* to come to church! The teachers received on-the-job training from the director."[17]

The third component of effective lay mobilization involves creating an environment where people feel empowered or enabled to do ministry. In many cases, empowerment occurs through preaching, teaching, and training. Don't expect people just to "get it." If you are like most of us, you want to ask people to do things and have them run off and do it. Comeback leaders understand that people have to be taught, trained, and encouraged to be effective ministers.

In the earlier sample responses, one comeback leader described taking three years to teach the congregation spiritual gifts, thoroughly and intentionally. The result was a very effective mobilization of people for ministry. It does not have to take that long, but people should be placed in ministries according to their giftedness. Ongoing training is provided, empowering people to do ministry and making them more effective.

The time it took to communicate, guide, recruit, and lead the process for mobilization highlights an important principle from comeback churches. We tend to overestimate what we can do in a year and underestimate what can happen in three years. Don't take a short-term view and don't quit if your vision isn't quickly fulfilled. We are in a marathon, not a sprint! So make sure you purposefully and deliberately put the processes and structures in place to maintain long-term growth.

Effective communication often seems like an elusive dream—something that can be conceptualized but never realized. Churches that improve their communication realize that communication is a process, not an event. There is hardly an instance when a church can communicate too much or too often. However, simply offering more communication that's not well planned and well presented doesn't help the church or its mission. Strive for ways to improve. Communicate effectively. Be engaging. Evaluate every printed, electronic, and oral communication as if you were the recipient. Does it make a good impression? Is it clear? Does it compel me to action?

John Kramp explains it well:

Trains will not run without fuel. Leaders cannot
lead and teams will not work without communication.

Compare the leadership process to a train, and communication becomes fuel in the train's fuel car.

Leaders communicate. They communicate the destination toward which they are moving. *Vision* and *personal planning* create a picture of the destination and a general plan to get there. However, only communication moves that picture from the mind of the leader to the minds of those who board the passenger car through enlistment.[18]

Comeback churches understand that communication is a big part of empowerment. Nothing is assumed—that the people understand their gifts, roles, or the expectations that God has for them. Comeback leaders take time to communicate the vision, expectations, and implementation of the plan.

In our study, the people were not only expected to be involved; they were shown how to be involved in a systematic way. As someone has said, "Structure breeds confidence." Comeback churches explain biblical guidelines, expectations for people in ministry, awareness and identification of gifts, and available training. They appreciate people in simple ways. They give people the confidence they need to minister effectively. The steps are simple, but essential; expectations are clear, equipping takes place, and encouragement is given.

Another important aspect of empowering people for ministry is to give them authority along with responsibility. As church members are encouraged to take responsibility for a ministry and exercise appropriate authority to get it done, they feel empowered to do more ministry. They take ownership of the ministry. Comeback leaders often describe situations where laypeople take active roles as servant leaders. As these laypeople exercise responsibility and authority, they become part of the ministry team, welcoming new opportunities for involvement.

A final aspect of empowerment is affirmation. Comeback churches make sure that people are appreciated for their ministry activity and involvement. Encouragement affirms people and supports them in their continued service. Be creative in appreciating others! A short handwritten "Thank You" from the pastor can keep people invigorated for weeks. A recognition or word of appreciation on Sunday mornings or a Wednesday night does wonders. Consider having a yearly "VIP Recognition Dessert." This is an inexpensive way to honor the "Volunteers in Partnership."

Harry Reeder, who understood the importance of creating an atmosphere of empowerment, said it well, "Those who influence others not only embody the truths they teach, but also empower others to succeed. Inspiration and motivation are their 'stock and trade.' One such leader was Douglas MacArthur."[19] Reeder goes on to tell the story of MacArthur, who as a brigadier general in World War I, was given the task of taking a well-fortified and well-armed enemy position. To motivate one of his majors, MacArthur showed him a medal of bravery MacArthur had won earlier in the war. The general told that major that he would receive one just like it once he completed this mission. As he turned to walk away, MacArthur suddenly did an about-face, walked back to the major and said, "Son, I know you are going to get there. So you go ahead and take mine now."[20] At that point, MacArthur pulled the medal out and handed it to him.

Like MacArthur on the battlefield, comeback leaders understand the importance of empowering people for spiritual warfare and ministry. They create an environment where laypeople are mobilized and empowered to do ministry.

Conclusion

As God's people discover their spiritual gifts and are mobilized for effective ministry, they need to be aware that the power for effective ministry comes from the indwelling presence of the Holy Spirit. When Christians are actively involved, utilizing their gifts for ministry, they must have the presence, power, and continuous in-filling of the Holy Spirit (Eph. 5:18). May God fill you and your church with His Holy Spirit as you create an atmosphere of expectation, equipping, and empowerment.

Suggestions for Further Study

Lawless, Chuck. *Membership Matters: Insights from Effective Churches on New Member Classes and Assimilation* (Grand Rapids: Zondervan, 2005).

Cordeiro, Wayne. *Doing Church as a Team* (Ventura, CA: Regal, 2001).

Network by Willow Creek Resources (www.willowcreek.com).

S.H.A.P.E. by Purpose Driven Ministries (www.purposedriven.com).

PLACE Ministries (www.placeministries.org/).

Connecting People through Small Groups

Jeremy Morton, pastor of Crosspoint Church, Perry, Georgia, recalls what happened when one young nonbeliever, Willie Taybor, began attending church with his girlfriend. As Willie participated in church activities, he served alongside Christians. The day that the church community worked together on a building project was the day that Willie committed his life to Christ.

Today, Willie mentors teenagers at the church, leads a young adult Bible study, heads a Tuesday night outreach gathering for young adults, and is enrolled in ministry training at a Christian college.

People frequently come to faith in Christ after they've been around Christians for some time. Research shows they're more likely to consider the claims of Christ when they are in community with His followers. We help them make the journey toward Christ when we invite them into our fellowship and demonstrate our relationship with Him.

This is the power of community. It influenced Willie to come to Christ and led him to reach others through mentoring and through a Bible study group. An effective way to build community is through small groups and Sunday school. Comeback churches used Sunday school, small groups, or both.

Surveys indicate the importance of a small-group structure in connecting people to the life of the church and providing a place of ministry for church members. There was an increased emphasis on building community and an expansion of the number of groups offered. To support these new groups, teacher training became a priority. One comeback leader indicated that an increased emphasis in Sunday school and increased teacher training were important factors in their comeback experience. The training gave teachers a clear set of priorities and showed them how to treat Sunday school classes as small groups.

Comeback leaders exemplified the power of small-group community. Most churches and leaders know they need small groups. More recently, the concept of utilizing a multiplying network of groups to promote church growth arose as an alternative to the more traditional model of Sunday school. However, Sunday school has been used very effectively and is compatible with church growth. Thom Rainer speaks to the power of Sunday school in his book *High Expectations,* "After nearly a decade of researching two thousand churches of different sizes, locations, and denominations, I cannot say that I am surprised that Sunday school was rated so highly as an assimilation tool. My surprise in this study, however, was the *intensity* by which the church leaders expressed their beliefs that Sunday school is the chief assimilation approach."[1]

We use the terminology of "small groups" in most cases, but the principles discussed apply to home groups and Sunday school groups. Though there are advantages to each approach, the point is that small groups are the place where community takes place. "We are not here reemphasizing the need for small groups, which have often been overlaid on already overfull and over-demanding church calendars. Rather we are arguing for basic communities to become the very building blocks on which the church is built and is able to expand."[2]

In this chapter, we will discuss how comeback churches developed an emphasis on small-group structures and started new groups. We will highlight the importance of connecting newcomers to the church family. In addition, we will share some of the tools, resources, and methods that can be used to develop this area of ministry.

Survey Responses

Pastor Gary Geesey of the Christian Center[3] in Desert Hot Springs, California, said, "*The Purpose-Driven Life* helped bring focus to what a balanced life for the believer looks like. The *40 Days of Purpose* helped us launch our small groups."[4] Survey results showed numerous examples of the impact *40 Days of Purpose* and *40 Days of Community* had on the churches and on their small groups.

Respondents indicated that small groups and/or Sunday school were the fifth strongest factor in the comeback. So, we asked this follow-up question: "If small group/Sunday school efforts had a major or vital effect, please describe how the efforts were increased and/or how they were changed (increased emphasis, new program, new materials, transition from one to the other, adding one to the other, etc.)." Here's what some comeback leaders said:

- We don't use artificial small groups; use natural small groups process → homogeneous and natural; intentional connectivity.
- Increased emphasis in Sunday school; increased teacher training → gave them a set of priorities and treated Sunday school class as small groups; small groups faded after a year.
- Zeroing in on this has increased worship.
- Placed a major emphasis on adults in SS; new education building.
- Forty Days of Community; just launched twenty new groups last week; six or seven in youth area and college groups.
- Increased number of classes; have just begun small groups.
- Moved to small groups; gained many new families as a result.
- Renewed emphasis on importance of Sunday school; added new classes.
- Starting new classes; increased emphasis on importance of small-group meetings.
- Added small-groups pastor.
- Increased groups and services → gave more people more flexibility in regards to being able to attend church.
- Increased emphasis; adding new groups and multiplying.
- New classes.
- New small groups added to Sunday school.
- Small groups started in place of Sunday school.
- Started small groups in different interest areas.

- Small groups in homes; Bible studies at apartment complexes; age-graded Sunday school.
- Started small groups—moved them to Sunday nights and saw dynamic growth.
- Increased emphasis; more classes; two services.
- New Sunday school classes; new materials; had no Sunday school program.
- New classes; classes for mentally handicapped—good number of people in the community.
- Adding one to the other; new classes; new age-graded structure; adding small groups to Sunday school.
- New program; new materials; changed how they conducted classes.
- Jesus model—picked twelve and focused on three; being an Acts church—small groups emphasize fellowship.
- (Small groups) aided in assimilation.

Four words stood out in the responses. "New" was stated 92 times, in 52.3 percent of the 176 responses; "new" referred to new space, new classes, new teachers, and other changes. "Increase" appeared 40 times (22.7% of responses). "Add" was used 31 times (17.6% of responses), with "start" being mentioned 27 times (15.3% of responses).

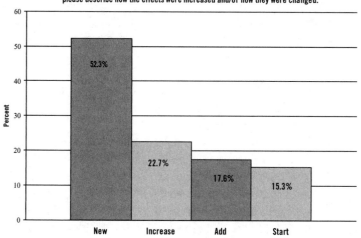

Words That Stood Out in Response to the Statement
"If small group/Sunday school efforts had a major or vital effect, please describe how the effects were increased and/or how they were changed."

Based on further analysis, several insights became apparent. First, comeback leaders had an intentional process or strategy for small groups and/or Sunday school. Second, a status quo did not exist. Changes were made. Whether these comeback churches added, replaced, or started new classes or groups, leaving this area of ministry the same was not an option. Third, comeback leaders utilized a training system to develop leaders for small groups or Sunday school. Fourth, comeback churches worked to create more space to accommodate new classes or groups.

The "Velcro Ability" of Small Groups

George Gallup found that 70 percent of Americans have said that the church is not meeting their needs. When asked what these needs were, there were six common responses:

1. To believe life is meaningful and has purpose.
2. To have a sense of community and deeper relationships.
3. To be appreciated and respected.
4. To be listened to and heard.
5. To grow in faith.
6. To receive practical help in developing a mature faith.[5]

These needs can be met in a variety of ways but are best met in a nurturing small group.

In my (Mike's) family, we just went through the process of teaching my five-year-old son how to tie his shoes—one of the many challenges of parenting. There were times when I really wanted to (and maybe did) get frustrated with him. It seemed like he just wasn't ever going to get it. At times, it was tempting to just go get some Velcro shoes and forget about the "shoe tying thing," but we persevered through five thousand loops and "rabbit ears." I am happy to say that my five-year-old can tie his shoes by himself now—at least most of the time.

Small groups are like Velcro shoes for little kids. Shoes that are secured by Velcro make it easier for little kids to get their shoes on and off their feet. It is easier for them to connect with Velcro than with shoelaces. In the same way, small groups make it easier for new people to connect with others in the life of the church. New people can feel like it's hard for them to fit into church life, get involved in ministry, or connect to other people in the church. This can be frustrating. But, when they can get involved with a smaller group of people, they are much more likely to "stick" to the church.

Building Relationships

Small groups give people an opportunity to build significant relationships with a smaller number of people. The groups are one way to encourage the development of spiritual community, or oneness. Unity among God's people reflects a part of the nature of God because He is a God of oneness.

In his book *Community 101,* Gilbert Bilezikian describes the biblical primacy of oneness: "Indeed, community finds its essence and definition deep within the being of God. Oneness is primarily a divine mode of being that pertains to God's own existence, independently from and prior to any of His works of creation. Whatever community exists as a result of God's creation, it is only a reflection of an eternal reality that is intrinsic to the being of God. Because God is eternally one, when He created in His image, He created oneness."[6] Deuteronomy 6:4–5 emphasizes God's oneness and His desire that His children connect with Him: "Hear, O Israel: The LORD our God, the LORD is one. Love the LORD your God with all your heart and with all your soul and with all your strength" (NIV).

Jesus described His desire for His followers' oneness in John 17:21–23: "May they all be one, as You, Father, are in Me and I am in You. May they also be one in Us, so the world may believe You sent Me. I have given them the glory You have given Me. May they be one as We are one. I am in them and You are in Me. May they be made completely one, so the world may know You have sent Me and have loved them as You have loved Me."

Intentionally connecting people in community is not an option for the church. It's a biblical mandate—the essence of what it means to be the body of Jesus Christ. Bilezikian goes on to expound on the nature of this mandate:

> In the meantime, it should become obvious that the primary application of the biblical mandate for communal life can only take place in a context of closeness and togetherness. Necessarily, this spells "small groups."

In the experience of many people, church is reduced to attendance at a service on Sunday morning. This is not really church. . . .

The biblical metaphor of "family" more appropriately describes what the church should resemble—a group of people, few enough in numbers to sit around in a circle, facing each other and sharing the joy and the benefits of togetherness. Every church that aspires to function as community must make a small group structure available to its constituency. . . .

It is in small groups that people can get close enough to know each other, to care and share, to challenge and support, to confide and confess, to forgive and be forgiven, to laugh and weep together, to be accountable to each other, to watch over each other, and to grow together. Personal growth does not happen in isolation. It is the result of interactive relationships. Small groups are God's gift to foster changes in character and spiritual growth.[7]

Developing a system of small groups builds biblical community and unwraps God's gift of oneness among His people. This is a basic component of training for new church plants, because the development of smaller groups is vital to the life of the church.

The early church, in Acts 2, paints the picture of large and small gatherings of people. Both were instrumental in the dynamic growth of the early church. Acts 2:42–47 illustrates this dual approach to growing disciples:

And they devoted themselves to the apostles' teaching, to fellowship, to the breaking of bread, and to prayers. Then fear came over everyone, and many wonders and signs were being performed through the apostles. Now all the believers were together and had everything in common. So they sold their possessions and property and distributed the proceeds to all, as anyone had a need. And every day they devoted themselves [to meeting] together in the temple complex, and broke bread from *house to house*. They ate their food with glad-

ness and simplicity of heart, praising God and having
favor with all the people. And every day the Lord added
to them those who were being saved (emphasis added).

As the story of the early church continued to unfold, this pattern is evident. "Every day in the temple complex, and *in various homes*, they [the apostles] continued teaching and proclaiming the good news that the Messiah is Jesus" (Acts 5:42, emphasis added). Paul describes his methodology of proclaiming the gospel of Jesus Christ and church planting in Acts 20:20–21: "and that I did not shrink back from proclaiming to you anything that was profitable, or from teaching it to you in public and *from house to house*. I testified to both Jews and Greeks about repentance toward God and faith in our Lord Jesus" (emphasis added).

As the early church expanded, it utilized a two-pronged approach, with large and small-group gatherings. Both helped carry out the basic functions of the church and expand the kingdom of Jesus Christ. Small groups were essential in meeting people's needs, drawing them to worship together as believers, praying for God's power to be unleashed, evangelizing the lost, encouraging the persecuted, and discipling new believers.

Think in terms of large and small groups fulfilling two purposes in the life of a believer: unity and intimacy. The celebration service (or worship service) is limited only by the size of the facility. The goal of the celebration service is unity—in doctrine, in mutual understanding of God and His glory expressed through the gospel of Jesus Christ, and in other important matters.

Most churches have a midsize group numbering between seventeen and seventy. This is the "congregation." The goal of this group is mutual care and fellowship. Regardless of the size of the church, most people only know about seventy people on a first-name basis. So, in a church of seventy or seven thousand, the average person will have a natural affinity group that will include no more than seventy people.

The third group is smaller, containing between five and seventeen people. This is the "cell." In the "small group" (or cell) the participants are able to know one another on a deeper level. This is especially true in "closed groups."

Inviting and Open to Newcomers

Closed small groups are those that meet for a specific length of time, usually around a certain topic or book of the Bible, and do not add new people after the first couple of meetings. These groups are ideal for *spiritual* growth in a church, but rarely do they help numerical growth.

In order for a church to grow numerically using small groups, the groups must be open, inviting, and welcoming to new people. Recall the word "new" from the comeback church pastors. These churches multiplied new, open groups, sometimes specifically targeting a segment in their community. Through a variety of new groups, the *number* of people involved increased.

In the life of a church, small groups can be an environment where people:

1. Learn more about God and what it means to be a follower of Jesus Christ.
2. Love others and experience God's love.
3. Minister to people in need, within the group as well as in the community.
4. Decide to grow deeper in faith.
5. Share the joys and stresses of life together.

All small groups exhibit these basic functions. The degree to which they emphasize these functions depends on the design or type of group. The healthiest groups will display all five functions.

Once a small-group system is implemented, a number of benefits accrue. Let's consider a few of those benefits:

- *Relationships*—Small groups allow people the opportunity to build significant friendships. That's not possible in larger groups—too many relational lines exist for everyone to feel like they are a significant part of things.
- *Reproducible*—Small groups are easier to reproduce or multiply than large groups. They do not require as much space or as many resources. In addition, they provide an excellent context to reproduce leaders and have the potential for unlimited growth.
- *Assimilation*—Small groups are an excellent way to get newcomers involved in the life of the church, and they

can help close the "back door." Small groups increase a church's ability to care for its members, realizing that the pastor can't meet everyone's needs.

- *Transformation*—Small groups are conducive to life change and spiritual formation. As people share their life experiences and journey of faith together, they can spur one another on to a deeper relationship with Jesus Christ.

- *Extension*—In some contexts, small groups can be an excellent way to start new churches. Whether it's done in a neighboring community, an apartment complex, or among a different people group, churches can be planted by developing smaller groups, meeting together as the beginning stage of a new church.

By briefly examining the biblical nature of small groups, how they function, and some of their benefits, we hope you will be encouraged to develop an expanding system, or network of groups, in your church context. If you already have a system in place, we hope this will help you renew your efforts at small-group expansion and experience greater benefits.

If your church has Sunday school instead of small groups, think about function instead of form. If the Sunday school class is consistently between five and seventeen people, and rarely are new people added, it is a closed small group. If the Sunday school class is bringing and including new people consistently, it is functioning as an "open small group." Most churches that have a Sunday night service have the function of a "small group" taking place after the service is over!

Now, let's look at two other important aspects of small groups according to comeback leaders.

Train and Identify New Leaders

Comeback leaders multiplied their ministry through small-group leaders. While everything rises and falls on leadership, it could be more accurate to say that everything rises and falls on leadership that develops other leaders. That's a mark of true leadership. Small groups are an excellent way to train leaders and identify new ones. This process must be built into a systematic, intentional strategy to develop more groups and train new leaders. This provides a foundation for sustainable growth.

Good leaders understand the biblical nature of leadership, the tasks and responsibilities of leadership, and the need for consistent spiritual growth. In his work *Leading Life-Changing Small Groups,* Bill Donahue outlines biblical leadership this way: leaders shepherd others, leaders work together, and leaders are lovers.[8]

Like spiritual shepherds, small-group leaders understand that those who follow Jesus are called to serve others. "For even the Son of Man did not come to be served, but to serve, and to give His life—a ransom for many" (Mark 10:45). They are not "Lone Rangers." They realize the need to work with others, function with a team mentality, and share leadership roles and responsibilities. They also learn to express genuine love and to speak the love languages of the people around them.

Effective leaders know that leadership isn't all fun and games. Along with their influence, they have responsibilities to fulfill and tasks to accomplish. In small groups, leaders need to involve everyone in the group, help them discover a sense of biblical oneness, encourage them to grow in Christ, and constantly develop new leaders. This is a great and life-changing responsibility.

Faithful leaders expend the effort to grow spiritually. They continually mature in Christ, realizing that they cannot rely on their past experiences with Him. It's a daily relationship. Jesus said, "If anyone wants to come with Me, he must deny himself, take up his cross daily, and follow Me" (Luke 9:23). To grow spiritually, these leaders spend time in the Word of God, listen for a word *from* God, pray fervently until they see God move, witness to those who are without Christ, and serve in the power of the Spirit. While very few have all of these characteristics, God uses what we offer Him to build our lives and the lives of those we reach, engage, coach, and train.

A good small-group system promotes healthy, biblical leadership. It provides a great environment to develop apprentice leaders. The greatest challenge is identifying potential apprentices. Donahue provides some helpful insights:

1. Look for group members who take the group seriously.
2. Consider people who challenge your leadership—maybe they're frustrated because they have no opportunity to lead.
3. Look for gifted people that you can recognize and affirm.
4. Pray regularly for new apprentices.
5. Look for people who embrace the small-group vision.
6. Observe people in your ministry as they perform tasks or work with people.
7. Try to look for people who exhibit good spiritual, emotional, and social qualifications.

Then, he concludes, "God's method for accomplishing His plan is people—humble, Spirit-led people."[9]

Once leaders identify apprentices, they can systematically develop them by gradually giving responsibilities, walking alongside them as they receive "on-the-job" training. The development of quality leaders and apprentices should be a priority in your small-group system.

Make Room for New Groups

Comeback churches made it a priority to start new groups. The ones that utilized Sunday school started new classes and carved out more space for them to meet. In some cases, they built. But in every case, comeback leaders found a way to connect more people in biblical community.

However, the biggest obstacles to connecting new people through small groups—building genuine biblical community—may not be space limitations. Obstacles that are less obvious impact our society and our churches. Randy Frazee identifies the problems of individualism, isolation, and consumerism in his book *The Connecting Church*. Overcoming these obstacles can be the greatest challenge to developing biblical oneness.

After realizing that there was a significant level of dissatisfaction with their existing small groups, Frazee identified three interconnected issues that prevented his own church from experiencing genuine biblical community. Frazee explained:

[C]onsumerism is not only a result of isolation, it also funds or fuels the continuation of the "sovereign individual" ideology. Consider this depiction of the effects of these cultural characteristics:

As a result, consumerism seeks to curb the negative feelings of isolation; we spend increasing amounts of money in an attempt to feel better. However, the more we are obsessed about applying consumerism as a solution to our loneliness, the more it feeds the individualism mind-set. It's a vicious cycle.[10]

Frazee goes on to identify the solution to those three problems—help people connect to a common purpose, a common place, and common possessions. This is what characterized the early church: "All the believers were united in heart and mind. And they felt that what they owned was not their own, so they shared everything they had. The apostles testified powerfully to the resurrection of the Lord Jesus, and God's great blessing was upon them all. There were no needy people among them, because those who owned land or houses would sell them and bring the money to the apostles to give to those in need" (Acts 4:32–35 NLT).

The concepts of a common purpose, a common place and common possessions were formulated into an acrostic based on the word "SERVICE." This describes the seven functions of biblical community utilized in Frazee's church:

> S—Spiritual Formation
> E—Evangelism
> R—Reproduction
> V—Volunteerism
> I—International Missions
> C—Care
> E—Extending Compassion[11]

Maybe this acrostic will be helpful as you develop a structure that connects people through small groups in your church. Or you may adopt or already have another structure. Regardless, one thing is certain—churches will not grow without an expanding system of small groups that promotes and develops biblical community.

Conclusion

Comeback leaders recognized and responded to a need for biblical unity and community in their churches. They were convinced that people needed to connect in smaller groups, and they were intentional in their efforts to provide for people to relate in this way. This not only led to the formation of new groups, but to a training system to develop existing leaders and recruit new ones.

Comeback leaders used the small-group system to identify and train new leaders. Small groups helped identify new leaders, and those leaders were trained through an apprenticeship process. Healthy small groups become like a "farm system" for discovering and developing leadership talent and potential.

Comeback churches added, replaced, or started new classes or groups. They were not willing just to maintain this area of ministry. Many of these churches were willing to make necessary changes to meet the demands and opportunities before them. If people need to connect in a significant way with several other people, then finding ways to start new smaller groups with different affinity points is vital. That is how new people will get Velcroed to the church family and continue to grow in their faith.

Comeback churches created more space to expand the number of small-group gatherings. In many cases, they understood that the more groups there are, the greater the number of people who can connect in community. They also understood that there are other obstacles to biblical community besides physical space limitations. The problems of individualism, isolation, and consumerism can stand in the way of connecting people in genuine biblical community. But these obstacles will be overcome through a system of small groups that engage in the functions of biblical community.

One caution: Move slowly and deliberately in empowering small-group leaders. Meet regularly with leaders in a ministry community, or one-on-one, for accountability, training, and coaching. Shepherding people is a major trust—one that God wants us to take seriously!

"So guard yourselves and God's people. Feed and shepherd God's flock—his church, purchased with his own blood—over which the Holy Spirit has appointed you as elders. I know that false teachers, like vicious wolves, will come in among you after I leave, not sparing the flock. Even some men from your own group will rise up and distort the truth in order to draw a following. Watch out! Remember the three years I was with you—my constant watch and care over you night and day, and my many tears for you. And now I entrust you to God and the message of his grace that is able to build you up and give you an inheritance with all those he has set apart for himself." (Acts 20:28–32 NLT)

Suggestions for Further Study

Donahue, Bill. *Leading Life-Changing Small Groups* (Grand Rapids: Zondervan, 2002).

Donahue, Bill, and Greg Bowman. *Coaching Life-Changing Small Group Leaders: A Practical Guide for Those Who Lead and Shepherd Small Group Leaders* (Grand Rapids: Zondervan, 2006).

Donahue, Bill, and Russ Robinson. *Building a Church of Small Groups: A Place Where Nobody Stands Alone* (Grand Rapids: Zondervan, 2005).

Donahue, Bill, and Russ Robinson. *The Seven Deadly Sins of Small Groups Ministry: A Troubleshooting Guide for Church Leaders* (Grand Rapids: Zondervan, 2005).

Frazee, Randy. *The Connecting Church: Beyond Small Groups to Authentic Community* (Grand Rapids: Zondervan, 2001).

Galloway, Dale, with Kathi Mills. *The Small Group Book: The Practical Guide for Nurturing Christians and Building Churches* (Grand Rapids: Revell, 1995).

Other Comeback Factors

If you are a seasoned pastor in a declining church situation, you have probably read *Comeback Churches* to this point and thought to yourself, *Yeah, but . . . there are other factors contributing to our decline that have not been addressed yet. These comeback churches you surveyed are in a growing area . . . are a newer church with younger people willing to change . . . had the finances to hire more staff,* etc. Now, imagine being able to sit down with one of the pastors of a comeback church and discussing with him how your church could stop the downward decline—including your *Yeah, but . . .* you were thinking earlier.

In the survey process, we collected information on a variety of other topics and issues. This collection of data will help you as you contemplate marketing, facilities, helpful books, influential people, church age and size, and other relevant matters. It gives a more comprehensive view of other contributing factors to revitalization from churches and leaders caught in the trap of plateau and decline.

Facilities

Comeback churches often changed their facilities to help facilitate their growth. We have seen and experienced the frustration of inadequate facilities that hindered church growth. While this is never the sole factor, insufficient meeting space or poor configuration of rooms can limit growth potential. Think of it like the bonsai tree. The reason the bonsai stays as small as it does is because the pot dictates the size of the tree. Certain bonsai trees may grow much larger in the wild. But because the pot confines the roots, and the roots determine the growth, the tree remains a dwarf as long as it is in the pot.

Both of us have been in churches that would exhibit significant growth potential but could never realize that potential. The numbers would rise to a certain level and then slowly drift back down, only to rise again and then drop—just like the waves of the ocean surge onto the shore and then recede back into the ocean. One of many reasons this occurs is inadequate facilities.

It is better to be in a smaller meeting place initially and have to get more chairs to accommodate the crowd. As the church begins to grow, leave a few empty seats. Most people in a church do not like to see empty seats. They will invite their friends until the church is filled to 85 percent of its capacity. Once the room appears "full," people begin to think that there is no longer any room, so they stop bringing others. One way to catch the wave of momentum is to begin multiple services.

Over half of the comeback leaders surveyed believed this was a significant factor in providing for comeback growth. They recognized that facilities can be a critical tool for growth.

Effective facilities—not just more—are like the difference between a hand drill and a cordless power drill. This past Father's Day I (Mike) decided to use a gift card to purchase one of those power drills. Wow . . . what a great invention! Guys like having their toys, but the difference in what you can accomplish with a power drill versus a hand drill is phenomenal. The same is true with regard to facilities. You can make do with what you have, but better facilities are a more effective tool for ministry and growth.

Those who changed their facilities were asked, "If facility changes had a major or vital effect, please describe what facility changes took place (e.g., remodeled existing structures, moved into new facilities, rented different meeting space, built new facilities)." Here is a short list with some of their responses:

- Four years ago we began to address how we can more effectively reach our city with a different facility in location and design; began to look for land; we are intentional about Jesus Christ; building is a good tool.

- Added new floor space → Starbucks; "edged up" campus → ultracontemporary; exploded with growth in Starbucks and concert hall.
- Built new facilities—multipurpose; remodeled SS classes and offices; allowed more classes to start.
- Remodeled children's wing; built recreation building; wing on sanctuary.
- Moved to multimedia format; moved to chairs; multiuse facilities.
- Total remodeling of buildings which were built in 1940s.
- Remodeled existing structures; bigger classrooms; moved offices to modular buildings.
- Moved into new facilities; believes this was number-one reason for growth.
- Remodeled existing structures; added new wing and made handicap accessible.
- Remodeled existing structures; landscape maintenance; currently in building program.
- Remodeled existing structures; turned parsonage into youth house.
- Remodeled existing structures; new playground and children's wing.
- Remodeled existing structures; new youth facility.
- Remodeled existing structures; repainted children's/day care area; new carpet; interpretation system (bilingual services—Spanish to English).
- Moved facilities twelve miles and planted a neighborhood (Hispanic and African American) church in old facility.
- Remodeled and renovated worship center and education space.
- Remodeled existing structures; new floors/carpet; general remodeling.
- Remodeled existing structures; added coffee house; multimedia.
- Built a community center.

As in our other survey responses, four words stood out. "Remodeled" was used 107 times (61.5% of responses). "New" was listed in 70, or 40.2 percent of responses. "Moved" was recorded 31 times (17.8% of the responses). "Built" was stated in 21, or 12.1 percent, of the responses.

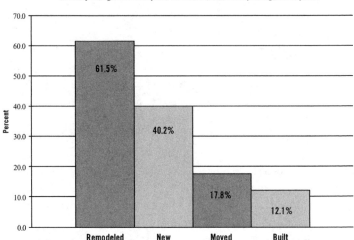

Responses to the Question
"If facility changes had a major or vital effect, what facility changes took place?"

Remodeled Facilities

Most churches (61.5%) remodeled, which is significant because it indicates that most of the churches encouraged revitalization without moving, buying new land, or building new buildings. Churches were able to upgrade their existing facilities by creating more space, making that space more functional, landscaping, expanding parking, upgrading their technological capabilities, and other improvements. Some comeback churches did add secondary buildings to support growth.

Built for Children and Youth

A noticeable number of the respondents remodeled or added new facilities to enhance worship, or youth, or children's ministry. This finding points to a correlation between buildings and ministries. Many comeback leaders saw their buildings as tools to enhance their ministry. They were a means to a more effective ministry end.

Facilities Helped Them Grow

We asked the question, "Did facility changes cause growth and revitalization, or were facility changes a result of growth?" One respondent stated, "We are intentional about Jesus Christ; the building is a good tool." Other respondents asserted, "We moved into new facilities; this was the number one reason for growth," and "Excitement about the new building brought growth." In some cases, facilities were perceived to be a result of growth, and in other cases, they were perceived to be a cause of growth. Either way, a positive correlation was noted between church facilities and revitalization.

In follow-up interviews, two comeback leaders described their churches' facility changes. Adam Dooley, pastor of Red House Baptist Church in Richmond, Kentucky, asserted, "A new building program brought excitement and growth to the church. People could see our vision for the new building and the ministry we could accomplish, and they wanted to be a part of it."[1] The church built entirely new facilities, including a worship center, education building, and a gym/fellowship hall.

Robert Eby, pastor of Calvary Christian Center in Lake Villa, Illinois, said, "Our growth spurred our remodeling."[2] This church totally renovated its worship center, replacing pews with chairs, putting in a new sound system, replacing the carpet, and giving the building a new paint job. The education space saw changes too—new carpet, paint, and classrooms.

Notice the cause-and-effect cycle—the vision to reach new people or a segment in the community led to new or remodeled facilities, which helped cause the growth. The resultant effect on the people who began supporting the vision financially had a tremendous impact on the church being excited about the new ministry opportunities, which led to more people, and the church becoming a comeback church.

That leads to a very important principle: *Let your vision determine your facilities. Never allow facilities to dictate your vision.*

As a God-loving, God-honoring, vision-driven pastor of spiritually minded leaders, you know more about what your facilities need to be than the architects and contractors the church may hire.

In a spirit of prayer, craft your vision to reach your community for Christ. Then, out of the overflow of that vision, design your facilities. Shop around for an architect and contractor who will really listen to your vision instead of purchasing a prepackaged set of plans. God may use your facilities in an entirely new, creative way that will serve as a model for other comeback churches!

Marketing

Marketing is a big issue in our society and in our churches. Some have embraced marketing concepts and applied those principles for reaching people in the community. They've decided that marketing can be used if done appropriately. Others believe that utilizing such concepts makes the church too much like the world.

We found that many of our surveyed comeback leaders had mixed feelings as well. Some were enthusiastic about marketing, and some were not. (We tend to be in favor of discerning marketing. Ed has recently published a manual called *Strategic Outreach: A How-to Marketing Manual for Pastors and Church Leaders,* available at Outreach.com.)

When you think about "marketing," try to do it without any emotional baggage. Every church markets itself in some way. Even the early church used "word-of-mouth" marketing effectively (see Acts 2, 3, 6, etc.). Every person who speaks about your church to someone in the community, every piece of literature you produce, every sign at the church building or rented facilities makes a statement about your view of yourself, the Lord, and the people you are striving to reach. Why not do it with a high degree of excellence?

We asked comeback leaders, "Was your church's comeback affected by increased marketing efforts?" and most said it was not a part of their strategy. However, it appears to us that more comeback churches used advertising than the church population as a whole. According to one informed guess, 10 percent of all American churches use advertising. However, 38 percent of comeback churches indicated that marketing had a significant impact upon their revitalization, rating it a 4 or 5.

Moreover, comeback leaders who rated this highly were asked to describe the impact of increased marketing. Listed below is a sampling of those responses:

- Personal invitations; more people can invite more people.
- Personal invitations—people have been going one-on-one, more intentionally inviting people, but not as part of a defined strategy.
- Direct mail and personal invitations—in-house publishing → two advertising guys on staff who produce and then mail; created campaign that backed up our people's ministry in the community; two sets of invitation cards by people.
- Personal invitations—Friend Day on occasion; constantly reminding people to invite friends.
- Personal invitations—word-of-mouth invitational part; as people's attitudes changed within the church, they engaged in inviting others.
- Direct mail caused growth and personal invitations.
- Door to door; TV ministry.
- Personal invitations, direct mail for events, newspaper ads.
- Targeted community through surveys and personal invitations.
- Community mailings; invitation cards to prospects; special seasonal events (Christmas, etc.).
- Radio, newspaper, billboards, flyers, personal invitation.
- Direct mail (23,000 pieces two times per year); Web site; newspaper; radio; invitation cards.
- Web site, TV, radio, newspaper, personal invitations.
- Flyers in community; personal invitations; door to door.
- Web site; flyers, door hangers, direct mail.
- Personal invitations; direct mail (150 pieces two to three times per year).
- Phone book; Chamber of Commerce member; billboards; personal invitations; involved in schools (band boosters, sponsorships, etc.).
- Personal invitations; telemarketing; gift packages.
- Personal invitations; direct mail (15,000 to 30,000 pieces quarterly); Web site.

- Word of mouth by members.
- Personal invitations; Web site; press articles; Mothers of Preschoolers (MOPS); Upward Basketball; became part of neighborhood watch groups to meet and reach people.

Those who used marketing found it helpful and used it frequently. Two interesting patterns were noted. First, nearly two-thirds (64%) of those who used marketing techniques as an intentional strategy used at least two different methods of marketing. Second, personal invitations were more commonly used than any other method.

Responses showed seven marketing priorities. "Personal invitations," appeared in 128 (74%) of the 173 responses. Other methods commonly noted were "newspaper"—stated 47 times (27.2% of responses); "Web site"—recorded 43 times (24.9% of responses); "mail"—used 38 times (22% of responses); "radio"—appeared 26 times (15% of responses); "television"—used 18 times (10.4% of responses); and "door to door"—mentioned 16 times (9.9% of response).

Seven Marketing Priorities

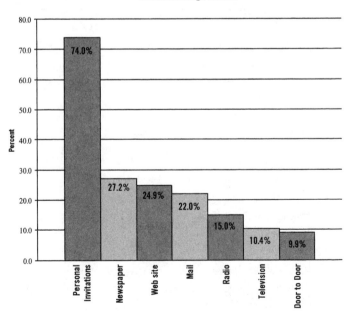

Comeback churches engaged in a variety of methods to communicate their presence to the people in their communities, but, as noted above, "personal invitations" overwhelmingly had the greatest impact. Comeback leaders utilized a "word-of-mouth" strategy, and one leader stated that he "constantly reminded people to invite friends." Another comeback leader asserted, "As people's attitudes changed within the church, they engaged in inviting others." Revitalization for many of these churches was based more upon an intentional focus of inviting people rather than on indirect marketing.

Both personal invitations and direct mail have a role in healthy church growth. Ultimately, they are about "marketing" the church. When people give personal invitations to friends, family members, neighbors, coworkers, or strangers to come to church, they are engaged in marketing. They're excited about what God is doing in the life of their church, and they want to share that excitement with others.

Helpful Books/Resources

The last section of the survey asked four summary questions. The first asked, "What three books (other than the Bible) were the most helpful in your transition?" Over thirteen pages of responses were recorded. With 297 (91.7% of 324 total surveys) responses, they provided a large number of suggested books and authors.

It might not come as a surprise, but the most recommended resources were connected to the Purpose Driven model. *The Purpose-Driven Church* was stated 99 times (33.3% of responses) and *The Purpose-Driven Life* was recorded 64 times (21.5% of responses). Combined, these books were mentioned 148 times, in 49.8 percent of the responses. And they appeared together 15 times. It is hard to overstate the impact of Purpose Driven resources. Most comeback leaders believed that the Purpose Driven resources helped the process of revitalization.

According to Pastor Kenneth Dyal of the Church at Argyle, Warren's books helped them refocus their ministry strategy and processes for the entire Jacksonville, Florida area. "*The Purpose-Driven Church* served as the basis for a total shift in focus for the church. We made major changes in our bylaws, allowing most decisions to be made by our deacons and staff. We also initiated the Membership 101 class, including the signed member covenant."[3]

After Rick Warren's books, Thom Rainer's were mentioned most often. References to Rainer and his works occurred in 26, or 8.8 percent, of the responses. *Surprising Insights from the Unchurched* was cited 13 times. John Maxwell's books were also popular among respondents, appearing 25 times (8.4% of responses). Maxwell's *The 21 Irrefutable Laws of Leadership* was recorded 21 times.

Three other authors received mention in over 5 percent of the responses: Henry Blackaby, Andy Stanley, and Jim Cymbala. Blackaby was referenced in 22, or 7.4 percent, of the responses. His works *Experiencing God* and *Spiritual Leadership* were cited in 15 and 7 responses, respectively. Stanley's works were mentioned in 21, or 7.1 percent, of the responses. His books *Can We Do That?* (coauthored with Ed Young Jr.) and *7 Practices of Effective Ministry* were each cited in 9 responses. Jim Cymbala's *"Fresh"* books were recorded in 18, or 6.1 percent, of the responses.

Several other authors or books were mentioned multiple times, though they represented less than 5 percent of the responses. *Good to Great* by Jim Collins (14 times); George Barna (12 times); John MacArthur (10 times); Bill Hybels (9 times); Max Lucado (7 times); Erwin McManus (7 times); Dallas Willard (6 times); John Bevere (5 times); Bob Russell (5 times); and Charles Stanley (4 times).

Comeback leaders took time to learn. Almost 92 percent of all the church leaders surveyed listed books or resources that had been helpful to them in ministry. These leaders didn't just rely on what they already knew. They continued to learn, read, study, and grow. Effective leaders make the commitment to be lifelong learners.

We also found that *comeback leaders practically applied* insights from books and resources strategically in the ministries of their churches. What they learned from reading, they applied in their ministry contexts. They were not interested in learning without purpose.

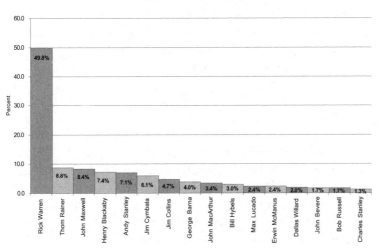

Helpful Books/Resources

Are You Ready to Be a Learner?

1. How focused and intense are you about your own learning habits?

Toward the end of his life, the apostle Paul wrote to his young friend, Timothy, "When you come, bring the cloak I left in Troas with Carpus, as well as the scrolls, especially the parchments" (2 Tim. 4:13). Even though Paul knew he was going to die, he was still learning all the way to the end. What a great model for all of us!

2. Have you read the books mentioned by comeback leaders or have you just read about them?

We've noticed a troubling thing over the years. Frequently people share opinions about books or paradigms they've never even read or studied! We have been in meetings, in a wide range of settings, when pastors shared negative comments about a specific book, pastor, author, or way of "doing church." And they shared strongly. As they continued to talk, it was obvious that they had not read the book—the pastors were parroting what others had said. We need to be very careful about this. "The one who gives an answer before he listens—this is foolishness and disgrace for him" (Prov. 18:13).

3. Why not take the next six months and actually read six of the books mentioned by comeback leaders?

Set a goal to apply at least one principle from each book to your ministry context. That could prove to be a valuable part of helping your church turn around.

Church Age

With all the information before us, what are some characteristics of comeback churches? Did those characteristics influence their growth? There were two general factors considered: the age of participating churches and average attendance. Churches surveyed ranged from several years to more than two hundred years old. The average age of a participating church was sixty-three years and the median age (the number in the middle of all the responses) was fifty-three years. Older churches, as well as younger churches, experienced revitalization.

Established churches that are experiencing plateau or decline should be encouraged by the discovery that older churches experience growth and revitalization. Over 83 percent of the surveyed churches were more than twenty years old; 72 percent were more than thirty years old.

In an insightful article entitled "Renewing Older Churches," Fred Oaks states:

> Research indicates that three-fourths of all U.S. congregations are at least 40 years old. Daunting challenges await those of us who would transition long-established churches from decline to health. A few foundation principles are key. . . .
>
> *Don't dodge the real issues.* Determining what matters is something persistent leaders must do continually.
>
> *Patiently keep the heat on.* A congregation's potential is like an egg. You can't hatch an egg with a blowtorch. You must wait for the egg to mature. But it is also true that unless the eggs are warmed continuously, they will never hatch. . . .
>
> *Connect past to present.* Sometimes the way forward is first a creative look back. Take time to research your

congregation's history. Your church's heritage can be a goldmine with cobwebs strewn across the entrance. You can emerge with nuggets in the form of stories. When these stories are told and retold, corporate identity is enriched. . . .

Farewells and fruitfulness. Our job as leaders is to focus on one overriding concern: restoring the fruitfulness of our churches. Many long-established congregations have enjoyed wonderful seasons of productive ministry in times past. Renewal leaders are filled with anticipation that there are more such times to come.[4]

Church Size

Comeback churches came in all sizes. This study included churches ranging from 18 in attendance to 7,000 in attendance. Higher-attendance churches were not the sole focus of this study, nor did they comprise the majority of churches surveyed. Sixty-five percent of the churches that participated averaged less than 200 in attendance. Twelve churches with more than 1,000 in attendance participated, but 312 churches averaged less than 1,000 in attendance. The average size of comeback churches' attendance was 266, and the median size was 138.

Smaller and larger churches can find good news in this outcome. For smaller churches that might be struggling to overcome a "small church" mentality, this reveals that even smaller churches can be revitalized and grow. They don't have to be stagnant, feel defeated, or think that they can't compete with larger churches. God works with any church that really wants to grow and change.

Conversely, larger churches do not have to accept a "slow growth" mentality. They can grow and experience continued revitalization, even when size makes it more difficult to achieve a significant growth rate (membership to baptism or conversion ratio).

What makes this study exceptionally encouraging is that the 312 comeback churches that averaged less than 1,000 had as great or a greater impact (by percentage) than the churches of more than 1,000. Maybe you're a pastor who's never joined the "K-Club" (average attendance more than 1,000). Possibly, you're in a rural setting or a midsize town that doesn't have huge growth potential. Regardless, your church can have just as profound an impact (percentage of people reached) as a large church in a metropolitan area. Our goal is always to hear our Lord's "Well done, good and *faithful* servant" (Matt. 25:21, 23 NIV). And that's true wherever He has placed us.

Conclusion

Let's return to the *Yeah, but . . .* reason you thought of to explain why your church will have difficulty in becoming a comeback church.

While the factors discussed in this chapter are not the most significant issues in church revitalization, they still provide nuggets of information from the gold mine of revitalization.

"Yeah, but . . . our facility." Does it need to be remodeled? Overhauled? Started over? Facilities can contribute significantly to a comeback, depending on your context. Maybe your church doesn't need to move or build new buildings. But, you may need to remodel or revitalize what you already have. Whatever the condition, size, or configuration of your facilities, make certain you're vision driven and values guided in their use!

"Yeah, but . . . our marketing." Why not try an "Outreach Day," with excellent invitations and direct mail? You will be surprised at the number of people who will bring and include others if they are just given the tools and encouragement to do it.

"Yeah, but . . . I don't have time to read." You don't have time *not* to read. Readers are leaders and leaders are readers. It will prove beneficial to pay attention to the books and resources used by comeback leaders. If they discovered principles that helped in their churches' revitalizations, you'll find help in those resources as well.

"Yeah, but . . . if my people were more responsive to growth." Spend some time getting to know them and their sphere of influence. If you really care about people and their needs, it will tremendously influence them to invite others to your church.

Furthermore, people are important. Comeback leaders know this, and they carefully, prayerfully, and intentionally identify people who can make a positive impact in their churches. May that remind us to place a higher value on the people we serve—and those with whom we serve.

"Yeah, but . . . our church has no resources . . . no opportunities . . . too mired in tradition . . . not in the right area . . . strong-willed people . . . history of conflict . . . troublesome deacons or elders . . . doesn't want change." While these are certainly formidable problems, remember that we serve a mighty and invincible God. Others faced seemingly insurmountable problems in ministry, yet became comeback churches.

"Yeah, but . . . it's not going to be easy." Of every "yeah, but . . ." that paralyzes our minds and our hearts, this is the only one that has merit. Nothing that's worthwhile ever is easy. When did God ever call anyone to an easy task? He calls us to a worthy task. Jesus didn't take the easy way, and neither should we.

Whether young or old, large or small, any church can experience revitalization and renewal. *Your* church can experience a comeback—and it begins with you. Trust God to do the impossible one more time!

Suggestions for Further Study

Arn, Charles. *How to Start a New Service: Your Church Can Reach New People* (Grand Rapids: Baker Books, 1997).

Bowman, Ray, and Eddy Hall. *When NOT to Build (exp. ed.): An Architect's Unconventional Wisdom for the Growing Church* (Grand Rapids: Baker Books, 2000).

Callahan, Kennon L. *Building for Effective Mission: A Complete Guide for Congregations on Bricks and Mortar Issues* (San Francisco: Jossey-Bass, 1997).

McIntosh, Gary L. *One Size Doesn't Fit All: Bringing Out the Best in Any Size Church* (Grand Rapids: Fleming H. Revell, 1999).

Reising, Richard. *Church Marketing 101* (Grand Rapids: Baker, 2006).

Comeback Change Agents: New or Renewed Leaders

When I (Ed) have led churches to consider change, I often start by telling them about my shoe. I have freakishly wide feet. Usually when I get new shoes, I have a hard time "breaking them in," and it hurts for awhile. However, once I get them "worn right," I wear them as long as I can. When the heels wear out, I replace them. When they get tattered, I get them polished. I do whatever I can to make them last and not change.

Eventually, the middle of the shoe starts to wear a hole. I put up with it for awhile, but then winter comes. The water starts to leak through the hole—and it is cold and not comfortable. Finally, after putting it off as long as I can, I get new shoes. But . . .

NOBODY CHANGES UNTIL THE PAIN OF STAYING THE SAME IS GREATER THAN THE PAIN OF CHANGE.

Comeback leaders know that change is necessary and change is painful. Change is a challenging thing. Below, we document some of the bigger changes—changes involving leaders.

One of the things you will see below is that we believe all comeback churches need a new pastor—either one brought in from the outside or one changed from the inside. Then, it will often need new or changed staff and other leaders. Change requires change agents—and that can be hard.

New (or Renewed) Pastors

Every movement needs a leader, and we discovered that God led comeback churches to call a new pastor, or God renewed the pastors who were currently leading the church. We believed that all the pastors were new pastors, just not all of them changed jobs. Some of them changed their leadership approach. We intentionally did not exclude churches that changed pastors and staff, and we found that the churches frequently did, and that change became a catalyst for comeback.

We asked about pastor and staff changes by posing the question, "Did the turnaround coincide with any significant pastoral or staff changes? If yes, please briefly describe the changes without mentioning specific names of people." Almost eleven pages of responses were recorded in response to this question. Out of 324 total surveys, 276 (85.2%) respondents answered "YES" to this question, which also means that 48 (14.8%) respondents answered "NO" to this question.

Comeback churches changed staff. Let that sink in—six of seven comeback churches experienced staff change prior to their comeback. It is an inescapable fact that most comeback churches changed staff.

That does not mean that all of the comeback churches had new pastors. As the graph illustrates, most, but not all, of them did. At least one-third did not indicate a change in pastor, but the pastors overwhelmingly indicated that they changed. In other words, the one-third that were not newly hired pastors decided to grow and change into being the kind of leader the church needed in order to be a comeback church.

Comeback churches had new or renewed pastors or staff. First, 95 (29.3%) responses recorded just the lead pastor being changed. Second, 111 responses recorded a senior pastoral change along with other staff changes (34.3%), which means overall that 63.6 percent of the respondents indicated that the church's turnaround coincided with a change in the role of lead or senior pastor. Third, 70 (21.6%) respondents indicated that only other staff or lay ministry changes had been made.

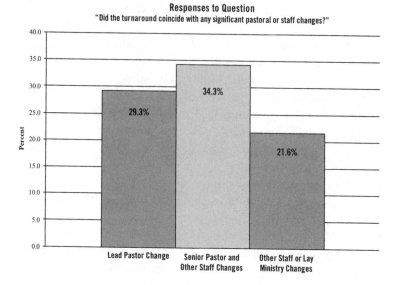

Responses to Question
"Did the turnaround coincide with any significant pastoral or staff changes?"

Almost 40 percent of comeback churches changed without changing their senior pastor. It is possible to lead a turnaround church as an established pastor, but it is more challenging. It means changing yourself while you transform the congregation. The process is simple to understand but difficult to implement. It is like telling a group of kindergartners what it will take to be in the Baseball Hall of Fame. The process is simple to understand; be a phenomenal athlete who works hard at your craft. But implementing that simple strategy is not easy.

All pastors will have to ask themselves if they are willing to do whatever it takes to be used of God to be the kind of leaders needed to lead churches to be comeback churches. For many pastors, that may mean changing leadership style, preaching style, shepherding style, and doing some of the hard work of ministry. It will take work, and we should remember the words of Scripture, "But you should keep a clear mind in every situation. Don't be afraid of suffering for the Lord. Work at telling others the Good News, and fully carry out the ministry God has given you" (2 Tim. 4:5 NLT).

New Staff in Key Ministry Areas

Many of the churches indicated that they changed staff, sometimes after a new pastor came, but frequently with the same pastor. The most common pastoral change was youth leadership, but worship pastor was also frequent. The graph below will illustrate the types of staff changes that were made.

In regard to this factor, four areas of ministry stood out in relationship to pastoral or staff changes. "Youth" was cited in 102, or 37 percent, of the 276 responses. "Worship/music" was recorded in 70, or 25.4 percent, of the responses. "Children" was mentioned in 38, or 13.8 percent, of the responses. Also, "secretary/administration" was listed in 33, or 12 percent, of the responses to this question.

Four Areas of Ministry Related to Staff Changes

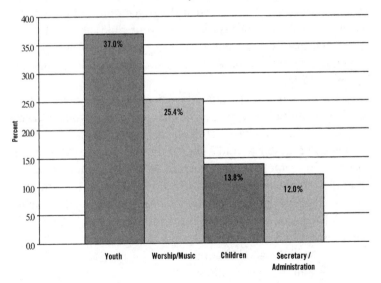

Why Change the Staff?

We have mixed feelings about the fact that more than 60 percent of the comeback churches changed pastors. As Thom Rainer's study seemed to indicate in his excellent book *Breakout Churches* (which we recommend you read), longevity appears to be a positive factor in regard to church growth scenarios. However, in this study on church revitalization, the situation seems to be different. Most of these churches changed with a new leader in the senior pastor's role.

We believe that the reason for a change in pastoral leadership is that these churches needed change in general, and in some cases a complete overhaul, because the church was in a pattern of plateau and decline. Most pastors are either unable or unwilling to make the change, but a good number of pastors were able to reinvent themselves to lead the comeback. Not all of the comeback churches required a new pastor, but all of them required a *changed* (renewed) pastor.

My friend Bill Easum has written a new book called *Put on Your Own Oxygen Mask First*. It's a great metaphor. Everyone who has flown a commercial flight has heard the flight attendant remind the passengers that when the oxygen masks fall from the ceiling, you should not rush to put on your child's mask—but put your own mask on first and then help your child. Why? Because if you don't put your mask on first, you may be unconscious and unable to help.

The same is true in church life. If you as a leader are so busy dealing with the "mundaneness of maintenance" or you are always putting out fires and have not sharpened your leadership potential, you will not be able to lead a church through change. Most comeback leaders came in wearing their oxygen masks, but a significant number put theirs on as they were already leading the church as pastor. They caught a vision and got a passion for church change.

What John Wesley wrote as his *Rule* is a good guide for the challenge of leading a comeback church:

> Do all the good you can,
> By all the means you can,
> In all the ways you can,
> In all the places you can,
> At all the times you can,
> To all the people you can,
> As long as ever you can.[1]

Bill Hybels, founding and senior pastor of the largest church in America, has had to reinvent himself and his leadership many times. Listen to how he describes the challenges he had in learning this principle from *Courageous Leadership*:

> I'll never forget the day three wise advisors came to me on behalf of the church. They said, "Bill, there were two eras during the first twenty years of Willow Creek's history when, by your own admission, you were not at your leadership best: once in the late 1970's and again in the early 1990's. The data shows that Willow Creek paid dearly for your leadership fumble. It cost all of us more than you'll ever know."
>
> Then they said the words I'll never forget: "The best gift you can give the people you lead here at Willow is a healthy, energized, fully surrendered, and focused self. And no one can make that happen in your life except you. It's up to you to make the right choices so you can be at your best." While they were talking the Holy Spirit was saying, "They're right, Bill. They're right."[2]

These "new" pastors, either coming from the outside or transformed on the inside, changed their focus from maintenance to mission. For most pastors and church leaders reading this book, they need *a change in their thinking not a change in their leader.* Too many churches are focused on maintenance and not strategic growth—and a new pastor or a changed pastor can make the difference, if they can change to strategic thinking.

Basic Elements of Strategic Thinking vs. Maintenance Thinking[3]

Strategic Thinking	Maintenance Thinking
Effective	Efficient
Success Seeker	Failure Avoider
Proactive	Reactive
Dynamic	Static
Flexible	Inflexible
Innovative	Traditional
Confronts	Avoids
Coordinated	Fragmented
Interdependent	Independent

This entire study was a crash course in change. All these churches made or experienced change in regard to their comebacks. As in sports, organizations often have found it easier to change the coach rather than figure out how to transform the players or other organizational dynamics. And in many cases, making a coaching change altered the overall dynamics of the team in a positive way. In addition, maybe fewer changes could be made in regard to the role of senior or lead pastor if more pastors could be trained to make the right kinds of personal and organizational changes.

Our hope is that if you have a new pastor, this book will help with the needed process. But, if your pastor has been at your present church awhile, we hope God will use this book to help you assist that pastor in leading the church to change. The best predictor of your future behavior is your past—we need churches and comeback leaders who are willing to do whatever it takes to make a dramatic and God-honoring comeback.

Why Some Avoid Change

Why is it so difficult for established church leaders to make the change? Two reasons surfaced from our study and our own experience:

Comeback leaders understood that change is hard. According to a fascinating article in *Fast Company* magazine, 90 percent of heart patients who are told to change their lifestyle habits or die, choose death over change.[4] Our churches and leaders seem to be no different. Changed leaders lead changing churches. Yet, the vast majority of time people and churches choose death over change.

Pastor Mark Canipe used to believe that people didn't want pastors to lead, so he didn't. Then, God spoke to him through the story of Joshua taking over after Moses' death (Deut. 34–Josh. 1). Pastor Canipe realized he had been a "fireman," always trying to keep the peace in the church. That passage of Scripture led him to change his attitude about leadership—he began to see that people do want to be led. So, starting with the deacons, the pastor started changing his leadership style. When the Lord told him to do something, he did it. At times, he agreed with the deacons that something should wait. The deacons began to see the effects of their pastor's change in attitude regarding leadership—how the Lord began to bless his efforts and the results of new things being done. This helped change their attitudes, which filtered down through the congregation. Now, they trust the pastor.[5] Additionally, they provide finances and worship leaders for their church plant's Saturday night service.[6]

If you are an established church pastor, you can make the transition if you will take the time to lead your people well—more "How to's" on this below.

Comeback leaders created a climate in which change is expected—and welcomed.

Here are some tips that might help in creating a climate of change:

- Develop a trust with the people that you serve.
- Make personal changes before asking others for change (i.e., "model change").
- Understand the history of the church; good leaders don't take the fence down until they know the reason it was put up.
- Place influencers in leadership positions.
- Check the "change in your pocket," the amount of trust people put in your leadership; you can increase your change, through compassion, competence, and consistency.
- Use this book with your congregation to help them through the process.

When to Make Changes?

There is more than one school of thought on when to make changes. Some tell new pastors not to make a change for one year. That was the case in comeback churches at times. Others made changes immediately.

Comeback leaders often took it slow with older congregations. At Centreville Baptist Church in Centreville, Nova Scotia, pastor Mark Potvin says that getting the older members of the church to buy into the vision is a difficult task. He explained that it took time and a change in focus. He explained, "One challenge of revitalizing a small church is getting older people to understand the need for change. One major key for us has been the willingness of our older generation members to change and accept change. We began doing things differently, like making young people a key focus of the church. If it hadn't been for the willingness of those older members, we might be declining or already dead."[7]

Comeback leaders took time to disciple people before they made changes. "One of the key things to our growth has been the change in our leaders' attitudes about their spiritual growth," says George Showers, pastor of the Seville Community Church of God in Elwell, Michigan. "They have come to a point where they participate in weekly Bible studies together, as well as participating in group discipleship studies. One particular example of leaders coming from the laity has occurred in our youth group. We have a couple that has stepped up and become key mentors, chaperones, and whatever else we need them to be to our youth. Also, when we began our building program, we had two guys who are contractors give resources and time to help with the cost of the building. They had never done anything like that before."[8]

My (Ed) own experience has been that the leaders in most declining churches have lost their passion. If you want to lead them, lead them first to Christ and spiritual maturity. When you lead them to Christian maturity, they will be more open for you to lead them to church revitalization.

Comeback leaders helped people to see the reality of the situation. If people won't change until the pain of staying the same is greater than the pain of change, your job is to inflict some pain. Churches need to experience the pain of the fact that they are not living up to their potential. They need to feel the hurt that their children no longer come to the church of their parents. In a loving way, we must help them see that the current situation is too painful not to change.

"Tom Landry, the coach of the Dallas Cowboys, defined *coaching* as 'making men do what they don't want, so they can become what they want to be.' An apt description of the pastoral task is to call people to do what they don't want so they can become what they want to be."[9] Ultimately, it is our task to help churches see what they *need* to do not what they *want* to do. That's leadership.

From our study, we have learned that there is not a "perfect" time to make change, but instead it is about "timing." God's Word reminds us,

There is an occasion for everything,
and a time for every activity under heaven:
a time to give birth and a time to die;
a time to plant and a time to uproot;
a time to kill and a time to heal;
a time to tear down and a time to build;
a time to weep and a time to laugh;
a time to mourn and a time to dance;
a time to throw stones and a time to gather stones;
a time to embrace and a time to avoid embracing;
a time to search and a time to count as lost;
a time to keep and a time to throw away;
a time to tear and a time to sew;
a time to be silent and a time to speak;
a time to love and a time to hate;
a time for war and a time for peace.
What does the worker gain from his struggles? I have seen
the task that God has given people to keep them occupied.
(Eccles. 3:1–10)

The point from the wisest man who ever lived is that wisdom is not always making war; wisdom is not always making peace; wisdom involves developing the skill of knowing **what time** it is!

Seven Principles for "Timing"

The following principles will help any pastor know if it is the right time to proceed with change.

Principle #1: Prayerfully determine what God wants you to change. This should go without saying, but it still must be stated. "Therefore I will always remind you about these things, even though you know them and are established in the truth you have" (2 Pet. 1:12).

Principle #2: Clearly define the change that needs to be made. Are there values that need changing first? Are there behaviors, or structures, or other spiritual issues that need to be changed?

Two cautions here: avoid loaded terms that slant issues in your favor, and always define change in terms of meeting more needs in a better way.

Principle #3: Look at the change objectively and clearly define the positive and negative forces that are presently holding the situation in stasis. Every situation has forces pushing for it and forces pushing against it—and all of them are holding it in place where it is right now. As you define these forces, you will see that the issue of change may be much bigger and broader than you first imagined. (See Lyle Schaller's *The Change Agent* for more information about this principle.)

Principle #4: Consider other issues of timing—like how much support you have for the change; who the key influencers are versus who the positional influencers are; how long the situation has been lying "in state"; how long you have been at the church and if people look to you as a key leader, etc.

Principle #5: Since the situation needing change is "frozen" in place, unfreeze it by creating healthy discontent; determine who will play needed roles to help the change, as well as determine your own role. Often in the Old Testament a prophet would be sent by God to tell His people of a change that needed to take place. There was also someone on the inside who would "pull" for the change that the prophet was "pushing." Then, there would be the shepherd/king who would help the people with the change. It is important to remember that as pastor you cannot fulfill all three roles! Remember, the difference between leadership and martyrdom can be about two steps or one wrong role!

Principle #6: Plan your approach and prepare for resistance to the change. Make sure you are including key decision makers in the process for change. You may need to empower implementers and release resources for the change. You can call the change an "experiment" or a "trial run" to give people an opportunity to warm up to the change. Just because you may have received an initial "no" vote does not mean the issue is dead.

Principle #7: Refreeze the situation so that the change stays in place. This may mean creating a structure to support the change, as well as implementing a process for conflict resolution (if necessary). Continually train leaders to continue the change once it has begun.

Who Is a Comeback Pastor?

It would be impossible and unwise to say that a "Comeback Pastor" is a certain personality, gift mix, or profile. The reality is that these pastors came from many backgrounds, educational experiences, and denominational affiliations. However, there were some surprising trends.

Older Pastors

We saw an interesting pattern regarding the number of older pastors in these revitalized churches. In this study, a positive correlation seemed to exist between being somewhat older and leading a comeback church. While the ages of pastors in this study ranged from twenty-six years old to eighty-six years old, the average pastor's age was forty-eight. Seventy-five percent of these comeback pastors were more than forty years of age.

It is interesting that many pastors at midlife decide to ride out the rest of their ministry. One insightful book, *Your Ministry's Next Chapter,* explains a common situation:

> Occasionally we hear about ministers whose careers crash and burn at mid-life. Often the tragedies are the result of foolish or immoral choices—pastors who at fifty act as though they were still sixteen. There are, however, other mid-life tragedies, perhaps no less destructive but likely more widespread, that never get reported: ministers who have slowed down, retired on the job, or stopped growing. They deliver previously delivered sermons. They live off the glow of the spiritual passion of their youth. They have stopped dreaming dreams. They dream only when they push the replay button on their memory file. Their careers, families, and churches gradually become diseased. Since the only symptom is a low-grade temperature, no one calls for help.[10]

Comeback leaders got a new vision and clear direction at any age. While it was evident that younger pastors led churches to make comebacks, pastors over forty years of age achieved this task more frequently in this study. Perhaps older pastors have a seasoned perspective that churches do not identify in younger pastors. Whatever the cause, the pattern was clear and encouraging—not every church needs a younger pastor; they often just need a better leader.

Educated Pastors

In this area, a positive correlation existed between a pastor having more education and being the leader of a comeback church. Ninety-five percent of those surveyed had more than a high school education. Seventy-nine percent had at least a college degree, and fifty-one percent had more than a college degree. While it was evident that pastors with less than a high school education were comeback leaders, over three-quarters of the comeback churches surveyed had pastors with at least a college degree. Thus, a majority of the churches surveyed had pastors that moved beyond a college degree in the area of education.

It is interesting to note that about half of those we surveyed did not have a seminary degree. The other half did. Thus, education did matter, but it was not always present, particularly at the seminary level, for all leaders.

Bivocational Pastors

We did not limit these churches by size, so we found that a larger number of the leaders of small to medium-sized churches were led by pastors with another employment. These are often called bivocational pastors, and 11 percent of our surveyed churches were led by bivocational pastors. When looking at only smaller churches, that number increased to 15 percent.

"One unique challenge [of being bivocational]," says Michael Rivera, associate pastor at Iglesia Evangelica Hispana AcyM in New York City, where both he and senior pastor Enrique Ruiz are bivocational, "is that there never seems to be enough time to do ministry."[11] One of the ways he and Pastor Ruiz have overcome the time challenge is making themselves as accessible as possible to their people. They both have cell phones and e-mail so the people have easier access to them. "I think another key is showing people that you are available to them. It's easy to become focused on our secular jobs. Sometimes we have to break some of those commitments when a pressing church need arises. Our people see that we really do care about them, and that we want to serve them in whatever way we can. That goes a long way in establishing meaningful relationships with people."[12]

"Time management!" That's the first thing that came out of Pastor Terry Bess's mouth when we asked him what was the biggest challenge of being a bivocational pastor. He is the pastor of the Glendale Assembly of God in Glendale, Oregon. "I like being bivocational because I get to minister to a lot of people. I've even had my foreman (at the mill) refer people to me for counseling."[13] Pastor Terry served as full-time pastor at Glendale for twelve years. He initially took the graveyard shift at the mill so he could raise some money for the church's mission trip to Africa. That was in 2001. He has remained bivocational because of the ministry opportunities it provides. When asked how he overcame the challenges that come with being bivocational, Terry said, "My boss allows me to be off whenever and for however long I need to be when it is church related. This has been a big help for me. Also, I have challenged my church members to step up and take a larger ministry role. They have responded wonderfully."[14]

Derek Spain, pastor of Lake Placid Baptist Church in Lake Placid, New York, said he struggles to balance time between two jobs and family. (Pastor Derek also is a North American Mission Board resort missionary at the U.S. Olympic Training Center in Lake Placid, so he says it ends up being two full-time jobs.) The only way he has been able to balance it is through prayer (from family, church leaders, friends), teamwork, and efficiency in both ministries.

One key to the church's growth came in the summer of 2003. The leaders in the church felt God was calling them to remodel their existing facilities and add to what they had. They added four new classrooms, missionary housing (for teams to come in and help with the church and the resort), and new recreational facilities for the church and community outreach. The church members were focused on depending on God for money and resources, and they also took an active role in sharing the workload. In fact, several members in the church are contractors, and they gave of their time and money (through donating resources) to help build these facilities. Also, mission teams came from Georgia, North Carolina, Virginia, and Mississippi, just to name a few. These teams helped with the building process as well. The original estimated price tag was a half million dollars. But, with all the donations from people, the church built these facilities for $300,000—and they completed the project debt free. Of the thirty-four baptisms that year, twenty came to Christ during that summer. Pastor Derek says, "It wasn't the building that caused our growth. It was our people learning to depend on God to provide for the needs we had. I don't think we would've grown if we hadn't had that time of stepping out on faith."[15]

Conclusion

"What people celebrate as tradition is usually a thing that's been changed by time. All things that resist change are changed by that resistance in ways undesired and undesirable," says Garry Wills. "The tradition must be repristinated if it is to be worth following."

What this means for leaders is that even preservation requires growth, learning and continual renovation. [Billy] Graham board member Bill Pollard said, "Everything—including relationships—tends to deteriorate with time unless the new, the improved, the changed is added."[16]

As the current pastor or church leader in a congregation desiring a comeback, you will have to renew and reinvent your role in order to catalyze necessary change. That means you need to ask some important questions such as:

1. Is there any evidence that I am disengaging spiritually or emotionally from ministry? How?

2. Have I seriously thought about leaving the ministry in the last three years? If so, what issues triggered the thoughts?

3. In one sentence, how would I describe the next chapter of my ministry?

4. Who in my ministry setting would be delighted to know I am reading a book about my next chapter? Why?

5. Do I truly believe my most effective years are in front of me?[17]

If your church leadership is not committed to change, work, and stay, the whole endeavor is doomed to failure. It requires a shared vision and willingness among the leaders.

Whichever role you are in, a new or a renewed pastor or church leader, change must happen if the church is to make a profound eternal mark that will not be erased.

Suggestions for Further Study

Hybels, Bill. *Courageous Leadership* (Grand Rapids: Zondervan, 2002).

London, H. B., Jr., and Neil B. Wiseman. *Pastors At Risk: Help for Pastors, Hope for the Church* (Wheaton, IL: Victor Books, 1993).

McIntosh, Gary L. *Staff Your Church for Growth: Building Team Ministry in the 21st Century* (Grand Rapids: Baker Books, 2000).

Myra, Harold, and Marshall Shelley. *The Leadership Secrets of Billy Graham* (Grand Rapids: Zondervan, 2005).

CHAPTER 11

Top Ten Most Common Transformations for Comeback Churches

In order to get a snapshot of the most significant comeback dynamics among these churches, we asked comeback leaders to rate seventeen areas arranged in a random fashion. Based upon their responses, there are ten areas that rated 3 or above in change during comebacks. We are calling these the Top Ten Typical Transformations found among comeback churches. The chart on the next page helps paint a picture of the ten big areas of change that occurred during 324 comebacks. The higher the rating, the greater the number of changes that were made in that area of ministry during these comebacks.

Top Ten Areas of Change

Since we have already discussed most of these issues throughout the course of this book, let's summarize briefly the importance of the "Top Ten List":

1. Prayer

In many different areas of response, it was evident that prayer permeated the revitalization process for most of the comeback churches and their leaders. Earlier in this book, comeback leaders made it clear—prayer was not just something they did before they started making changes, but it was also something they did more strategically as they were making a turnaround.

Change during Comeback

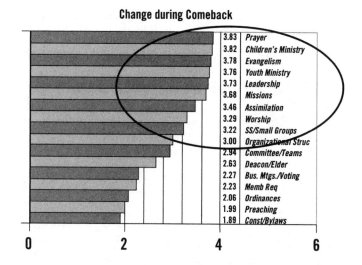

3.83	Prayer
3.82	Children's Ministry
3.78	Evangelism
3.76	Youth Ministry
3.73	Leadership
3.68	Missions
3.46	Assimilation
3.29	Worship
3.22	SS/Small Groups
3.00	Organizational Struc
2.94	Committee/Teams
2.63	Deacon/Elder
2.27	Bus. Mtgs./Voting
2.23	Memb Req
2.06	Ordinances
1.99	Preaching
1.89	Const/Bylaws

**(1) No Change (2) Little Change (3) Some Change
(4) Many Changes (5) Drastic Changes**

It is essential that we pray and hear from God when we seek to lead our churches through change. We should expect to hear from God. "Why is it, when we talk to God, we call it prayer, but when God talks to us, we call it schizophrenia?"[1] We need to hear from God for His guidance. When we hear from God, our faith is strengthened. "Few things provide our faith with a more thorough workout than a divinely-ordered vision."[2] You receive such vision only through prayer. We spent time dealing with "Three Faith Factors" and would encourage you to review those principles which include more strategic prayer effort.

2. Children's Ministry

While it was no surprise that prayer was the number one area that changed during the comeback, we found it fascinating that children's ministry and youth ministry were in the top five. We didn't necessarily expect to find them rated that high, but once the comebacks started taking place, comeback churches saw the need to make changes in regard to children's and youth ministry.

When surveyed, a significant majority of comeback leaders indicated that the area of children's ministry changed in many ways during the comeback. In follow-up interviews, some comeback churches were asked to describe the changes that took place in their children's ministries. Why was this area of ministry rated in such a significant way among comeback churches and their leaders?

Aylesford United Baptist Church in Aylesford, Nova Scotia, had a dynamic children's ministry that took off in the last several years. Pastor Clyde Lowe was a musician as well as a pastor. He utilized a band comprised of members in the church, which formed when he first came as pastor. Forming that band influenced the children to form their own worship band, which was made up of people from age nine to adult and was geared specifically toward children. Children learned to play instruments on their own and gained practical experience as they participated in the worship services. Other children's ministry events included a yearly emphasis focused on children in the Sunday morning worship service, summer VBS, and activities on Saturdays during the summer based on themes.[3]

Pastor Chad Current of Living Hope Community Church in Centerville, Ohio, explained in an e-mail:

> The children's ministry here is based on the team concept, which is why I think it has been so successful. Instead of one or two people running it, each age group has a team of leaders and a team of helpers that serve in a rotation. We have about 50 people in the rotation. This takes the weight off any one person and allows many people to take ownership for the ministry. Next, the children's team has made a focus on safety . . . we publicize to the church that we do background checks on all serving the children, we have windows in the doors, we have check-in and check-out systems and a parent paging system in the worship area if the parents are needed. Most important, the children's team is dedicated to making the children's ministry fun, interactive, and high energy. Every child worker has a love for kids and seeing them know Jesus. We also budget money for children's ministry. Finally, the team does special events throughout the year just for kids . . . Easter Party, Mud Party, etc.

Their emphasis on children has helped to transform their church.

Don Emerson, pastor of Maranatha Baptist Church in Logan, Utah, said children's ministry "has been extremely important for us. We have used this avenue to reach people in a predominately Mormon community who came because their children had first attended one of our events."[4] Pastor Emerson saw the need for a more effective children's ministry. They tried many different programs and found that AWANA worked best for them. They have children from families who are members, regular attenders, sporadic attenders, and some whose families don't come at all. In regard to Sunday, there are two couples who have done an excellent job with the children's worship. There is a certain level of enthusiasm from the adult leaders and a passion for reaching children. That kind of passion has helped change this church, and it can help renew yours as well.

3. Evangelism

We have spent much time dealing with issues of evangelism—but it bears repeating, comeback churches have a fresh and new passion for evangelism. It is important for all churches desiring a comeback to remember, "'Follow me and I will make you fish for people,' was the challenge Jesus gave the Galilean fishermen. *Following* and *fishing* are inseparably linked."[5]

4. Youth Ministry

Fourth on the Top Ten list of comeback changes is youth ministry. Many of the comeback churches realized that there was a need to change how youth ministry was done. In relationship to staffing, this was one of the top areas mentioned. In regard to staff changes made by the churches that were surveyed, 37 percent added or changed youth ministers. Obviously, churches that started to turn around discovered that being more effective in ministering to youth was a key to continuing the revitalization process. In some cases, this also included making facility changes to enhance youth ministry potential.

5. Leadership

Leadership is more than just telling people what to do. It is helping them to understand what they should do, developing a shared strategy, and then leading the church to "own" the plan. John Maxwell explains, "Once you have your strategy in place, make sure your people line up with your strategy. Ideally, all team members should know the big goal, as well as their individual role in achieving it."[6]

We have dealt extensively with leadership issues in chapter 2 and other places throughout the book. We encourage you to review these areas and focus a lot of time and energy on developing your leadership potential; this will be critical to making a comeback and keeping it going.

6. Missions

As we have explained in chapter 0, we believe that being on mission, or being missional, is foundational to church health, growth, and renewal. Comeback leaders often described that developing a renewed belief in Jesus Christ and the mission of the church as vital to making a comeback, and they led their churches to live out a missional focus. Many comeback leaders described an increasing sense of excitement and anticipation as the people in their congregations engaged in strategic outreach, church planting, or international missions. Being on mission with Jesus Christ will change people's lives in your church as well.

7. Assimilation

As we discussed in chapters 5, 6, 7, and 8, having an effective assimilation process is a key component of renewal and growth. Comeback churches made changes in this area and often raised expectations in regard to membership and ministry involvement. This helped create an atmosphere for revitalization and growth. Creating a system of effective assimilation will help transform guests and attenders into active, on-mission followers of Jesus Christ who are engaged in ministry.

8. Worship

Praise and worship have the ability to connect believers with the renewing presence of God and attract nonbelievers to Jesus Christ. Comeback leaders and churches understood that inspiring and relevant worship was a significant aspect of renewal in their churches. In chapter 4, we explained that the majority of churches in this study definitely leaned in the direction of having a more contemporary style, which often required making changes in worship. Making a comeback will probably require churches to take a long and hard look at how they do worship, and then make some changes.

9. Sunday School/Small Groups

An effective system of small groups can be the Velcro that holds the revitalization process together. Comeback leaders realized that changes were necessary in order to develop an expanding network of small groups. So, they added classes, created new groups, and developed leaders. This gets more people involved in building community, a sense of biblical oneness. Having smaller groups of people meeting together allows new people to connect in an environment where they can be appreciated and encouraged in a meaningful way.

10. Organizational Structure

Some comeback churches discovered that they were not organized for growth, and therefore, had to make some changes in structure to prepare for growth and renewal. Sometimes that involved getting the right people in the right places. Sometimes that meant doing things differently. Sometimes that meant comeback churches had to stop expending time and energy on ineffective ministries. In most situations, this will involve leading people to change their attitudes about ministry and refocus their priorities on the most important areas of service. As Mark Mittelburg explained, "The mission of an organization is an extension of the mission of the leaders. So if you want to reshape the priorities of the organization, you're going to have to reshape the priorities of the men and women who guide it."[7]

Conclusion

As we have stated many times, making a turnaround requires making changes. That's just the way it is. It's not always easy to make changes, but it's necessary. Comeback leaders led their churches to make changes in order to begin the process of revitalization, and they continued to make changes as renewal began to take place. We hope that you will begin to evaluate at least three areas where change needs to take place in your church, then begin to implement necessary changes gradually with your people.

Suggestions for Further Study

Gibbs, Eddie. *ChurchNext: Quantum Changes in How We Do Ministry* (Downers Grove, IL: InterVarsity Press, 2000).

Maxwell, John C. *Thinking for a Change: 11 Ways Highly Successful People Approach Life and Work* (New York: Warner, 2003).

McIntosh, Gary L. *Church That Works: Your One-Stop Resource for Effective Ministry* (Grand Rapids: Baker Books, 2004).

Patterson, Ben. *Deepening Your Conversation with God: Learning to Love to Pray* (Minneapolis: Bethany House, 2001).

Making a Comeback— Top Factors and Biggest Challenges

In this chapter, we are going to take a brief look at two summary issues. We thought it would be important to ask comeback leaders to boil down the nature of their churches' comebacks in two ways:

1. Ask each respondent to reflect on all that has happened to turn the church around. What are the top three factors that made an impact upon each church's revitalization?
2. Ask each respondent to identify the barriers that were impediments on the road to revitalization. If a pastor can get a handle on these overarching issues, then the pastor can begin to build a foundation for renewal.

Before you see how the pastors of the comeback churches responded, take just a moment to write down your reaction to these two questions:

1. What do you believe to be the top three factors that could revitalize your church?
2. What would you say are the major barriers to your church experiencing a comeback?

Go ahead—write it down. We'll wait.

Top Three Factors: Prayer, Evangelism, and Preaching

Respondents were asked to identify the top three factors that led to their church being revitalized. Overall, the top three responses were "prayer," "evangelism/outreach," and "preaching." These words were identified in 44.7 percent, 37.2 percent, and 25 percent of the responses, respectively.

Three Key Factors to Church Revitalization

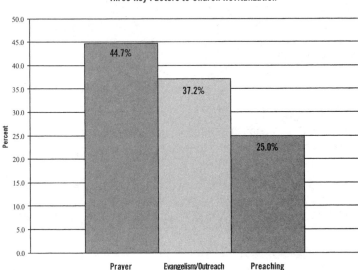

At first, these responses can seem to be too simplistic. It is easy to think, "There has got to be more to it than that!" It's easy to assume, "Well, that makes sense. After all, this is just a bunch of pastors giving the answers that they think everybody wants to hear. They're just being spiritual."

However, we can definitely find support for these practices in the Bible. Really, the whole reason a meeting was called in Acts 6 was so that a solution could be found to the problem of how to handle the early church's benevolence funds so that the spiritual leaders could keep doing what the spiritual leaders were supposed to do—pray, share the Word, and lead the church in kingdom expansion: "Then the Twelve summoned the whole company of the disciples and said, 'It would not be right for us to give up preaching about God to wait on tables. Therefore, brothers, select from among you seven men of good reputation, full of the Spirit and wisdom, whom we can appoint to this duty. But we will devote ourselves to prayer and to the preaching ministry.' . . . So the preaching about God flourished, the number of the disciples in Jerusalem multiplied greatly, and a large group of priests became obedient to the faith" (Acts 6:2–4, 7).

It is also important to reflect on the nature of prayer as it was described in this study. Comeback leaders reported that prayer permeated many aspects of ministry within their churches. In addition, the survey pointed out that revitalization was impacted by strategic prayer. Many comeback leaders described that praying in their churches was systematic and intentional. Of course, systematic and strategic prayer leads to effective outreach: "Devote yourselves to prayer; stay alert in it with thanksgiving. At the same time, pray also for us that God may open a door to us for the message, to speak the mystery of the Messiah—for which I am in prison—so that I may reveal it as I am required to speak" (Col. 4:2–4).

Comeback churches also engaged in strategic outreach efforts. They didn't just make evangelistic efforts; they made outreach efforts that connected with people in their communities. In addition, numerous comeback leaders reported that church members were methodically and intentionally trained to engage in outreach efforts, and events were planned that allowed people to reach out to friends and neighbors.

Also, when comeback leaders discussed their preaching, quite a few related that their preaching was strategic as well. They didn't just preach the Word of God; they preached the Word in such a way that motivated people to action, and they cast vision regularly within the context of their preaching.

Therefore, identifying prayer, outreach, and preaching as the top three comeback factors for comeback churches may be a simple and spiritual formula for renewal, but that does not mean that it's a simplistic formula. Making a comeback isn't easy; comeback leaders made the effort to be strategic and intentional in prayer, outreach, and preaching.

Even though we have already discussed these three issues more thoroughly in the course of the book, we asked several comeback pastors to describe how these elements were emphasized and/or combined in their churches' comeback processes. This might help you catch a vision for implementing these components in your church, if you have not been able to do so to this point in your ministry.

The Sumter Wise Drive Church of the Nazarene in Sumter, South Carolina, had grown through an increase in evangelistic zeal, experienced by Pastor William Watts and the members themselves. They conducted outreach events, weekly visitation, and evangelism training. Pastor Watts also emphasized the importance of the church's weekly prayer meetings with prayer for salvation, healing, and other needs.[1]

Mark Hoult, of the Gaylord Church of the Nazarene in Gaylord, Michigan, explained the need to be sensitive to his congregation because he came on staff immediately following a split in the church. Hoult immediately set the church's priorities as (1) prayer, (2) leadership, and (3) evangelism. Most often these priorities were conveyed through his sermons.[2]

This, of course, surfaces the spiritual principle we find in Revelation 3. When a church realizes it is poor, blind, and naked, and they need help desperately, then the church is ready for God's renewal. In response to sincere repentance and a desire to stay in step with what the Spirit of God wants to do in their church, the comeback leaders took steps necessary for revitalization. "Look! I stand at the door and knock. If you hear my voice and open the door, I will come in, and we will share a meal together as friends" (Rev. 3:20 NLT).

Living Hope Assembly of God in Camden, New York, established a relationship with three churches of other denominations. One major evangelistic event sponsored by the four churches was a joint showing of *The Passion of the Christ*. Living Hope has also participated in Assembly of God evangelism events. In addition to these large group events, the church conducted in-house witnessing seminars as well. One resource that helped Living Hope become more evangelistic was *Contagious Christians* by Bill Hybels, according to Pastor Aaron Gravett.[3]

Biggest Challenges: Attitudes, Finances, and Facilities

After being asked about top factors that led to new life, survey respondents were asked to identify the biggest challenges their churches faced in making a comeback. Three major issues surfaced—attitudes, finances, and facilities. Since the issue of facilities has already been discussed and was placed third after attitude and finances, let's turn our attention now to the top two items mentioned as the biggest challenges.

When examining the nature of challenges and obstacles to growth, the spiritual climate in the church cannot be ignored. The church is in the middle of a spiritual battle (Eph. 6:10–20). So, God's people will face challenges and obstacles just because of *who* we are, children of God, and because of *what* we are doing, seeking to build God's kingdom at the expense of God's adversary, Satan. As Martin Luther declared, "For where God built a church, there the Devil would also build a chapel."[4]

That being said, the spiritual conflict will often manifest itself indirectly. Hence, churches deal with challenges like people's negative attitudes, lack of financial provisions, and inadequate facilities, not directly with Satan and his demon cohorts. The churches' spiritual adversaries will use those issues to distract, discourage, and deter God's people from being all they can be in Christ and will keep churches from fulfilling their God-given purpose of kingdom expansion.

As we face the challenges of ministry, we need constantly to remember who our true enemy is and who we are fighting against. Facing challenges will often involve people who have different views and difficult attitudes, but ultimately, people are not the enemies we face. As we face the challenges and obstacles of ministry and leading churches to face the obstacles of renewal, David Nixon offered some helpful advice:

1. *Know what you believe and why* . . . Don't try to undermine the faith and practice of others who may differ from you.

2. *Understand that conflict can't always be avoided.* You may prefer to be perceived as helpful and friendly and to

have everyone like you, but correction is part of a leader's job . . . confrontation is often necessary and may lead to positive results.

3. Acting right is as important as being right. Often this is as simple as staying calm in the midst of the storm of controversy . . . being like Jesus is the goal.

4. Refuse to demonize believers who differ from you.

5. Never attempt to change another denomination's theology. Find one that fits what you believe.

6. Clarify only what is essential. Don't try to answer every criticism.

7. Do no harm . . . If you can't put out the fire, at least don't fan it.[5]

These insights may help you face the obstacles and challenges of leading a comeback in your church. Now with that backdrop, we are ready to discuss the specific challenges of attitude and finances.

Attitudes

Attitude surfaced as the biggest challenge among comeback respondents through words and phrases like *"change," "tradition," "mind-set," "mentality," "disunity," "small church,"* and *"small town."* Comeback churches often had to overcome attitude obstacles. In his book *One Size Doesn't Fit All,* Gary McIntosh lists the growth obstacles that small churches often face:

Small-church image,
Ineffective evangelism,
Inadequate programming,
Downward momentum, and
Ingrown fellowship.[6]

Every single one of the items in that list can relate to attitude. Maybe that's the reason Paul reminded believers to watch their attitudes: "Do nothing out of rivalry or conceit, but in humility consider others as more important than yourselves. Everyone should look out not [only] for his own interests, but also for the interests of others. Make your own attitude that of Christ Jesus" (Phil. 2:3–5).

Being unwilling to change, when change is necessary in order to grow, is the wrong attitude. Traditions are a necessary part of church life and ministry; every church has them. However, when people choose to hold on to traditions at the expense of being effective in reaching the lost, that is the wrong attitude. If a church wants to hold on to the warm, fuzzy feelings of small church intimacy instead of "making room" for new people who need Christ, then that church has adopted the wrong attitude. Churches that make the decision not to develop new ministries, and do them well, may have accepted an attitude of defeat.

The essence of this book is that churches can change. Churches can overcome their attitude challenges and start growing again. Things don't have to be small, ineffective, inadequate, downward, and ingrown. Attitudes can be renewed.

In follow-up interviews, some comeback leaders were asked to describe how they overcame attitude challenges. Pastor Jeff LeBert of the New Hope Church of the Nazarene in Rogers, Arkansas, said his church organized a community carnival called "Family Fest" in which they had games and activities for kids, music, and door prizes for adults. Those who came had to register for the door prizes, which gave the church a prospect list. The church did excellent follow-up on those prospects, which resulted in a new attitude. A by-product of the attitude change came in the form of a new youth and children's building (the church was mostly older couples with no youth or children). The church had overcome a poor attitude, in part, by sponsoring the outreach event.[7]

Bluff Avenue Baptist Church in Fort Smith, Arkansas, used focused campaigns to spur its attitude change. "Several things led to our new attitude," said Pastor Robert Berry. "Two major events were the *40 Days of Purpose* and *40 Days of Community* campaigns. Also, we make our services positive and inviting, which helped with visitors."[8] Two other contributors to the attitude change were FAITH and a strong Vacation Bible School.

According to Samuel Macri of Clinton Road Baptist Church in New Hartford, New York, "*Experiencing God* and *The Purpose-Driven Church* helped in our change. They both helped us see clearly Christ's mission for the church." The empowerment of layleaders, increased reconciliation, service, and missions involvement helped the people of Clinton Road change their prevailing attitude. Concerning missions involvement, Macri offered, "God really blessed us when we became a mission-minded church."[9]

Finances

After attitude, comeback respondents cited finances as the next biggest challenge to a comeback. More than 21 percent of the respondents mentioned a lack of financial resources as one of their biggest challenges in making a comeback. That fits into the list of growth obstacles cited by Gary McIntosh for medium-sized churches:

> Inadequate facilities,
> Inadequate staff,
> Inadequate finances,
> Poor administration, and
> Increasing complexity.[10]

All the items listed can relate to a lack of finances. Inadequate facilities and staff can be the result of not having enough money to build or remodel or hire more staff. Increased finances can allow for better administration and can sure make things less complex in a hurry.

So, how did comeback leaders address the challenge of finances? In follow-up interviews, some comeback leaders were asked to describe how they overcame this revitalization challenge. Pastor Jerry Hurley of the New Banklick Baptist Church in Walton, Kentucky, brought the church's financial needs before the people. Also, financial needs were placed in the church's newsletter, which circulates to 175 nonmember, prayer, and support partners in and out of the state. The financial needs of the church were met through prayer and the practical steps of informing those who can help financially.[11]

David Cleveland, pastor of Broadway Baptist Church in Tampa, Florida, said, "Broadway is unique in that we are debt free. Whenever a need arises, we seek counsel from the Lord and our church leaders. When the decision is made that the need is legitimate, we put forth a campaign, challenging our people to give to the need. The Lord has always allowed us to raise the money to pay for the needs immediately. It is a great challenge because most of our members are in the low income bracket. But our theme verse is Philippians 4:19."[12]

Paul Poole, pastor of the First Assembly of God in Beaver Falls, Pennsylvania, said, "We don't stop doing the things that need to be done. We just become more creative in our approach." One example of creative financing was the church's Valentine's Banquet, which required substantial financial resources. Rather than paying for items, the church asked businesses to donate decorations, candy, and other related items. In addition, rather than underwriting the costs of mission trips, the church required its members to raise money for the mission trips which they took. Pastor Poole said, "This makes the trip more meaningful for everyone involved."[13] Finally, this church family discussed and prayed for its financial needs during the weekly age-graded prayer meetings.

Facilities

Comeback churches addressed facility needs when they became a hindrance. It is an interesting paradox. Most churches that grew did not focus on their buildings to do so. However, their building soon became a hindrance once they started to grow. In the helpful book, *When NOT to Build,* the authors explain: "Churches with consistent growth were churches determined to keep their focus on people. To keep that focus, they had left behind some traditional ways of thinking about and using their facilities. As a result, facilities demanded less of their members' time, money, and energy, and those resources were available for meeting people's needs."[14]

There came a tipping point for the churches in our study that required them to address building needs. See chapter 9, "Other Comeback Factors," for more information on facilities.

Conclusion

Making a turnaround may not be easy, and it is not. But, it does not have to be complex either. Comeback leaders affirmed that it can start with simple things like strategic and intentional prayer, outreach, and preaching. Every church should be able to find a way to do these basic spiritual disciplines fervently.

In addition, every church is going to face challenges. That is the nature of being in a spiritual organization with a spiritual purpose and having a spiritual enemy. Whether it is the challenge of attitude or finances or facilities, churches can find a way, with God's help, to overcome their growth obstacles and start growing again. There are 324 comeback churches that have proved it's possible. May God help you get to or stay on the path of revitalization.

Suggestions for Further Study

Goodwin, Steven J. *Catching the Next Wave: Leadership Strategies for Turn-Around Congregations* (Minneapolis: Augsburg Fortress, 1999).

Klopp, Henry. *The Ministry Playbook: Planning for Effective Churches* (Grand Rapids: Baker Books, 2002).

McNeal, Reggie. *The Present Future: Six Tough Questions for the Church* (San Francisco: Jossey-Bass, 2003).

Nixon, David F. *Leading the Comeback Church: Help Your Church Rebound from Decline* (Kansas City: Beacon Hill Press, 2004).

Rainer, Thom S. *Breakout Churches: Discover How to Make the Leap* (Grand Rapids: Zondervan, 2005).

Southerland, Dan. *Transitioning: Leading Your Church through Change* (Grand Rapids: Zondervan Publishing House, 2000).

Comeback Conclusions

> *The Church must be forever building, and always decaying, and always being restored. . . . The Church must be forever building, for it is ever decaying within and attacked from without; for this is the law of life. . . .*
>
> *Much to cast down, much to build, much to restore. Let the work not delay, time and the arm not waste. Let the clay be dug from the pit, let the saw cut the stone, let the fire not be quenched in the forge.*[1]

From its inception, the church has followed this very pattern throughout its history—growing, decaying, and being restored. As we asserted in chapter 1, the state of the North American church is currently in a period of time in which it is decaying. Segments of the North American church have been in a pattern of plateau and decline. What would it take for a significant number of those churches to be restored, renewed, and revitalized? Is there a process that plateaued or declining churches can follow to make a comeback, to move from being stuck and stagnant to vibrancy and growth?

The answer from history and the cheers of the comeback churches we surveyed is a resounding "YES!" We have been blessed to lead churches through revitalization. And, we have been encouraged by the stories of 324 churches that made the change.

Comeback churches gained a new sense of purpose. It is a temptation that is common to all pastors, people, and churches (1 Cor. 10:13). The church begins with a vibrant vision and an outward focus toward reaching the community for Christ, but then a subtle shift begins to happen. The church's focus turns inward instead of outward. The church would declare on paper that it is concerned about the community, but by the way the church invests its finances, efforts and time, an objective observer would conclude that the church is more interested in maintenance and not mission. The goal switches from meeting the needs of those outside of Christ to asking what's in it for the average person already attending—how can we keep them happy and coming. This natural tendency to slide toward a "me focus" instead of a mission focus is why churches need to have an intentional strategy to help with the God-ordained command for outreach. "He said to them, 'Go into all the world and preach the gospel to the whole creation'" (Mark 16:15).

What will it take to build an ongoing strategy to keep the fire for outreach stoked? Paul told Timothy, "For this reason I remind you to fan into flame the gift of God, which is in you through the laying on of my hands. For God did not give us a spirit of timidity, but a spirit of power, of love and of self-discipline" (2 Tim. 1:6–7 NIV). How can you and your church stay on the missional edge of church life and be relevant in reaching out to the people in the communities where you live? Let us share a few thoughts with you on some vital things to keep in mind as God leads you in planning for the bright, hopeful future He has in mind for you and your church.

Comeback Process

In this study, 324 comeback churches were surveyed in order to seek answers to the questions of what and how to make a comeback from a trend of spiraling downward, both spiritually and numerically. How did 324 churches start growing again after experiencing a pattern of plateau or decline? Based upon the information gathered in this study, some church change factors were perceived to be more important than others by comeback leaders.

Guidelines to Attain Revitalization

1. Leadership is the most important factor in making a comeback. Leadership is rated as the factor having the highest impact by comeback leaders. Leadership is about influence.

Churches that are in a pattern of plateau or decline need strong leaders who will point the way to revitalization. Comeback leaders illustrated the truth that church renewal, in many ways, does occur based on strong, effective leadership.

But what kind of leadership does the church need? Comeback leaders identified several important components of leadership in their responses—the development of an attitude of growth, intentionality and proactivity, shared ministry, and the activation of a shared vision. Comeback leaders are not willing to settle for a slow or no-growth mentality; maintaining a small-church mind-set is not an option. They are willing to identify and make necessary changes and set growth goals. Survey respondents describe an environment where the ministry is shared with the people based upon a common vision.

2. Vibrant faith is a significant factor in revitalization, particularly in three faith factors: renewed belief in Jesus Christ and the mission of the church, servanthood, and strategic prayer. If the percentages hold true in the larger picture of North American churches, then what churches believe about the person and power of Jesus and about God's mission for the church, how you follow Him as a servant leader, and your prayer relationship really matter. Creating a renewed focus and emphasis on Jesus is vital to making a comeback. Believers need to experience the reality of Jesus Christ in their everyday lives. Then, in order to create an atmosphere of renewed belief, comeback leaders will want to find ways to translate that belief into practical activity.

3. Laypeople becoming actively involved in meaningful ministry is a significant factor in church renewal. Creating an atmosphere of lay mobilization is very important in the revitalization process. Increased expectations, equipped people, and empowered people are key components of developing an atmosphere of lay ministry involvement.

4. Churches will want to be more intentional about their evangelistic efforts. Those churches that make plans to reach out to the people in and around their communities, and then, prepare people to engage in those outreach efforts will be more likely to experience renewal. In addition, churches should not necessarily expect to discover only one effective evangelistic strategy. These 324 comeback churches used many different strategies and methods of outreach. Thus, the discovery of evangelistic methods or strategies that work best for a given church may take awhile to discover. Those churches that have the desire to be revitalized will want to engage in intentional outreach efforts, become active agents of community service, and pray for the Spirit of God to draw people to Jesus.

5. A "celebrative" and "orderly" mood of worship is a huge factor in revitalization. If worship in a church cannot be described as "celebrative" and "orderly," then that church might want to consider exploring some ways to gradually introduce some new energy, enthusiasm, and contemporary flavor into its worship experience.

In some cases, churches and pastors might want to consider making changes in regard to other factors such as small groups, facilities, and marketing, but these factors are not as important or influential as leadership, vibrant faith, lay ministry, evangelistic efforts, and worship, according to the findings of this study. Overall, the most significant aspect of this study is that it proves revitalization can occur; 324 churches are comeback congregations. Revitalization can happen, and this study reveals some insights that will help churches that want to get on the comeback pathway.

Comeback Obstacles

In one of the summary questions, survey respondents were asked to identify the biggest challenges they had faced in regard to making their comebacks. The two most prominent issues identified by comeback leaders were attitude and finances.

If a comeback movement is going to take place in North America, these same issues will likely be obstacles for many other churches as well. Many other plateaued or declining churches will probably struggle with a small church mind-set, a slow growth mentality, a no-growth mentality, a maintenance mind-set regarding traditions, or a fear of change. The issue is, "Do the people in plateaued or declining churches really want to grow?"

According to some of the comeback leaders interviewed, these attitude issues can be addressed in practical ways. In many cases, an attitude of growth can be created by utilizing good tools and resources like the Purpose Driven materials. In all cases, an attitude adjustment toward growth will involve influencing people to change. Comeback leaders believe that attitudes can change.

In regard to finances, money is always a necessary resource to conduct ministry and live life. Some plateaued and declining churches will perceive that a lack of finances is a major obstacle to revitalization. Some of the follow-up interviews reveal the need for prayer and creativity in overcoming the obstacle of finances.

Other Suggestions

Churches can address comeback obstacles and create a movement toward revitalization by making changes, and consequently, reverse the overall trend toward decline and stagnation. Healthy church growth will require that churches not live in denial of their problems; stagnant churches will need to change their mind-set.

Churches will have to clearly and specifically acknowledge that they are in a pattern of plateau and decline, and then, seek to discover the reasons behind that pattern. Before plateaued and declining churches can be revitalized, they will need to realize the unhealthy patterns which exist in their midst. Here are some specific suggestions that will help you address these comeback challenges:

Grab for What Lies Ahead

Keep thinking and reaching forward (Phil. 3:14). Don't get stuck in the past, whether that means traditions or accomplishments. Too many churches choose their past over their future, their heritage over their growth, and their traditions over their children.

Simply put, churches need a fresh new vision because some ways of doing evangelism just do not work the same as they once did, and wise churches realize that. That may bother you, but it shouldn't. You probably already know it to be true. That's why, if you're like most churches, you ended the morning radio show in the 1940s, quit doing Sunday school enrollment campaigns in the '50s, and stopped the bus ministry in the '80s. God uses different approaches at different times. Our task is to find new ways to reach people with the unchanging message. Ultimately, it is just the gospel—and the gospel transforms, but God has led us to use different strategies over the years to help us share the gospel broadly and widely. Our churches need to press ahead toward God's plan to reach their communities today, not the plan that was used in 1954.

Here are some suggestions:

- Set some God-sized goals and go for it. Every church needs to be dissatisfied with its current condition, not because it needs more numbers, but because each community is made up of people without Christ who need to be reached. John Knox cried, "Give me Scotland or I die." We need to pray the same for Selma, Sellersburg, and Seattle.
- Remember Jesus has commissioned you for this purpose. According to Ephesians 3:10, the instrument that God uses to make known His "manifold wisdom" is the church—your church. He placed you where you are for such a time as this.
- Stick with it. Not everything you try is going to work, but don't quit. One of the keys to success is perseverance, not necessarily following the latest ideas and fads.

Gauge Your Progress

Don't be afraid to evaluate. Winston Churchill once said, "However beautiful the strategy, you should occasionally look at the results." It's important to set some specific growth goals and then determine whether or not you're reaching those goals. Don't sugarcoat your situation. Ask the tough questions like:

- How many unchurched people are we reaching?
- When was the last time I witnessed to someone?
- Are the programs and events we're doing producing effective results?
- Do we need to sacrifice some "sacred cow" ministries?

Ron Shrum at Bayless Baptist Church in St. Louis, Missouri, has had experience in leading several churches through revitalization. He believes that getting people to see a bigger vision is key. They have to see what lies ahead. Ron explains, "You have to convey a vision of possibility. You have to let the people see that it (growth and health) can be achieved. You must set goals. You must have great celebrations over small victories so people are encouraged, excited and energized about the growth God has in store." Bayless Church started realizing its potential for growth when small goals were set and met. They've been in a healthy growth pattern for three years and are averaging over 300 in attendance (up from 150 in 2001 after four years of steady decline).

Give Ministry Away

Are you trying to do it all yourself or are you seeking to involve others as much as possible? Are you stirring up the gifts and talents of the people God has placed around you? Are you building leaders so they also can build leaders? One of the factors that led many of those churches to renewal and revitalization was mobilizing the laity. The study made it clear—you cannot turn around a church alone. It takes a team effort.

Grow as a Leader

If you're not growing and developing as an *on mission* leader, how can you be an influencer in stirring the waters? Pastor Moss, who's led Oak Ridge Baptist Church in Salisbury, Maryland, through five years of healthy growth and reached more than 450 in attendance (after stagnancy around 50 for almost all of the 1990s), says this about leadership, "If you don't have a strong leader with strong leadership skills, you'll go nowhere." When asked how he sees himself as a leader, he says, "It's terrifying to see a church grow under your leadership and then go home and realize your own shortcomings." The most important gift a pastor can give is not to be present at everything, but to be there for the right things.

Too many pastors have too many excuses why the church has declined—sometimes we are the reason for the decline. Our first priority should be to grow close to the Lord and grow as a godly leader. Then, we can help others in the process of renewal as well.

Change Your Focus

If pastors are going to lead their churches through church revitalization, a change of focus will be required. Far too many churches are focused on maintenance and not vision. That means a change in calendar, strategy, and plans is needed.

Comeback pastors and their best leaders needed to focus their time on two groups: leaders and the lost. Too many pastors and *on mission* leaders have filled their calendars with "deciding" rather than "doing." We're amazed at how many churches will put their best leaders on boards to decide things that one person should be empowered to do.

Comeback churches took risks. We need churches to take biblically informed risks to reach people for the Kingdom. Unfortunately, there's often a long line of experts to tell you what you're doing wrong—but our focus needs to be on pleasing the Lord and reaching those in whom He is already at work. What a privilege! And God will reward us for our faithful ministry for Him: "So whether we are here in this body or away from this body, our goal is to please him. For we must all stand before Christ to be judged. We will each receive whatever we deserve for the good or evil we have done in this earthly body" (2 Cor. 5:9–10 NLT).

Comeback churches changed plans. I'm not here to tell you what you're doing is right or wrong. But if you're a pastor or leader from nine out of ten of our churches, your church is not experiencing healthy evangelistic growth. The best predictor of your future behavior is your past—we need churches and *on mission* leaders who are willing to do whatever it takes to make a dramatic and God-honoring comeback. If the horse is dead, it's time to dismount.

Why is it so hard? . . . Because change is hard. Leaders have to encourage their churches to embrace change. That may take time. You can increase your change through compassion, competence, and consistency.

Leading a comeback church is hard work—but it's God's work. God wants His churches filled with life again. That often involves a future that looks different from the past, but it can happen. So, come on, jump in! Do what it takes to be the kind of leader that can guide a comeback church—grab for what lies ahead, gauge your progress, give ministry away, grow as a leader, and change your focus.

Don't settle for stagnation and decline—there are few things as exciting as new believers coming into the life of a once declining church. It will be difficult to make a comeback. That we can promise. But, if you have the heart for it, God can work in ways that you cannot imagine.

If you don't have the heart for it, maybe it is time for a new one.

To be effective pastors, we must enlarge our love and make ourselves vulnerable. And when we do that, it is inevitable that we will experience a godly angina, a deep and piercing pain of the heart. As C. S. Lewis observes in *The Four Loves,* a heart that loves is a heart that knows pain:

> To love at all is to be vulnerable. Love anything, and your heart will certainly be wrung and possibly be broken. If you want to be sure of keeping it intact, you must give your heart to no one, not even to an animal. Wrap it carefully round with hobbies and little luxuries; avoid all entanglements; lock it up safe in the casket or coffin of your selfishness. But in that casket—safe, dark, motionless, airless—it will change. It will not be broken; it will become unbreakable, impenetrable, irredeemable. The alternative to tragedy, or at least the risk of tragedy, is damnation. The only place outside Heaven where you can be perfectly safe from all the dangers and perturbations of love is Hell.[2]

There is a great risk here. But there is a greater risk in living a mediocre life in a dying church while the world goes on without a Spirit-filled church to help them know the one true God.

Conclusion

Three hundred and twenty-four comeback churches from ten denominations participated in a phone survey about revitalization. Comeback leaders described a process of intentional change, especially in the areas of leadership, renewed belief, lay ministry, and evangelism. In addition, they described their worship as celebrative, orderly, informal, and contemporary.

While segments of the North American church are in a period of decline or stagnation, this study reveals that there is hope for struggling and declining churches. Churches can be restored, renewed, and revitalized. We hope this study in revitalization will help many churches and their leaders recognize that some things need to be torn down (slow or no-growth attitudes) and some things need to be built and restored (leaders, laity, and a path to revitalization).

Take a moment and imagine your church transformed. Imagine how the community might respond. Imagine how God would be glorified:

Can you imagine the community in which you live being genuinely thankful for your church?

Can you imagine city leaders valuing your church's friendship and participation in the community—even asking for it?

Can you imagine the neighborhoods around your church talking behind your back about "how good it is" to have your church in the area because of the tangible witness you've offered them of God's love?

Can you imagine a large number of your church members actively engaged in, and passionate about, community service, using their gifts and abilities in ways and at levels they never thought possible?

Can you imagine the community actually changing (Proverbs 11:11) because of the impact of your church's involvement?

Can you imagine many in your city, formerly cynical and hostile toward Christianity, actually praising God for your church and the positive contributions your members have made in Jesus' name?

Can you imagine the spiritual harvest that would naturally follow if all this were true?[3]

If you are a pastor or a church leader, that change begins with you. Get your life revitalized and get your focus right. Lewis and Cordeiro explain, "The most important lesson I've learned over the years is that you teach what you know, but you reproduce what you are through your character and example."[4]

May the work of revitalization not be delayed by us. Instead, may the work of God flow through us.

> Now to Him who is able to do above and beyond
> all that we ask or think—according to the power that
> works in you—to Him be glory in the church and in
> Christ Jesus to all generations, forever and ever. Amen.
> (Eph. 3:20–21)

Suggestions for Further Study

Dale, Robert. *Leadership for a Changing Church: Charting the Shape of the River* (Nashville: Abingdon Press, 1998).

Frazee, Randy, with Lyle E. Schaller. *The Come Back Congregation: New Life for a Troubled Ministry* (Nashville: Abingdon Press, 1995).

Reeder, Harry L., III, with David Swavely. *From Embers to a Flame: How God Can Revitalize Your Church* (Phillipsburg, NJ: P & R Publishing, 2004).

Notes

Preface

1. Because this is a NAMB research project, Ed's royalties will be returned for more research of this kind to help churches know how to do more effective ministry.

Chapter 0: Foundations

1. Michael Slaughter and Warren Bird, *Unlearning Church: Just When You Thought You Had Leadership All Figured Out* (Loveland, CO: Group Publishing, 2001), 15.

2. Tim Keller, "The Missional Church," Article online, June 2001, 1.

3. My thinking here is influenced by Frost and Hirsch's *The Shaping of Things to Come*, an excellent book seeking to apply missiological principles in a Western context. Although I see the process as more of an interaction than a progression, they challenged us to think missionally with a theological foundation of Christology, missiology, and ecclesiology. Dr. Gailyn Van Rheenen's "Missional Helix" (http://missiology.org/mmr/mmr25.htm) helped us to see the process as an ongoing conversation and interaction of theological disciplines. Hence, the idea is a Missional Matrix: engaging all three theological disciplines in conversation and interaction. Alan Hirsch tells me he has moved in a similar direction himself.

4. John Mark Terry, *Church Evangelism* (Nashville: Broadman & Holman Publishers, 1997), 16.

5. We are indebted to Richard Smith, Director of Missions for the Spurgeon Association in Kansas, for many items in this list.

6. H. B. London, *Refresh, Renew, Revive* (Colorado Springs: Focus on the Family, 1996), 1.

7. George Barna, *Leaders on Leadership* (Ventura, CA: Regal Books, 1997), 18.

8. Quoted by Donald S. Whitney, *Spiritual Disciplines for the Christian Life* (Colorado Springs: NavPress, 1991), 237.

9. Oswald Chambers, *Prayer—A Holy Occupation* (Grand Rapids: Discovery House, 1992), 97.

Chapter 1: Why Consider Becoming a Comeback Church?

1. http://www.ctlibrary.com/le/2005/fall/8.24.html.

2. Lyle Schaller, *Activating the Passive Church* (Nashville: Abingdon Press, 1986), 126.

3. Win Arn, *The Pastor's Manual for Effective Ministry* (Monrovia, CA, Church Growth, 1988), 16.

4. C. Peter Wagner, *Leading Your Church to Growth* (Ventura, CA: Regal Books, 1984), 31–32.

5. Aubrey Malphurs, *Vision America: A Strategy for Reaching a Nation* (Grand Rapids: Baker Books, 1994), 62.

6. Sherri L. Doty, Assemblies of God Statistician (2006, October 5). E-mail from Doty to authors. Doty noted: "These U.S. stats do not include the new churches opened 2001–2005 that may have grown during that time period, nor the churches closed, which would have shown losses. Nor do they include churches which did not give us

a report in both 2000 and 2005. That being said, we had 8,563 churches submitting reports for both years. Of those, churches ranked 1–3,151 grew 10.1+% or more in Sunday AM worship attendance; churches ranked 3,152 – 5,059 changed +/- 10.0% (1907); and churches 5,060 – 8,563 lost 10.1% or more (3503)." More statistics can be viewed online at www.gensec.ag.org.

7. Dale Jones, Director of Research Center, Church of the Nazarene (2006, September 21). E-mail sent from Jones to authors. "This was a quick version deliberately ignoring some of those finer points. It shows net change very well, which is what I thought you were looking for. But the report can be adapted to meet your needs. I chose some 'normal' growth and decline rates (5%, 10%, 25%) and applied them to one-year, ten-year, and twenty-five-year periods for USA Churches of the Nazarene. This shows the numbers of newly reported churches and those that are no longer active for each of the time periods. The 'new' and 'no longer' categories represent 'in comparison to our beginning and ending dates.' That is, a church that began in 1998 and became inactive in 2003 would not be counted at all rather than being counted as both 'new' and 'no longer.' The 'at least 5%' numbers always include the 10% and 25% figures, so the three should not be added to get a total number. That is, the 413 churches that grew at least 25% in the last year also grew at least 10%. Therefore, they are included in the 1,062 churches that grew at least 10% in the last year." More statistics for the Church of the Nazarene can be found in the Research Center section of their Web site, http://www.nazarene.org/ministries/administration/researchcenter/display.aspx

Nazarene Churches since 2004:		Since 1995:	
New churches	103	New churches	673
Existing grew at least 5%	1,593	Existing grew at least 5%	1,735
Existing grew at least 10%	1,062	Existing grew at least 10%	1,551
Existing grew at least 25%	413	Existing grew at least 25%	1,164
Churches no longer active	139	Churches no longer active	675
Existing declined at least 5%	1,723	Existing declined at least 5%	2,154
Existing declined at least 10%	1,144	Existing declined at least 10%	1,945
Existing declined at least 25%	354	Existing declined at least 25%	1,334

Since 1980:			
New churches	1,190	Churches no longer active	994
Existing grew at least 5%	1,463	Existing declined at least 5%	2,084
Existing grew at least 10%	1,367	Existing declined at least 10%	1,947
Existing grew at least 25%	1,110	Existing declined at least 25%	1,511

8. Ed Stetzer, "Stirring the Waters," *On Mission* (Winter 2005), [on-line], accessed Fall 2005; available from http://www.onmission.com/site/c.cnKHIPNuEoG/b.830521/k.D281/Stirring_the_waters.htm; Internet.

9. Ed Stetzer, "The Missional Nature of the Church and the Future of Southern Baptist Convention Churches," presented to the Baptist Center for Theology and Ministry conference, New Orleans Baptist Theological Seminary, February 12, 2005.

10. George Barna, *Grow Your Church from the Outside In* (Ventura, CA: Regal Books from Gospel Light, 2002), 23.

11. Ibid., 23. Barna stated, "We define a person as unchurched if he or she has not attended a Christian church service at any time during the past six months, other than special events such as weddings and funerals." Many other people exist somewhere between that definition and active membership in a particular local church.

12. George Barna, "Number of Unchurched Adults Has Nearly Doubled Since 1991," The Barna Update (4 May 2004), [on-line]; accessed 15 January 2006; available from http://www.barna.org/FlexPage.aspx?Page=BarnaUpdateNarrow&BarnaUpdateID =163; Internet.

13. http://www.christianitytoday.com/outreach/articles/americanchurchcrisis.html.

14. Ibid.

15. George Hunter, III, *To Spread the Power: Church Growth in the Wesleyan Spirit* (Nashville: Abingdon Press, 1978), 32.

16. E-mail to Ed Stetzer from George Hunter, September 15, 2006.

17. Erwin McManus, *Seizing Your Divine Moment: Dare to Live a Life of Adventure* (Nashville: Thomas Nelson, Inc., 2002), 104.

18. Aaron Blache, Interview by NAMB Research Team, January 26, 2006.

19. John F. MacArthur Jr. and Master's Seminary Faculty, *Rediscovering Pastoral Ministry: Shaping Contemporary Ministry with Biblical Mandates* (Dallas: W Publishing Group, 1995; electronic ed., Logos Library Systems, 3); Richard L. Mayhue, and Robert L. Thomas, *The Master's Perspective on Pastoral Ministry* (Kregel Academic & Professional, 2002).

Chapter 2: Rising with Leadership

1. "Back from the Brink," *Leadership Journal* (Fall 2005): 25.

2. The Arbinger Institute, Inc., *Leadership and Self-Deception* (San Francisco: Berrett-Koehler Publishers, Inc., 2000, 2002), vii.

3. www.firstassemblyda.com.

4. Maurice Seneca, Interview by NAMB Research Team, February 3, 2006.

5. Ibid.

6. Lyle E. Schaller, "Schaller: Courageous Leaders Can Say It Ain't Workin'," *Penn-Jersey Baptist,* February 2006.

7. J. W. McLean and William Weitzel, in their book *Leadership: Magic, Myth or Method* cited in Stephen A. Macchia, *Becoming a Healthy Church* (Grand Rapids: Baker Books, 1999, 2006), 120–21.

8. Stephen Sinclair, Interview by NAMB Research Team, February 1, 2006.

9. www.lakeshorechurch.net.

10. Eugene McBride, Interview by NAMB Research Team, February 2, 2006.

11. Bobb Biehl, *30 Days to Confident Leadership* (Nashville: Broadman & Holman, 1998), 75.

12. www.gbchurch.net.

13. Tony Haefs, Interview by NAMB Research Team, February 2, 2006.

14. Vernon Johnson, Interview by NAMB Research Team, February 2, 2006.

15. www.briarwoodchurch.net.

16. John Shamblin, Interview by NAMB Research Team, February 2, 2006.

17. Brian Moss, Interview by NAMB Research Team, February 2, 2006.

18. Harry Austin, Interview by NAMB Research Team, February 2, 2006.

19. Andy Stanley, *Visioneering* (Sisters, OR: Multnomah Publishers, Inc., 1999), 17.

20. Ed Stetzer, *Planting New Churches in a Postmodern Age* (Nashville: Broadman & Holman, 2003), 306.

21. Ron Yost, Interview by NAMB Research Team, February 2, 2006.

22. Aubrey Malphurs and Will Mancini, *Building Leaders* (Grand Rapids: Baker Books, 2004), 23.

23. Mark Canipe, Interview by NAMB Research Team, February 2, 2006.

24. Richard Jueckstock, Interview by NAMB Research Team, January 30, 2006.

25. John Boquist, Interview by NAMB Research Team, February 4, 2006.

Chapter 3: Three Faith Factors

1. "Back from the Brink," *Leadership Journal* (Fall 2005): 26.
2. Dave Banfield, Interview by NAMB Research Team, February 1, 2006.
3. Richard Culpepper, Interview by NAMB Research Team, February 7, 2006.
4. Stephen Willis, Interview by NAMB Research Team, January 27, 2006.
5. Harold Stanfill, Interview by NAMB Research Team, January 31, 2006.
6. Jeff LeBert, Interview by NAMB Research Team, February 7, 2006.
7. Al Byrom, Interview by NAMB Research Team, February 7, 2006.
8. John Brokopp, Interview by NAMB Research Team, January 31, 2006.
9. Bill Bright, His Final Interview, Video from Campus Crusade for Christ.
10. John Ortberg, *The Life You've Always Wanted: Spiritual Disciplines for Ordinary People* (Grand Rapids: Zondervan, 2002), 96.
11. Paul Grigsby, Interview by NAMB Research Team, January 27, 2006.
12. Iain Murray, *Revival and Revivalism: The Making and Marring of American Evangelicalism, 1750–1858* (Edinburg: Banner of Truth Trust, 1994), 17.
13. Thom S. Rainer, *The Book of Church Growth—History, Theology, and Principles* (Nashville: Broadman & Holman Publishers, 1993), 183–84.
14. Roger Lipe, Interview by NAMB Research Team, January 31, 2006.
15. William Watts, Interview by NAMB Research Team, February 7, 2006.
16. http://www.stonetablets.com/reach.htm.
17. Kenn Gangel, *Coaching Ministry Teams* (Nashville: Word Publishing, 2000), 65.
18. Donald A. McGavran, *Understanding Church Growth*, ed. C. Peter Wagner, rev. 3rd ed. (Grand Rapids: William B. Eerdmans Publishing Company, 1970; reprint, 1991), 278–80.
19. "Back from the Brink," *Leadership Journal* (Fall 2005): 26.
20. Mac Brunson and Ergun Caner, *Why Churches Die: Diagnosing Lethal Poisons in the Body of Christ* (Nashville: Broadman & Holman, 2005), 204–5.

Chapter 4: Worship and Preaching Matters

1. Stephen A. Macchia, *Becoming a Healthy Church* (Grand Rapids: Baker Books, 1999, 2006), 44.
2. Richard Culpepper, Interview by NAMB Research Team, February 7, 2006.
3. Steven Fletcher, Interview by NAMB Research Team, February 3, 2006.
4. Virgil Grant, Interview by NAMB Research Team, February 3, 2006.
5. Steven Fletcher, Interview by NAMB Research Team, February 3, 2006.
6. Johnny Agnew, Interview by NAMB Research Team, February 2, 2006.
7. http://www.onmission.com/site/c.cnKHIPNuEoG/b.830489/k.D6A3/Vitals.htm.
8. Scott Sampson, Interview by NAMB Research Team, January 27, 2006.
9. Stephen Willis, Interview by NAMB Research Team, January 27, 2006.
10. Keith Thompson, Interview by NAMB Research Team, February 1, 2006.
11. Fred Lund, Interview by NAMB Research Team, February 1, 2006.
12. Larry Brinkley, Interview by NAMB Research Team, February 3, 2006.
13. Chip Garrison, Interview by NAMB Research Team, February 3, 2006.
14. Ibid.
15. Thom S. Rainer, *High Expectations: The Remarkable Secret for Keeping People in Your Church* (Nashville: Broadman & Holman Publishers, 1999), 75.

Chapter 5: Intentional and Strategic Church Evangelism

1. Elmer Towns, Friendship Evangelism Training Course, 1987.
2. Dale Fitch, Interview by NAMB Research Team, January 26, 2006.

3. www.stcharlesassembly.org.
4. www.outreach.com.
5. Jerry Harris, Interview by NAMB Research Team, January 31, 2006.
6. www.willardcma.org.
7. Richard Jueckstock, Interview by NAMB Research Team, January 30, 2006.
8. http://www.cmacpd.bc.ca/.
9. http://www.cmacpd.bc.ca/churchhealth/growing-healthy-church.htm.
10. Rick Warren, CLASS 101 Participant's Notes, 1998, page 12.
11. Mark Hoult, Interview by NAMB Research Team, February 3, 2006.
12. Robert Lewis and Wayne Cordeiro, *Culture Shift* (San Francisco: Jossey-Bass, 2005), 155.

Chapter 6: Connecting People to Spiritual Maturity

1. Stan Toler and Larry Gilbert, *The Pastor's Playbook* (Kansas City, MO: Beacon Hill Press of Kansas City, 2000), 11.
2. E-mail to authors, October 10, 2006.
3. Mark Mittlelburg, *Building a Contagious Church: Revolutionizing the Way We View and Do Evangelism* (Grand Rapids: Zondervan, 2000), 92.
4. E-mail to authors, October 10, 2006.
5. Rob Morris, Interview by NAMB Research Team, February 2, 2006.
6. Thom S. Rainer, *High Expectations: The Remarkable Secret for Keeping People in Your Church* (Nashville: Broadman & Holman Publishers, 1999), 104–5.
7. Bob Gilliam, TNet International Training Seminar, June 13, 1998.
8. George Stevenson, Interview by NAMB Research Team, January 26, 2006.

Chapter 7: Motivating and Mobilizing People Out of the Pews

1. Tim Payne, Interview by NAMB Research Team, January 27, 2006.
2. "Back from the Brink," *Leadership Journal* (Fall 2005): 26.
3. Robert Berry, Interview by NAMB Research Team, February 7, 2006.
4. Keith Raderstorf, Interview by NAMB Research Team, February 7, 2006.
5. SHAPE stands for Spiritual Gifts, Heart, Abilities, Personality, and Experiences. You can find SHAPE resources by contacting Purpose Driven Ministries. In fact, the SHAPE materials were organized in a small-group format recently.
6. E-mail to authors, October 11, 2006.
7. PREPARE: 2677 καταρτισμός *Strong's #2677*: A making fit, preparing, training, perfecting, making fully qualified for service.
8. J. H. Moulton and George Milligan, *The Vocabulary of the Greek Testament: Illustrated from the Papyri and other Non-Literary Sources* (Grand Rapids: Eerdmans, 1974), 1,034.
9. J. I. Packer, *A Quest for Godliness: The Puritan Vision of the Christian Life* (Wheaton, IL: Crossway Books, 1990), 117.
10. Chuck Lawless, "Churches that people join," *Membership Matters: Insights from Effective Churches on New Member Classes and Assimilation* (Grand Rapids: Zondervan, 2005), 107.
11. David Gehret, Interview by NAMB Research Team, February 1, 2006.
12. Harry L. Reeder III and David Swavely, *From Embers to a Flame: How God Can Revitalize Your Church* (Phillipsburg, NJ: P & R Publishing, 2004), 195.
13. Network is the system used by Willow Creek Church. You can find these resources by contacting the Willow Creek Association in Chicago.
14. http://placeministries.org/.
15. Wayne Cordeiro, *Doing Church as a Team* (Ventura, CA: Regal, 2001), 72.

16. Chuck Lawless, *Membership Matters: Insights from Effective Churches on New Member Classes and Assimilation* (Grand Rapids: Zondervan, 2005), 106.

17. Keith La Fountain, Interview by NAMB Research Team, February 7, 2006.

18. John Kramp, *On Track Leadership* (Nashville: B & H Publishing Group, 2006), 51.

19. Reeder, *From Embers to a Flame,* 121.

20. Ibid., 122.

Chapter 8: Connecting People through Small Groups

1. Thom S. Rainer, *High Expectations: The Remarkable Secret for Keeping People in Your Church* (Nashville: Broadman & Holman Publishers, 1999), 29.

2. Eddie Gibbs, *ChurchNext: Quantum Changes in How We Do Ministry* (Downers Grove, IL: InterVarsity Press, 2000), 232.

3. www.christiancenterofdhs.org.

4. Gary Geesey, Interview by NAMB Research Team, February 3, 2006.

5. Dale Galloway with Kathi Mills, *The Small Group Book: The Practical Guide for Nurturing Christians and Building Churches* (Grand Rapids: Fleming H. Revell, 1995), 17.

6. Gilbert Bilezikian, *Community 101: Reclaiming the Church as Community of Oneness* (Grand Rapids: Zondervan Publishing House, 1997), 16.

7. Ibid., 54.

8. Bill Donahue, *Leading Life-Changing Small Groups* (Grand Rapids: Zondervan, 2002), 37–38.

9. Ibid., 68.

10. Randy Frazee, *The Connecting Church: Beyond Small Groups to Authentic Community* (Grand Rapids: Zondervan, 2001), 179.

11. Ibid., 82–83.

Chapter 9: Other Comeback Factors

1. Adam Dooley, Interview by NAMB Research Team, February 2, 2006.

2. Robert Eby, Interview by NAMB Research Team, February 2, 2006.

3. Kenneth Dyal, Interview by NAMB Research Team, February 3, 2006.

4. Fred Oaks, "Renewing Older Churches," *Leadership Journal* (Fall 2005): 47–49.

Chapter 10: Comeback Change Agents: New or Renewed Leaders

1. John Wesley in his *Rule.* John Bartlett, *Bartlett's Familiar Quotations* (Boston: Little, Brown and Company, 1855, 1980), 346.

2. Bill Hybels, *Courageous Leadership* (Grand Rapids: Zondervan Publishing, 2002), 184.

3. This is taken from "A Strategy Development Process" by Hugh Townsend at NAMB. It is a Church Planter Network Resource.

4. http://www.fastcompany.com/magazine/94/open_change-or-die.html.

5. Mark Canipe, Interview by NAMB Research Team, February 2, 2006.

6. Sunshine Community Church, Graniteville, South Carolina.

7. Mark Potvin, Interview by NAMB Research Team, January 30, 2006.

8. George Showers, Interview by NAMB Research Team, February 2, 2006.

9. Bill Hull, *The Disciple-Making Pastor* (Old Tappan, NJ: Fleming H. Revell, 1988), 91.

10. G. Fenton, *Vol. 8: Your Ministry's Next Chapter,* The Pastor's Soul Series; Library of leadership development (Minneapolis: Bethany House Publishers, 1999), 9.

11. Michael Rivera, Interview by NAMB Research Team, February 1, 2006.

12. Ibid.

13. Terry Bess, Interview by NAMB Research Team, February 1, 2006.

14. Ibid.

15. Derek Spain, Interview by NAMB Research Team, January 31, 2006.

16. Harold Myra and Marshall Shelley, *The Leadership Secrets of Billy Graham* (Grand Rapids: Zondervan Publishing, 2005), 285–86.

17. G. Fenton, *Your Ministry's Next Chapter,* 12.

Chapter 11: Top 10 Most Common Transformations for Comeback Churches

1. B. Patterson, and D. L. Goetz, *Vol. 7: Deepening Your Conversation with God,* The Pastor's Soul Series; Library of Leadership Development (Minneapolis: Bethany House Publishers, 1999), 121.

2. Andy Stanley, *Visioneering* (Sisters, OR: Multnomah Publishers, Inc., 1999), 63.

3. Clyde Lowe, Interview by NAMB Research Team, February 3, 2006.

4. Don Emerson, Interview by NAMB Research Team, February 3, 2006.

5. Eddie Gibbs, *ChurchNext: Quantum Changes in How We Do Ministry* (Downers Grove, IL: InterVarsity Press, 2000), 56.

6. John C. Maxwell, *Thinking for a Change: 11 Ways Highly Successful People Approach Life and Work* (New York: Warner Books, 2003), 247.

7. Mark Mittlelburg, *Building a Contagious Church: Revolutionizing the Way We View and Do Evangelism* (Grand Rapids: Zondervan, 2001), 89.

Chapter 12: Making a Comeback—Top Factors and Biggest Challenges

1. William Watts, Interview by NAMB Research Team, February 7, 2006.

2. Mark Hoult, Interview by NAMB Research Team, February 3, 2006.

3. Aaron Gravett, Interview by NAMB Research Team, February 7, 2006.

4. Martin Luther, *Table Talk* in *Catching the Next Wave: Leadership Strategies for Turn-Around Congregations* by Steven J. Goodwin (Minneapolis: Augsburg Fortress, 1999), 107.

5. David F. Nixon, *Leading the Comeback Church* (Kansas City: Beacon Hill Press, 2004), 97–98.

6. Gary L. McIntosh, *One Size Doesn't Fit All: Bringing Out the Best in Any Size Church* (Grand Rapids: Fleming H. Revell, 1999), 180.

7. Jeff LeBert, Interview by NAMB Research Team, February 7, 2006.

8. Robert Berry, Interview by NAMB Research Team, February 7, 2006.

9. Samuel Macri, Interview by NAMB Research Team, February 7, 2006.

10. McIntosh, *One Size,* 180.

11. Jerry Hurley, Interview by NAMB Research Team, February 7, 2006.

12. David Cleveland, Interview by NAMB Research Team, February 7, 2006.

13. Paul Poole, Interview by NAMB Research Team, February 7, 2006.

14. Ray Bowman and Eddy Hall, *When NOT to Build* (Grand Rapids: Baker Books, 1992, 2000), 43.

Chapter 13: Comeback Conclusions

1. T. S. Eliot, *Collected Poems 1909–1962* (New York: Harcourt Brace & Company, 1991), 153–54.

2. P. A. Cedar, R. K. Hughes, and B. Patterson, *Mastering the Pastoral Role.* Series statement from jacket. Mastering ministry (Portland, OR: Multnomah; Christianity Today, Inc., 1991), 139.

3. Robert Lewis, *The Church of Irresistible Influence* (Grand Rapids: Zondervan Publishing, 2001), 13–14.

4. Robert Lewis and Wayne Cordeiro, *Culture Shift* (San Francisco: Jossey-Bass, 2005), 91.